Classic
Main Courses

Classic
Main Courses

Best-loved recipes for every meal: over 180 timeless dishes
with step-by-step instructions shown in 800 photographs

Jenni Fleetwood

southwater

This edition is published by Southwater, an imprint of Anness Publishing Ltd,
108 Great Russell Street, London WC1B 3NA; info@anness.com

www.southwaterbooks.com; www.annesspublishing.com

If you like the images in this book and would like to investigate using them for publishing, promotions or advertising,
please visit our website www.practicalpictures.com for more information.

© Anness Publishing Ltd 2014

A CIP catalogue record for this book is available from the British Library.

Publisher: Joanna Lorenz
Editorial Director: Helen Sudell
Editor: Joy Wotton
Production Controller: Mai-Ling Collyer
Designers: Nigel Partridge, Steers McGillan Ltd and Sarah Williams
Recipes: Alex Barker, Carla Capalbo, Lesley Chamberlain, Jacqueline Clark, Roz Denny, Patrizia Diemling, Matthew Drennan,
Joanna Farrow, Valerie Ferguson, Jenni Fleetwood, Silvano Franco, Yasuko Fukuoka, Shirley Gill, Brian Glover, Nicola Graimes,
Juliet Harbutt, Deh-Ta Hsiung, Christine Ingram, Manisha Kanani, Emi Kasuko, Lucy Knox, Gilly Love, Lesley Mackley, Norma
MacMillan, Jane Milton, Sallie Morris, Anne Sheasby, Marlena Spieler, Linda Tubby, Laura Washburn, Kate Whiteman
Photographers: Nicki Dowey, Michelle Garrett, Amanda Heywood, Janine Hosegood, David Jordan, Dave King, William Lingwood,
Thomas Odulate, Craig Robertson and Sam Stowell

NOTES
Bracketed terms are intended for American readers.
For all recipes, quantities are given in both metric and imperial measures and, where appropriate, in standard cups and spoons.
Follow one set of measures, but not a mixture, because they are not interchangeable.
Standard spoon and cup measures are level. 1 tsp = 5ml, 1 tbsp = 15ml, 1 cup = 250ml/8fl oz.
Australian standard tablespoons are 20ml. Australian readers should use 3 tsp in place of 1 tbsp for measuring small quantities.
American pints are 16fl oz/2 cups. American readers should use 20fl oz/2.5 cups in place of 1 pint when measuring liquids.
Electric oven temperatures in this book are for conventional ovens. When using a fan oven, the temperature will probably need to be
reduced by about 10–20°C/20–40°F. Since ovens vary, you should check with your manufacturer's instruction book for guidance.
The nutritional analysis given for each recipe is calculated per portion (i.e. serving or item), unless otherwise stated. If the recipe gives
a range, such as Serves 4–6, then the nutritional analysis will be for the smaller portion size, i.e. 6 servings. The analysis does not
include optional ingredients, such as salt added to taste.
Medium (US large) eggs are used unless otherwise stated.

PUBLISHER'S NOTE

CONTENTS

INTRODUCTION	6
Preparing and Cooking Ahead	8
Choosing Accompaniments	10
HEARTY SOUPS	12
EGG AND CHEESE DISHES	32
SALADS	50
RICE AND RISOTTO	70
PASTA, GNOCCHI AND NOODLES	90
PAN-FRIED DISHES	110
STEWS, CASSEROLES AND CURRIES	130
STOVE-TOP DISHES	150
GRILLS AND GRIDDLED DISHES	170
ROASTS	190
BAKED DISHES	212
PIZZAS, TARTS AND PIES	232
Index	254

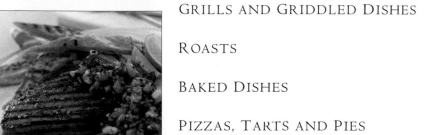
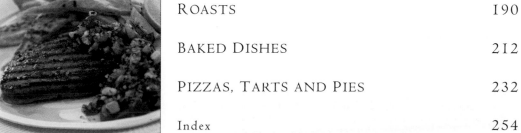

INTRODUCTION

Fifty years ago, main dishes were just that – the most important part of any meal and the course around which all others revolved. Most cookbooks of that era focused on the roast, the casserole or the mixed grill, paying scant attention to any other dishes. Then came the food revolution. People started eating out more and, as they dwelt on the delights of appetizers and desserts, main dishes started to take second place. In some restaurants, main courses disappeared entirely. Now it appears as though the pendulum has swung again. Nostalgia, coupled with nutritional advice that stresses the importance of eating small amounts of protein with plenty of vegetables, has put the main course back where it rightfully belongs – as the pivotal part of every meal.

However, the main course still has something of an image problem. Appetizers and desserts are seen as enticing and exciting, but main courses seem to have earned adjectives like "comforting", "robust", "satisfying" and "rib-sticking". When it comes to planning a special occasion meal, most of us have no difficulty in deciding what to serve for the first and final courses – it's what comes between the first and the last that proves to be the most problematic.

That's where this book comes in. With over 185 recipes you need never struggle for inspiration again. In fact, the difficulty will lie in deciding what to choose from this superb collection, whether it be a colourful healthy salad, a stunning soufflé, a pasta dish or the full works in the form of a meat or chicken roast or a hearty casserole.

BREAKING THE RULES

The days of the marathon meal – with an appetizer or soup leading to the fish course, followed by a main dish, a sorbet (sherbet), dessert, crackers and cheese and, finally, coffee – have largely disappeared. And today it is perfectly acceptable simply to serve guests a satisfying stew with lots of deliciously crusty bread for mopping up the juices, a beautiful baked fish with a pile of buttery new potatoes or a home-baked pie with a crisp salad. The rule is that there are virtually no rules, so that when you are entertaining at home, you can dispense with soups and appetizers altogether, if you like, or you can simply offer guests canapés with their drinks as they arrive.

The classic meat-and-two-veg theme has also vanished as more people have either become vegetarians or simply chosen to limit the amount of meat they eat. Today, a main course can be a roulade, a pie, a risotto, a substantial soup – or anything else you choose to serve. A curry with a cooling raita and plump Peshwari naan would go down well, as would a home-made pizza with a stylish marinara topping. It is even perfectly acceptable to serve sausages and mash and, if you prop the sausages on a mound of spicy mashed sweet potato and surround them with caramelized onions, you'll be recreating a fashionable restaurant dish that will delight your guests.

You don't necessarily have to serve vegetables alongside your chosen main dish either. Instead, they can star in the appetizer or appear in a salad, served French-style as a separate course. When serving vegetables, consider a fresh medley of steamed batons of carrots, leeks and celery, for instance, or a mixture of roast vegetables. That way you cut down on last-minute cooking, and avoid the flurry in the kitchen when your guests have just arrived. You'll have time to make them welcome.

Although the rules may have been relaxed somewhat, some of the old suggestions remain intact, simply because they make good sense. Whatever you choose to serve, the

Left: A filling risotto made with fresh seafood is an elegant and delicious alternative to a traditional meat-and-three-vegetable main meal.

meal should always be balanced in terms of flavours, colours and textures. For example, it wouldn't be a good idea to serve a creamy mousse as a main course then follow it with a silky-smooth dessert, or to serve a juicy Thai stew or curry after a soup. If the main course is quite dry, for example a country meat loaf, it should be accompanied by a succulent side dish, such as creamed leeks or mushrooms. It also makes good sense to try and avoid using the same ingredients in successive courses as repeatedly encountering the same flavours and textures can be boring.

THE FINER DETAILS

The appearance of the food on the plate has become just as important as the actual dish itself, so do give some thought to the colours and shapes of the ingredients used in the dish. Although the ubiquitous sprig of parsley seems to have been consigned to the great herb garden in the sky, more interesting garnishes, such as tiny bunches of redcurrants, braided chives or cucumber ribbons can add colour and shape to any plate. Just make sure

Left: Casseroles and curries are best served as a main course when they are not preceded by soups.

Above: Beautifully presented and elegantly garnished food will create a sophisticated look.

the garnish is appropriate – try lemon wedges with a fish dish, a fresh sprig of herbs on a vegetable stew, or spring onion curls with an Asian curry.

STRESS-FREE COOKING

When planning any meal, make life easy for yourself by preparing or cooking as much as possible ahead of time. Ease a heavy workload by using kitchen appliances such as the microwave oven, food processor and any other time-saving appliances you may have. Make use of your fridge and freezer – many dishes are even better when made ahead of time and reheated.

Most importantly, enjoy yourself – cooking and sharing good food with friends and family is one of life's greatest pleasures, so master these main dishes and you'll have many wonderful meals in store.

Preparing and Cooking Ahead

The marvellous thing about many main dishes is that they can be prepared in advance and cooked when required. Not only does this keep stress levels low but it also ensures that success levels remain high. Slow-cooked dishes, such as casseroles and stews, are also a boon as they need little attention and reward the cook by quietly gaining in flavour as they simmer in the oven. At the other end of the spectrum are dishes such as stir-fries and salads, which need little or no cooking. This time, careful preparation is the key. Salad leaves can be washed and dried, then bagged and put in the refrigerator. Not only will they be ready to toss together at the last minute, but they will also become crisper on standing. Stir-fry vegetables should all be cut to a similar size. Although it is not a good idea to do this too far ahead, because valuable nutrients will be lost, such advance preparation is helpful when you know you will be in a hurry later.

COOKING IN ADVANCE

Dishes such as stews, curries and casseroles often benefit from being made the day before they are to be served. This allows time for the flavours of the different ingredients to meld. If it is more convenient, you can cook dishes like this even further ahead,

Right: The components of a salad can be prepared in advance, ready for last-minute assembly when required.

freeze them and defrost them when you need to. The food must be cold before being placed in the freezer. Let it cool for a little, then place the dish or pot in a sink of very cold or iced water to accelerate the chilling process. Some china is designed to withstand extremes of temperature and can be used in both the oven and the freezer, but it is not recommended that you switch between the two without either allowing the hot food to cool, or the frozen food to thaw completely. It is best to thaw dishes overnight in the refrigerator. If you use a microwave for thawing, always follow the instructions in your handbook, and stir the stew or casserole frequently as it thaws, to make sure the item thaws evenly. When thawing a large block of frozen food in the microwave, it is a good idea to defrost it in short bursts, with a resting time between each, so that the heat that is generated spreads throughout the defrosting food and is not concentrated only in certain areas.

Rather than tie up a favourite straight-sided casserole or gratin dish by transferring it to the freezer for several weeks, tip the contents into a pan or dish, then wash the casserole or

dish and line it with microwave-proof film (wrap). Return the casserole or stew to the dish, and place it in the freezer. Lift out the contents when frozen, then double wrap and label the block and return it to the freezer. When you want to serve the food, just unwrap the block and return it to the original dish for thawing and reheating.

LEFTOVERS

As with freshly cooked food intended for the freezer, leftovers should be cooled quickly if they are to be kept for another meal. Leaving leftovers in their original dishes to cool slowly in a warm kitchen could encourage harmful bacteria to multiply in the food, causing illness. So transfer leftovers to clean, cold dishes and as soon as they have cooled, cover them and place them in the refrigerator. Use the next day and reheat thoroughly.

Leftovers can also be recycled, and the remains of dishes such as chicken, game or meat casseroles, can be used as a filling for a pie. A simple fish pie, topped with mashed potato, can easily be transformed into hot, crisp fish cakes. However, you should not rework ingredients more than once.

Left: Cooking casseroles and stews a day ahead is not only convenient, but also improves the flavour of the dish.

FREEZING TIPS AND TECHNIQUES

• Cool food rapidly, then wrap securely and label – with a description, the date and number of servings. If you are freezing several items at the same time, use the fast-freeze facility on your freezer.

• Hearty soups and stews freeze well, unless they contain chopped potatoes, rice, barley or pasta, which lose texture and become mushy on freezing. If these ingredients are included in the recipe, add them after thawing, then simmer the soup or stew until these ingredients are fully cooked.

• Stews and casseroles freeze well, but leave a little head room in the container to allow the liquid to expand during the freezing process.

• Blot the surface of a stew to remove surplus fat before freezing or chill so that fat solidifies and can be lifted off. Fat can become rancid, especially if a dish is frozen for a long time. Omit bacon unless you are freezing a composite dish for just a few weeks.

• Make sure that any pieces of meat or poultry in a dish that includes a sauce or gravy are fully submerged in the liquid, to reduce the risk of their drying out in the freezer.

• Although fish in sauce can be frozen, the thawed and reheated dish will not taste so good as when it was originally made, so it is better to cook such dishes on the day you serve them.

• Small items, such as meatballs, burgers and fish cakes, freeze well. Open-freeze them on trays, then wrap individually so that you can remove just as many as you need at any time.

Rice advice

Although rice can be cooked ahead of time and frozen or chilled for reheating, it is essential that it is cooled quickly and thoroughly before being stored. It should be reheated until it is very hot and served immediately. Never keep cooked rice warm for long periods. These precautions are necessary to avoid food poisoning.

STORAGE TIMES

• Meat casseroles and stews improve in taste if they are cooked ahead, but they should not be kept in the refrigerator for more than 2 days before being reheated and served.

• Soups can be frozen for a period of up to 3 months. Leave adequate space when wrapping the container to allow for expansion on freezing.

• Casseroles or stews containing bacon, pork or ham should not be frozen for more than 6 weeks. If these ingredients are not present, optimum freezing time is 2 months.

• Minced (ground) beef dishes, such as chilli con carne, freeze well. These can be stored for up to 2 months.

• Curries freeze well for up to 3 months, but the flavour of the spices deteriorates after this.

• Cooked pasta dishes, such as lasagne and cannelloni, can be frozen for up to 3 months.

• Cooked fish dishes in sauce can be frozen for up to 1 month only. Frozen fish cakes should be used within 2 months.

Above: Make the most of your freezer by batch-cooking suitable dishes, such as stews, casseroles and chilli con carne.

REHEATING

It is important always to make sure that a dish has thawed completely before reheating. Food should be piping hot all the way through before being served, especially if it contains meat on the bone. Timing will depend on the specific ingredients and the quantities being used, but as a guide, a chicken casserole that has been thawed to room temperature should be reheated for 45–60 minutes in an oven preheated to 200°C/400°F/Gas 6. Stir the casserole and check its temperature occasionally. Such delicate foods as fish should not be reheated for so long that their flavour and texture is spoiled. If you reheat foods in a pan on top of the stove, stir them frequently to prevent them from sticking to the base of the pan. If you use the microwave to reheat food, then follow the instructions in your handbook for the precise cooking time.

CHOOSING ACCOMPANIMENTS

The decision about what side-dishes to serve with your chosen main dish will depend very much on whatever else is on the menu. You don't have to serve a vast array of vegetable accompaniments, especially if you've started the meal with a salad or a fruit appetizer, such as grapefruit cocktail or a slice of melon. It is, however, traditional (and sound nutritional sense) to offer a carbohydrate of some sort alongside the main dish. Obvious choices would be rice, potatoes, pasta and bread, but you could also choose grains such as couscous, polenta and lentils or even quinoa (pronounced keen-wa), an extremely nutritious and tasty South American grain, that is cooked in a similar way to rice.

RICE

If you choose rice, make sure that it complements the main course. Basmati rice, with its slightly nutty flavour, is perfect for Indian dishes, whereas Thai fragrant rice is the first choice for a green or red curry from that country. Try to experiment with the more unusual rices, too, such as the red rice from the Camargue and California. Brown rice makes a good accompaniment to vegetable casseroles and stews, or it can be cooked, cooled and made into a salad to serve with kebabs and grilled meat.

Left: Mashed potato is a versatile accompaniment, whether served plain or flavoured with herbs or mustard.

POTATOES

Mashed or creamed potato tastes great with creamy fish dishes, fried liver and sausages and pork casserole. The modern trend is to flavour the mash with garlic, mustard or herbs. You could try a mixture of mashed potato and celeriac, or mashed potato and swede (rutabaga). Sweet potato mash tastes great, too – for extra interest, stir in a few spoonfuls of a hot Mexican tomato salsa. For smooth results, use a ricer, potato masher or fork.

Roast potatoes and baked layered potatoes are great served with roasts, baked fish or pot roasts, while potato chips (French fries) or fried potatoes are often partnered with steak.

Baked potatoes, split and topped with butter, cream cheese, Stilton or crème fraîche are delicious with grills (broils). When the first new potatoes arrive in the shops, they are a special treat, especially if you toss the boiled or steamed potatoes with butter and chopped fresh parsley or finely grated lemon rind. For flap-free main courses, consider potato dishes that don't require any last-minute attention.

GRAINS AND PULSES

Couscous is an excellent partner for Moroccan tagines and similar dishes that have quite a lot of liquid. It is readily available from supermarkets and the latest pre-cooked forms of couscous are exceptionally quick and easy to prepare. Polenta is an Italian staple and is a very good alternative to mashed potato. Soft polenta can be served with stews and casseroles and when polenta is grilled, it is an excellent alternative to bread. Quinoa, which is available from health food stores, is a nutty-flavoured grain that goes well with vegetable stews, such as ratatouille, and bean pots. Although lentils are usually included as an ingredient in a recipe, Puy lentils are a classic French accompaniment. Serve them hot with braised meat and game.

Above: Serve piping-hot garlic bread with baked pasta dishes.

PASTA

There are many different forms of pasta, from Italian spaghetti and tagliatelle to the wide range of Asian egg and rice noodles. Choose the type that suits your dish, not just in terms of its origin, but also to reap maximum value from the shape. Slim or flat noodles are not only great with thin, creamy sauces, they also go well with stir-fried vegetables, while penne and rigatoni are sturdy enough for chunky sauces.

BREAD

If you are serving a rich casserole or stew that has plenty of gravy or sauce, a rustic loaf or a supply of freshly baked wholemeal (whole-wheat) rolls will not only suit the mood of the meal, but also give guests an excuse to mop up every last drop of gravy. There are dozens of delicious loaves available, so try some unusual varieties. Soda bread is perfect with an Irish stew, while lavash, a large flat bread that is torn into pieces at the table, is great with Middle Eastern dishes. Italian breads, such as focaccia, are ideal with hearty casseroles such as osso bucco. Garlic bread is delicious with fish brochettes, grilled (broiled) pork chops or lamb steaks cooked on the barbecue. For a change, make your own garlic butter and transform rolls into individual garlic and herb breads.

SALADS

Although substantial salads, such as Insalata di Mare or Salad Niçoise, make perfect main course dishes in their own right, those salads that are less elaborate and substantial are better served as accompaniments to main meals. Use really fresh ingredients as these have a far superior flavour and crisp texture.

Salads don't work particularly well with meat or chicken stews or very creamy dishes, but they are perfect partners for pizzas, cold pies, baked pasta dishes such as lasagne, roulades, fajitas and grilled (broiled) fish and meat dishes. A simple green salad tossed with fresh herbs picked from the garden or window box is ideal and not overly time-consuming to make. Salads based on tomatoes, with added ingredients such as red onion or orange segments, are not only versatile but also simple to prepare.

Salad dressings should be kept simple so as not to compete with the other flavours in the bowl. A mixture of lemon juice, olive oil, fresh herbs, salt and freshly ground black pepper proves ideal for most salads and takes minutes to prepare, and any dressing that you don't use can be stored in the refrigerator until needed.

Below: A crisp salad is easy to prepare and goes well with main courses that don't contain a lot of sauce.

VEGETABLES

The choice of which vegetables to serve as accompaniments depends on what is part of the main dish. A main dish that includes a selection of vegetables, such as escalopes of chicken with baby vegetables, would be good on its own, or with potatoes or a similar starch vegetable. However, you might wish to offer a selection of three or four different vegetables with roast lamb or pork. Try to balance crisp vegetables such as roast potatoes, lightly cooked broccoli and crunchy cabbage with creamy offerings such as puréed celeriac, carrot or parsnip.

Always imagine what the food will look like on the plate and aim to have a mixture of colours and textures. For example, baby carrots, puréed spinach and fried potatoes would add colour as well as texture to a main course, whereas mashed potato, cauliflower and braised celery would look – and taste – rather plain and dreary.

CONDIMENTS AND SAUCES

Many dishes are enhanced if they are served with a complementary relish or sauce. Roasts are traditionally served with rich-flavoured sauces: cranberry sauce with turkey, mint sauce with lamb and horseradish cream with beef. Spicy

Below: Braised leeks make a wonderful accompaniment when teamed with sweet carrots.

food is best with a cooling condiment. Curry, for instance, is complemented by a cucumber raita. When serving chilli dishes, piquant relishes and tomato salsas are perfect, adding colour and texture to the meal. Classic Italian salsa verde is a natural partner for sautéed fish or grilled steak, while a rich onion gravy goes well with sausages, liver, pork chops or toad-in-the-hole. Dark rich gravies are also good with mounds of creamy mashed potato.

Classic vegetable companions

Some vegetables seem to go particularly well with specific meat, poultry or fish dishes.
• The slightly tart flavour of braised red cabbage with apples is excellent with roast pork or baked ham.
• Fennel, with its delicate, almost aniseedy flavour, is the perfect partner for fish or chicken.
• Sweet-tasting corn and smoked haddock go well together, but it is better to use naturally-coloured haddock to avoid overdoing the yellow theme.
• Mashed swede (rutabaga) is the classic accompaniment for haggis, but also tastes great with herbed sausages or spicy minced (ground) beef patties.
• Spinach is classically served with veal dishes and it also goes well with fish dishes.
• Sweet potatoes, especially when candied, are simply superb with baked ham. They are also the classic accompaniment for Thanksgiving turkey.
• Green beans frequently partner tomato-based stews, but they are also very good with grilled meats and fish.
• Roast vegetables, such as aubergines (eggplant), red onion, courgettes (zucchini) and celery, make a colourful bed for baked chicken breast portions or pork chops, and are also excellent with roast meats of all types.

HEARTY SOUPS

Whether you're cooking for the family, or having friends around for a casual supper, nothing beats a bowl of steaming soup on a chilly day. Soup spells comfort as well as flavour, and when the soup is a substantial one, such as Clam Chowder or Chunky Lamb and Chickpea Broth, there's no need for elaborate accompaniments. A little freshly grated Parmesan, if appropriate, some warm bread rolls, the salt cellar and pepper mill — and the meal is served. For a sophisticated occasion, serve Seafood Laksa or Bouillabaisse. The preparation may take a little longer, but the ease of serving will be just the same.

SPINACH AND RICE SOUP

USE VERY YOUNG SPINACH LEAVES TO PREPARE THIS LIGHT AND FRESH-TASTING SOUP.

SERVES FOUR

INGREDIENTS
675g/1½lb fresh spinach
  leaves, washed
45ml/3 tbsp extra virgin olive oil
1 small onion, finely chopped
2 garlic cloves, finely chopped
1 small fresh red chilli, seeded and
  finely chopped
225g/8oz/generous 1 cup risotto rice
1.2 litres/2 pints/5 cups
  vegetable stock
salt and freshly ground black pepper
shavings of pared Parmesan or
  Pecorino cheese, to serve

1 Place the spinach in a large pan with just the water that clings to its leaves after washing. Add a large pinch of salt. Heat gently until the spinach has wilted, then remove from the heat and drain, reserving any liquid.

2 Either chop the spinach finely using a large kitchen knife or place in a food processor and process the leaves to a fairly coarse purée.

VARIATION
You can substitute Swiss chard for the spinach, if you like.

COOK'S TIP
Buy Parmesan or Pecorino cheese in a piece from a reputable supplier, and it will be full of flavour and easy to grate or shave with a vegetable peeler.

3 Heat the oil in a large pan. Add the onion, garlic and chilli and cook gently for 4–5 minutes, until softened. Stir in the rice until well coated, then pour in the stock and reserved spinach liquid. Bring to the boil, lower the heat and simmer for 10 minutes.

4 Add the spinach and season with salt and pepper to taste. Cook the soup for a further 5–7 minutes, until the rice is tender. Taste and adjust the seasoning, if necessary. Ladle into heated bowls, top with the shavings of Parmesan or Pecorino and serve immediately.

Per portion: Energy 340Kcal/1431kJ; Protein 9.2g; Carbohydrate 52.3g, of which sugars 3.4g; Fat 11.9g, of which saturates 1.9g; Cholesterol 0mg; Calcium 320mg; Fibre 4g; Sodium 449mg.

LOBSTER BISQUE

BISQUE IS A LUXURIOUS, VELVETY SOUP, WHICH CAN BE MADE WITH ANY CRUSTACEANS.

SERVES SIX

INGREDIENTS
    500g/1¼ lb fresh lobster
    75g/3oz/6 tbsp butter
    1 onion, chopped
    1 carrot, diced
    1 celery stick, diced
    45ml/3 tbsp brandy, plus extra for
        serving (optional)
    250ml/8fl oz/1 cup dry white wine
    1 litre/1¾ pints/4 cups fish stock
    15ml/1 tbsp tomato purée (paste)
    75g/3oz/scant ½ cup long grain rice
    1 fresh bouquet garni
    150ml/¼ pint/⅔ cup double (heavy)
        cream, plus extra to garnish
    salt, ground white pepper and
        cayenne pepper

1 Cut the lobster into pieces. Melt half the butter in a large pan, add the vegetables and cook over a low heat until soft. Put in the lobster and stir until the shell on each piece turns red.

2 Pour over the brandy and set it alight. When the flames die down, add the wine and boil until reduced by half. Pour in the fish stock and simmer for 2–3 minutes. Remove the lobster.

3 Stir in the tomato purée and rice, add the bouquet garni and cook until the rice is tender. Meanwhile, remove the lobster meat from the shell and return the shells to the pan. Dice the lobster meat and set it aside.

COOK'S TIP
It is best to buy a live lobster, chilling it in the freezer until it is comatose and then killing it just before cooking. If you can't face the procedure, use a cooked lobster; take care not to over-cook the flesh. Stir for only 30–60 seconds.

4 When the rice is cooked, discard all the larger pieces of shell. Tip the mixture into a blender or food processor and process to a purée. Press the purée through a fine sieve placed over the clean pan. Stir the mixture, then heat until almost boiling. Season with salt, pepper and cayenne, then lower the heat and stir in the cream. Dice the remaining butter and whisk it into the bisque. Add the diced lobster meat and serve immediately. If you like, pour a small spoonful of brandy into each soup bowl and swirl in a little extra cream.

Per portion: Energy 406Kcal/1684kJ; Protein 20.3g; Carbohydrate 13.7g, of which sugars 3.1g; Fat 25.2g, of which saturates 15g; Cholesterol 153mg; Calcium 84mg; Fibre 0.7g; Sodium 365mg.

CLAM CHOWDER

IF FRESH CLAMS ARE HARD TO FIND, USE FROZEN OR CANNED CLAMS FOR THIS CLASSIC RECIPE FROM NEW ENGLAND. LARGE CLAMS SHOULD BE CUT INTO CHUNKY PIECES. RESERVE A FEW CLAMS IN THEIR SHELLS FOR GARNISH, IF YOU LIKE. TRADITIONALLY, THE SOUP IS SERVED WITH SAVOURY BISCUITS CALLED SALTINE CRACKERS. YOU SHOULD BE ABLE TO FIND THESE IN ANY GOOD DELICATESSEN.

SERVES FOUR

INGREDIENTS
100g/3¾oz salt pork or thinly sliced
   unsmoked bacon, diced
1 large onion, chopped
2 potatoes, peeled and cut into
   1cm/½in cubes
1 bay leaf
1 fresh thyme sprig
300ml/½ pint/1¼ cups milk
400g/14oz cooked clams, cooking
   liquid reserved
150ml/¼ pint/⅔ cup double
   (heavy) cream
salt, ground white pepper and
   cayenne pepper
finely chopped fresh parsley, to garnish

1 Put the salt pork or unsmoked bacon in a pan, and heat gently, stirring frequently, until the fat runs and the meat is starting to brown. Add the chopped onion and cook over a low heat, stirring occasionally, until softened but not browned.

2 Add the cubed potatoes, the bay leaf and thyme sprig, stir well to coat with fat, then pour in the milk and reserved clam liquid and bring to the boil. Lower the heat and simmer for about 10 minutes, until the potatoes are tender but still firm. Lift out the bay leaf and thyme sprig and discard.

3 Remove the shells from most of the clams. Add all the clams to the pan and season to taste with salt, pepper and cayenne. Simmer gently for 5 minutes more, then stir in the cream. Heat until the soup is very hot, but do not allow it to boil. Pour into a warmed tureen, garnish with the chopped fresh parsley and serve immediately.

CHINESE CRAB <u>AND</u> CORN SOUP

FROZEN WHITE CRAB MEAT WORKS AS WELL AS FRESH IN THIS DELICATELY FLAVOURED SOUP.

SERVES FOUR

INGREDIENTS
600ml/1 pint/2½ cups fish or
   chicken stock
2.5cm/1in fresh root ginger, very
   thinly sliced
400g/14oz can creamed corn
150g/5oz cooked white crab meat
15ml/1 tbsp arrowroot or
   cornflour (cornstarch)
15ml/1 tbsp Chinese rice wine or
   dry sherry
15–30ml/1–2 tbsp light soy sauce
1 egg white
salt and ground white pepper
shredded spring onions (scallions),
   to garnish

COOK'S TIP
This soup is sometimes made with whole kernel corn, but creamed corn gives a better texture. If you can't find it in a can, use thawed frozen creamed corn instead; the result will be just as good.

1 Put the stock and ginger in a large, heavy pan and bring to the boil over a medium heat. Stir in the creamed corn and bring back to the boil.

2 Turn off the heat and add the crab meat. Put the arrowroot or cornflour in a cup and stir in the rice wine or sherry to make a smooth paste, then stir this into the soup. Cook over a low heat for about 3 minutes, until the soup has thickened and is slightly glutinous in consistency. Add light soy sauce, salt and white pepper to taste.

3 In a bowl, whisk the egg white to a stiff foam. Gradually fold it into the soup. Ladle the soup into heated bowls, garnish each portion with spring onions and serve immediately.

VARIATION
To make prawn (shrimp) and corn soup, substitute 150g/5oz cooked peeled and deveined prawns for the crab meat. Chop the peeled prawns coarsely and add to the soup at the beginning of step 2.

Top per portion: Energy 439Kcal/1829kJ; Protein 25.6g; Carbohydrate 25.9g, of which sugars 8.8g; Fat 26.6g, of which saturates 15.2g; Cholesterol 136mg; Calcium 204mg; Fibre 1.8g; Sodium 1638mg.
Below per portion: Energy 201Kcal/852kJ; Protein 11.3g; Carbohydrate 33.8g, of which sugars 9.9g; Fat 3.2g, of which saturates 0.5g; Cholesterol 27mg; Calcium 17mg; Fibre 1.4g; Sodium 695mg.

MATELOTE

TRADITIONALLY THIS FISHERMEN'S SOUP IS MADE FROM FRESHWATER FISH, INCLUDING EEL, ALTHOUGH IN NORMANDY, THEY USE SEA FISH AND CONGER EEL. ANY FIRM FISH CAN BE USED, BUT TRY TO INCLUDE AT LEAST SOME EEL, AND USE A ROBUST DRY WHITE OR RED WINE FOR EXTRA FLAVOUR.

SERVES SIX

INGREDIENTS

1kg/2¼lb mixed fish, including
   450g/1lb conger eel if possible
50g/2oz/¼ cup butter
1 onion, thickly sliced
2 celery sticks, thickly sliced
2 carrots, thickly sliced
1 bottle dry white or red wine
1 fresh bouquet garni containing
   parsley, bay leaf and chervil
2 cloves
6 black peppercorns
beurre manié for thickening
   (see Cook's Tip)
salt and cayenne pepper
For the garnish
   25g/1oz/2 tbsp butter
   12 baby (pearl) onions, peeled
   12 button (white) mushrooms
   chopped flat leaf parsley

1 Cut all the fish into thick slices, removing any obvious bones. Melt the butter in a large pan, add the fish and sliced vegetables and stir over a medium heat until lightly browned. Pour in the wine and enough cold water to cover. Add the bouquet garni and spices and season. Bring to the boil, lower the heat and simmer gently for 20–30 minutes, until the fish is tender, skimming the surface occasionally.

2 Meanwhile, prepare the garnish. Heat the butter in a deep frying pan and sauté the baby onions until golden and tender. Add the mushrooms and cook until golden. Season and keep hot.

3 Strain the soup through a large sieve placed over a clean pan. Discard the herbs and spices in the sieve, then divide the fish among deep soup plates (you can skin the fish if you wish, but this is not essential) and keep hot.

4 Reheat the soup until it boils. Lower the heat and whisk in the *beurre manié* little by little until the soup thickens. Season to taste with salt and pepper and pour over the fish. Garnish each portion with the sautéed baby onions and mushrooms and sprinkle with chopped parsley. Serve immediately.

COOK'S TIP
To make the *beurre manié* for thickening, mix 15g/½oz/1 tbsp softened butter with 15ml/1 tbsp plain (all-purpose) flour. Add to the boiling soup, a pinch at a time, whisking constantly.

Per portion: Energy 305Kcal/1275kJ; Protein 32.1g; Carbohydrate 5.7g, of which sugars 4.6g; Fat 8.4g, of which saturates 4.6g; Cholesterol 94mg; Calcium 49mg; Fibre 1.6g; Sodium 169mg.

PROVENÇAL FISH SOUP

THE RICE MAKES THIS A SUBSTANTIAL MAIN MEAL SOUP. BASMATI OR THAI RICE HAS THE BEST FLAVOUR, BUT ANY LONG GRAIN RICE COULD BE USED. IF USING A QUICK-COOK RICE, COOK THE VEGETABLES FOR LONGER BEFORE ADDING THE RICE.

SERVES FOUR TO SIX

INGREDIENTS
450g/1lb fresh mussels
about 250ml/8fl oz/1 cup white wine
675–900g/1½–2lb mixed white fish
  fillets such as monkfish, plaice,
  flounder, cod or haddock
6 large scallops
30ml/2 tbsp olive oil
3 leeks, chopped
1 garlic clove, crushed
1 red (bell) pepper, seeded and cut
  into 2.5cm/1in pieces
1 yellow (bell) pepper, seeded and
  cut into 2.5cm/1in pieces
175g/6oz fennel, cut into
  4cm/1½in pieces
400g/14oz can chopped tomatoes
about 1.2 litres/2 pints/5 cups
  well-flavoured fish stock
generous pinch of saffron threads,
  soaked in 15ml/1 tbsp hot water
175g/6oz/scant 1 cup basmati
  rice, soaked
8 large raw prawns (shrimp), peeled
  and deveined
salt and ground black pepper
30–45ml/2–3 tbsp fresh dill,
  to garnish
crusty bread, to serve (optional)

1 Scrub the mussels and pull off the beards, discarding any shellfish that do not close when tapped with a knife. Place them in a heavy pan. Add 90ml/6 tbsp of the wine, cover tightly, bring to the boil over a high heat and cook, shaking the pan occasionally, for about 3 minutes or until all the mussels have opened. Strain, reserving the liquid. Set aside half the mussels in their shells for the garnish; shell the rest and put them in a bowl. Discard any mussels that have not opened.

2 Cut the fish into 2.5cm/1in cubes. Detach the corals from the scallops and slice the white flesh into three or four pieces. Add the scallops to the fish and the corals to the mussels.

3 Heat the olive oil in a pan and cook the leeks and garlic for 3–4 minutes, until softened. Add the peppers and fennel and cook for 2 minutes more.

4 Add the tomatoes, stock, saffron water, reserved mussel liquid and the remaining wine. Season well and cook for 5 minutes. Drain the rice, stir it into the mixture, cover and simmer for 10 minutes, until it is just tender.

5 Carefully stir in the white fish and cook over a low heat for 5 minutes. Add the prawns and cook for a further 2 minutes, then add the scallop corals and mussels and cook for 2–3 minutes more, until all the fish is tender. If the soup seems dry, add a little extra white wine or stock, or a little of both. Spoon into warmed soup dishes, top with the mussels in their shells and sprinkle with the dill. Serve with fresh crusty bread, if you like.

COOK'S TIP
To make your own fish stock, place about 450g/1lb white fish trimmings – bones, heads, but not gills – in a large pan. Add a chopped onion, carrot, bay leaf, fresh parsley sprig, 6 peppercorns and a 5cm/2in piece of pared lemon rind. Pour in 1.2 litres/2 pints/5 cups water, bring to the boil and simmer for 25–30 minutes. Strain through muslin (cheesecloth).

Per portion: Energy 544Kcal/2283kJ; Protein 55.9g; Carbohydrate 49.2g, of which sugars 11.7g; Fat 9.3g, of which saturates 1.4g; Cholesterol 143mg; Calcium 177mg; Fibre 5.6g; Sodium 325mg.

SEAFOOD LAKSA

A LAKSA IS A MALAYSIAN STEW OF FISH, POULTRY, MEAT OR VEGETABLES WITH NOODLES. AUTHENTIC LAKSAS ARE OFTEN VERY HOT, AND COOLED BY THE COCONUT MILK AND THE NOODLES. IF YOU WOULD PREFER A SPICY VERSION, ADD A LITTLE CHILLI POWDER INSTEAD OF SOME OF THE PAPRIKA.

SERVES FOUR TO FIVE

INGREDIENTS
  3 medium-hot fresh red
    chillies, seeded
  4–5 garlic cloves
  5ml/1 tsp mild paprika
  10ml/2 tsp fermented shrimp paste
  25ml/1½ tbsp chopped fresh root
    ginger or galangal
  250g/9oz small red shallots
  25g/1oz fresh coriander (cilantro),
    preferably with roots
  45ml/3 tbsp groundnut (peanut) oil
  5ml/1 tsp fennel seeds, crushed
  2 fennel bulbs, cut into thin wedges
  600ml/1 pint/2½ cups fish stock
  300g/11oz thin vermicelli
    rice noodles
  450ml/¾ pint/scant 2 cups
    coconut milk
  juice of 1–2 limes
  30–45ml/2–3 tbsp Thai fish sauce
  450g/1lb firm white fish fillet, such
    as monkfish, halibut or snapper
  450g/1lb large raw prawns (shrimp)
    (about 20), peeled and deveined
  small bunch of fresh holy basil or
    ordinary basil
  2 spring onions (scallions),
    thinly sliced

1 Put the chillies, garlic, paprika, shrimp paste, ginger or galangal and 2 shallots in a food processor, blender or spice grinder and process to a paste. Remove the roots and stems from the coriander and add them to the paste; chop and reserve the coriander leaves. Add 15ml/1 tbsp of the oil to the paste and process again until fairly smooth.

2 Heat the remaining oil in a large pan. Add the remaining shallots, the fennel seeds and fennel wedges. Cook over a medium heat, stirring occasionally, until lightly browned, then add 45ml/3 tbsp of the spice paste and stir-fry for about 1–2 minutes. Pour in the fish stock and bring to the boil. Reduce the heat and simmer for 8–10 minutes.

3 Meanwhile, cook the vermicelli rice noodles according to the packet instructions. Drain and set aside.

4 Add the coconut milk and the juice of 1 lime to the pan of shallots. Stir in 30ml/2 tbsp of the fish sauce. Bring to a simmer and taste, adding a little more spice paste, lime juice or fish sauce as necessary.

5 Cut the fish into chunks and add to the pan. Cook for 2–3 minutes, then add the prawns and cook until they turn pink. Chop most of the basil and add to the pan with the reserved coriander.

6 Divide the noodles among wide bowls, then ladle in the soup. Sprinkle with spring onions and the remaining whole basil leaves. Serve immediately.

Per portion: Energy 524Kcal/2199kJ; Protein 43.1g; Carbohydrate 65.1g, of which sugars 6.3g; Fat 10.1g, of which saturates 2g; Cholesterol 233mg; Calcium 162mg; Fibre 1.9g; Sodium 356mg.

BOUILLABAISSE

AUTHENTIC BOUILLABAISSE COMES FROM THE SOUTH OF FRANCE AND INCLUDES RASCASSE (SCORPION FISH) AS AN ESSENTIAL INGREDIENT. IT IS, HOWEVER, PERFECTLY POSSIBLE TO MAKE THIS WONDERFUL MAIN-COURSE SOUP WITHOUT IT. USE AS LARGE A VARIETY OF FISH AS YOU CAN.

SERVES FOUR

INGREDIENTS
45ml/3 tbsp olive oil
2 onions, chopped
2 leeks, white parts only, chopped
4 garlic cloves, chopped
450g/1lb ripe tomatoes, peeled
    and chopped
3 litres/5 pints/12 cups boiling fish
    stock or water
15ml/1 tbsp tomato purée (paste)
large pinch of saffron threads
1 fresh bouquet garni, containing
    2 thyme sprigs, 2 bay leaves and
    2 fennel sprigs
3kg/6½lb mixed fish, cleaned and
    cut into large chunks
4 potatoes, peeled and
    thickly sliced
salt, pepper and cayenne pepper
a bowl of Rouille and a bowl of
    Aioli, to serve
For the garnish
16 slices of French bread, toasted
    and rubbed with garlic
30ml/2 tbsp chopped fresh parsley

2 Simmer the soup for 5–8 minutes, removing each type of fish as it becomes cooked. Continue to cook until the potatoes are very tender. Season well with salt, pepper and cayenne.

3 Divide the fish and potatoes among individual soup plates. Strain the soup and ladle it over the fish. Garnish with toasted French bread and parsley. Serve with rouille and aioli.

1 Heat the oil in a large pan. Add the onions, leeks, garlic and tomatoes. Cook until slightly softened. Stir in the stock or water, tomato purée and saffron. Add the bouquet garni and boil until the oil is amalgamated. Lower the heat; add the fish and potatoes.

COOK'S TIP
Suitable fish for Bouillabaisse include rascasse, conger eel, monkfish, red gurnard and John Dory.

Per portion: Energy 814Kcal/3426kJ; Protein 142.3g; Carbohydrate 28.1g, of which sugars 10.8g; Fat 15.1g, of which saturates 2.2g; Cholesterol 345mg; Calcium 121mg; Fibre 4.9g; Sodium 895mg.

MEDITERRANEAN LEEK AND FISH SOUP WITH TOMATOES

THIS CHUNKY SOUP, WHICH IS ALMOST A STEW, MAKES A ROBUST AND WONDERFULLY AROMATIC MEAL IN A BOWL. SERVE IT WITH CRISP-BAKED CROÛTES SPREAD WITH A SPICY GARLIC MAYONNAISE.

SERVES FOUR

INGREDIENTS
30ml/2 tbsp olive oil
2 large thick leeks, white and green
  parts separated, both thinly sliced
5ml/1 tsp crushed coriander seeds
good pinch of dried red chilli flakes
300g/11oz salad potatoes, sliced
200g/7oz can Italian peeled
  chopped plum tomatoes
600ml/1 pint/2½ cups fish stock
150ml/¼ pint/⅔ cup fruity white wine
1 fresh bay leaf
1 star anise
strip of pared orange rind
good pinch of saffron threads
450g/1lb white fish fillets, such as
  monkfish, sea bass, cod or haddock
450g/1lb small squid, cleaned
250g/9oz uncooked peeled
  prawns (shrimp)
30–45ml/2–3 tbsp chopped parsley
salt and ground black pepper
To serve
1 short French loaf, sliced and toasted
spicy garlic mayonnaise

1 Gently heat the oil in a pan, then add the green part of the leeks, the coriander and chilli and cook for 5 minutes.

2 Add the potatoes and tomatoes and pour in the stock and wine. Add the bay leaf, star anise, orange rind and saffron.

3 Bring to the boil, reduce the heat and part-cover the pan. Simmer for 20 minutes, or until the potatoes are tender. Taste and adjust the seasoning.

4 Cut the fish into chunks. Cut the squid sacs into rectangles and score a criss-cross pattern into them without cutting right through.

5 Add the fish to the soup and cook gently for 4 minutes. Add the prawns and cook for 1 minute. Add the squid and the shredded white part of the leek and cook, stirring occasionally, for 2 minutes.

6 Stir in the chopped parsley and serve with toasted French bread and spicy garlic mayonnaise.

Per portion: Energy 326Kcal/1379kJ; Protein 49.7g; Carbohydrate 17.5g, of which sugars 4.4g; Fat 4.2g, of which saturates 0.9g; Cholesterol 421mg; Calcium 106mg; Fibre 2.9g; Sodium 333mg.

FISH SOUP WITH ROUILLE

MAKING THIS SOUP IS SIMPLICITY ITSELF, ALTHOUGH THE EXQUISITE FLAVOUR SUGGESTS IT IS THE PRODUCT OF PAINSTAKING PREPARATION AND COOKING.

SERVES SIX

INGREDIENTS
  1kg/2¼lb mixed fish
  30ml/2 tbsp olive oil
  1 onion, chopped
  1 carrot, chopped
  1 leek, chopped
  2 large ripe tomatoes, chopped
  1 red (bell) pepper, seeded
    and chopped
  2 garlic cloves, peeled
  150g/5oz/⅔ cup tomato
    purée (paste)
  1 large fresh bouquet garni,
    containing 3 parsley sprigs, 3 celery
    sticks and 3 bay leaves
  300ml/½ pint/1¼ cups white wine
  salt and ground black pepper
For the rouille
  2 garlic cloves, coarsely chopped
  5ml/1 tsp coarse salt
  1 thick slice of white bread, crust
    removed, soaked in water and
    squeezed dry
  1 fresh red chilli, seeded and
    coarsely chopped
  45ml/3 tbsp olive oil
  salt and cayenne pepper
For the garnish
  12 slices of baguette, toasted in
    the oven
  50g/2oz/½ cup grated Gruyère cheese

1 Cut the fish into 7.5cm/3in chunks, removing any obvious bones. Heat the oil in a large, heavy pan, then add the fish, onion, carrot, leek, tomatoes and red pepper. Cook over a medium heat, stirring occasionally, until the vegetables begin to colour.

2 Add all the other soup ingredients, then pour in just enough cold water to cover the mixture. Season well and bring to just below boiling point, then lower the heat to a bare simmer, cover and cook for 1 hour.

3 Meanwhile, make the rouille. Put the garlic and coarse salt in a mortar and crush to a paste with a pestle. Add the soaked bread and chilli and pound until smooth, or purée in a food processor. Whisk in the olive oil, a drop at a time, to make a smooth, shiny sauce that resembles mayonnaise. Season with salt and add a pinch of cayenne if you like a fiery taste. Set the rouille aside.

4 Lift out and discard the bouquet garni from the soup. Purée the soup in batches in a food processor, then strain through a fine sieve placed over a clean pan, pushing the solids through with the back of a ladle.

5 Reheat the soup without letting it boil. Check the seasoning and ladle into individual bowls. Top each serving with two slices of toasted baguette, a spoonful of rouille and some grated Gruyère.

COOK'S TIP
Any firm fish can be used for this recipe. If you use whole fish, include the heads, which enhance the flavour of the soup.

Per portion: Energy 513Kcal/2159kJ; Protein 41.3g; Carbohydrate 48.2g, of which sugars 11.7g; Fat 14.8g, of which saturates 3.6g; Cholesterol 85mg; Calcium 192mg; Fibre 4.4g; Sodium 642mg.

PUMPKIN, RICE AND CHICKEN SOUP

THIS IS A WARM, COMFORTING CHICKEN SOUP WHOSE SPICE AND ORANGE RIND GARNISH WILL BRIGHTEN THE DULLEST WINTER DAY. FOR AN EVEN MORE SUBSTANTIAL MEAL, ADD A LITTLE MORE RICE AND MAKE SURE YOU USE ALL THE CHICKEN FROM THE STOCK.

SERVES FOUR

INGREDIENTS

1 wedge of pumpkin, about 450g/1lb
15ml/1 tbsp sunflower oil
25g/1oz/2 tbsp butter
6 green cardamom pods
2 leeks, chopped
115g/4oz/generous ½ cup basmati
   rice, soaked
350ml/12fl oz/1½ cups milk
salt and freshly ground black pepper
generous strips of pared orange rind,
   to garnish
For the chicken stock
2 chicken quarters
1 onion, quartered
2 carrots, chopped
1 celery stalk, chopped
6–8 peppercorns
900ml/1½ pints/3¾ cups water

1 First make the chicken stock. Place the chicken quarters, onion, carrots, celery and peppercorns in a large, heavy pan. Pour in the water and bring to the boil over a low heat. Skim off any scum on the surface if necessary, then lower the heat, cover and simmer gently for 1 hour.

2 Strain the chicken stock into a clean, large bowl, discarding the vegetables. Skin and bone one or both chicken pieces and cut the flesh into strips. (If not using both chicken pieces for the soup, reserve the other piece for another recipe.)

3 Peel the pumpkin and remove all the seeds and pith, so that you have about 350g/12oz flesh. Cut the flesh into 2.5cm/1in cubes.

4 Heat the oil and butter in a pan, add the cardamom pods and cook for about 2–3 minutes, until slightly swollen. Add the leeks and pumpkin. Cook, stirring, for 3–4 minutes over a medium heat, then lower the heat, cover and sweat for 5 minutes more, or until the pumpkin is quite soft, stirring once or twice.

5 Measure out 600ml/1 pint/2½ cups of the stock and add to the pumpkin mixture. Bring to the boil, then lower the heat, cover and simmer gently for 10–15 minutes, until the pumpkin is soft.

6 Pour the remaining stock into a measuring jug (cup) and make up with water to 300ml/½ pint/1¼ cups. Drain the rice and put it into a pan. Pour in the stock, bring to the boil, then simmer for about 10 minutes, until the rice is tender. Add seasoning to taste.

7 Remove and discard the cardamom pods, then process the soup in a blender or food processor until smooth. Pour it back into a clean saucepan and stir in the milk, chicken and rice (with any stock that has not been absorbed). Heat until simmering. Ladle into warm bowls, garnish with the strips of pared orange rind and freshly ground black pepper and serve immediately with wholemeal (whole-wheat) bread.

Per portion: Energy 336Kcal/1406kJ; Protein 25.4g; Carbohydrate 33.9g, of which sugars 7.8g; Fat 11g, of which saturates 5g; Cholesterol 71mg; Calcium 168mg; Fibre 2.9g; Sodium 122mg.

CHICKEN AND LEEK SOUP WITH PRUNES AND BARLEY

THIS RECIPE IS BASED ON THE TRADITIONAL SCOTTISH SOUP, COCK-A-LEEKIE. THE UNUSUAL COMBINATION OF LEEKS AND PRUNES IS SURPRISINGLY DELICIOUS.

SERVES SIX

INGREDIENTS
 1 chicken, weighing about 2kg/4¼lb
 900g/2lb leeks
 1 fresh bay leaf
 a few each fresh parsley stalks and
    thyme sprigs
 1 large carrot, thickly sliced
 2.4 litres/4 pints/10 cups chicken or
    beef stock
 115g/4oz/generous ½ cup
    pearl barley
 400g/14oz ready-to-eat prunes
 salt and ground black pepper
 chopped fresh parsley, to garnish

1 Cut the breast portions off the chicken and set aside. Place the remaining carcass in a large pan. Cut half the leeks into 5cm/2in lengths and add them to the pan. Tie the bay leaf, parsley and thyme into a bouquet garni and add to the pan with the carrot and the stock. Bring to the boil, then reduce the heat and cover. Simmer gently for 1 hour. Skim off any scum when the water first boils and during simmering.

2 Add the chicken breast portions and cook for another 30 minutes, until they are just cooked. Leave until cool enough to handle, then strain the stock into a bowl. Reserve all the chicken meat. Discard all the skin, bones, cooked vegetables and herbs. Skim as much fat as you can from the stock, then return it to the pan.

3 Meanwhile, rinse the pearl barley thoroughly in a sieve under cold running water, then cook it in a large pan of boiling water over a medium heat for about 10 minutes. Drain, rinse well again and drain thoroughly.

4 Add the pearl barley to the stock. Bring to the boil over a medium heat, then lower the heat and cook very gently for 15–20 minutes, until the barley is just cooked and tender. Season the soup with 5ml/1 tsp salt and black pepper to taste.

5 Add the prunes. Slice the remaining leeks and add them to the pan. Bring to the boil, then simmer for 10 minutes, or until the leeks are just cooked.

6 Slice the chicken breast portions and add them to the soup with the remaining chicken meat, sliced or cut into neat pieces. Reheat if necessary, then ladle the soup into deep plates and sprinkle with chopped parsley.

Per portion: Energy 606Kcal/2533kJ; Protein 44.9g; Carbohydrate 40g, of which sugars 23.9g; Fat 30.8g, of which saturates 8.4g; Cholesterol 220mg; Calcium 45mg; Fibre 4.2g; Sodium 405mg.

POT-COOKED UDON IN MISO SOUP

UDON IS A WHITE WHEAT NOODLE, MORE POPULAR IN THE SOUTH AND WEST OF JAPAN THAN THE NORTH. IT IS EATEN WITH VARIOUS HOT AND COLD SAUCES AND SOUPS. HERE, IN THIS DISH KNOWN AS MISO NIKOMI UDON, THE NOODLES ARE COOKED IN A CLAY POT WITH A RICH MISO SOUP.

SERVES FOUR

INGREDIENTS

200g/7oz skinless, boneless chicken
  breast portions
10ml/2 tsp sake
2 abura-age (thin deep fried tofu)
900ml/1½ pints/3¾ cups dashi
  stock, or the same amount
  of water and 7.5ml/1½ tsp
  dashi-no-moto
6 large fresh shiitake mushrooms,
  stalks removed, quartered
4 spring onions (scallions), trimmed
  and chopped into 3mm/⅛in lengths
30ml/2 tbsp mirin
about 90g/3½oz aka miso or
  hatcho miso
300g/11oz dried udon noodles
4 eggs
seven spice powder (optional)

4 Put the mirin and miso paste into a small bowl. Scoop 30ml/2 tbsp soup from the pan and mix this in well.

5 To cook the udon, boil at least 2 litres/3½ pints/9 cups water in a large pan. The water should not come higher than two-thirds the depth of the pan. Cook the udon for 6 minutes and drain.

6 Put the udon in one large flameproof clay pot or casserole (or divide among four small pots). Mix the miso paste into the soup and check the taste. Add more miso if required. Ladle in enough soup to cover the udon, and arrange the soup ingredients on top of the udon.

7 Put the soup on a medium heat and break the eggs on top. When the soup bubbles, wait for 1 minute, then cover and remove from the heat. Leave to stand for 2 minutes. Serve with seven spice powder, if you like.

1 Cut the chicken into bitesize pieces and place in a shallow dish. Sprinkle with sake and leave to marinate in a cool place for 15 minutes.

2 Put the abura-age in a sieve and thoroughly rinse with hot water from the kettle to wash off the oil. Drain on kitchen paper and cut each abura-age into four squares.

3 To make the soup, heat the dashi stock in a large pan. When it has come to the boil, add the chicken pieces, shiitake mushrooms and abura-age and cook for 5 minutes over a medium heat. Remove the pan from the heat and add the spring onions.

Per portion: Energy 666Kcal/2781kJ; Protein 49.6g; Carbohydrate 61.9g, of which sugars 1.8g; Fat 24.4g, of which saturates 1.8g; Cholesterol 225mg; Calcium 1536mg; Fibre 0.7g; Sodium 655mg.

HOT AND SOUR SOUP

ONE OF CHINA'S MOST POPULAR SOUPS, THIS IS FAMED FOR ITS CLEVER BALANCE OF FLAVOURS. THE "HOT" COMES FROM PEPPER; THE "SOUR" FROM VINEGAR. SIMILAR SOUPS ARE FOUND THROUGHOUT ASIA, SOME RELYING ON CHILLIES AND LIME JUICE TO PROVIDE THE ESSENTIAL FLAVOUR CONTRAST.

SERVES SIX

INGREDIENTS
  4–6 dried shiitake mushrooms
  2–3 small pieces of wood ear (dried
    Chinese mushroom) and a few
    golden needles (lily buds) (optional)
  115g/4oz pork fillet (tenderloin), cut
    into fine strips
  45ml/3 tbsp cornflour (cornstarch)
  150ml/¼ pint/⅔ cup water
  15–30ml/1–2 tbsp sunflower oil
  1 small onion, finely chopped
  1.5 litres/2½ pints/6¼ cups beef or
    chicken stock, or 2 × 300g/11oz
    cans consommé made up to the full
    quantity with water
  150g/5oz drained fresh firm
    tofu, diced
  60ml/4 tbsp rice vinegar
  15ml/1 tbsp light soy sauce
  1 egg, beaten
  5 ml/1 tsp sesame oil
  salt and ground white or black pepper
  2–3 spring onions (scallions),
    shredded, to garnish

1 Place the shiitake mushrooms in a bowl, with the pieces of wood ear and the golden needles, if using. Add sufficient warm water to cover and leave to soak for about 30 minutes. Drain the mushrooms, reserving the soaking water. Cut off and discard the mushroom stems and slice the caps finely. Trim away any tough stem from the wood ears, then chop them finely. Using kitchen string, tie the golden needles into a bundle.

2 Lightly dust the strips of pork fillet with some of the cornflour. Mix the remaining cornflour to a smooth paste with the measured water.

3 Heat the oil in a wok or pan and cook the onion until soft. Increase the heat and cook the pork until it changes colour. Add the stock or consommé, mushrooms, soaking water, and wood ears and golden needles, if using. Bring to the boil, then simmer for 15 minutes.

4 Discard the golden needles, lower the heat and stir in the cornflour paste to thicken. Add the tofu, vinegar, soy sauce, and salt and pepper.

5 Bring the soup to just below boiling point, then drizzle in the beaten egg by letting it drop from a whisk (or to be authentic, the fingertips) so that it forms threads in the soup. Stir in the sesame oil and serve at once, garnished with spring onion shreds.

Per portion: Energy 169Kcal/709kJ; Protein 7.6g; Carbohydrate 19.7g, of which sugars 0.8g; Fat 7.2g, of which saturates 1.2g; Cholesterol 44mg; Calcium 141mg; Fibre 0.2g; Sodium 351mg.

MISO SOUP WITH PORK AND VEGETABLES

THIS IS QUITE A RICH AND FILLING SOUP. ITS JAPANESE NAME, TANUKI JIRU, MEANS RACCOON SOUP FOR HUNTERS, BUT AS RACCOONS ARE NOT EATEN NOWADAYS, PORK IS NOW USED.

SERVES FOUR

INGREDIENTS
    200g/7oz lean boneless pork
    15cm/6in piece gobo or 1 parsnip
    50g/2oz mooli (daikon)
    4 fresh shiitake mushrooms
    ½ konnyaku or ½ × 225–285g/
      8–10¼oz packet tofu
    a little sesame oil, for stir-frying
    600ml/1 pint/2½ cups dashi stock, or
      the same amount of water and
      10ml/2 tsp dashi-no-moto
    70ml/4½ tbsp miso
    2 spring onions (scallions), chopped
    5ml/1 tsp sesame seeds

1 Press the meat down on a chopping board using the palm of your hand and slice horizontally into very thin long strips, then cut the strips crossways into small pieces. Set the pork aside.

2 Peel the gobo using a potato peeler, then cut diagonally into 1cm/½in thick slices. Quickly plunge the slices into a bowl of cold water to stop them discolouring. If you are using parsnip, peel, cut it in half lengthways, then cut it into 1cm/½in thick half-moon-shaped slices.

3 Peel and slice the mooli into 1.5cm/⅔in thick discs. Cut the discs into 1.5cm/⅔in cubes. Remove the shiitake stalks and cut the caps into quarters.

4 Place the konnyaku in a pan of boiling water and cook for 1 minute. Drain and cool. Cut in quarters lengthways, then crossways into 3mm/⅛in thick pieces.

5 Heat a little sesame oil in a heavy cast-iron or enamelled pan until purple smoke rises. Stir-fry the pork, then add the tofu, if using, the konnyaku and all the vegetables except for the spring onions. When the colour of the meat has changed, add the stock.

6 Bring to the boil over a medium heat, and skim off the foam until the soup looks fairly clear. Reduce the heat, cover, and simmer for 15 minutes.

7 Put the miso in a small bowl, and mix with 60ml/4 tbsp hot stock to make a smooth paste. Stir one-third of the miso into the soup. Taste and add a little more miso if required. Add the spring onion and remove from the heat. Serve very hot in individual soup bowls and sprinkle with sesame seeds.

Per portion: Energy 114Kcal/475kJ; Protein 15.8g; Carbohydrate 1g, of which sugars 0.8g; Fat 5.2g, of which saturates 1.1g; Cholesterol 32mg; Calcium 306mg; Fibre 0.4g; Sodium 41mg.

CHUNKY LAMB AND CHICKPEA BROTH

THIS JEWISH DISH OF SAVOURY MEATS AND BEANS IS BAKED IN A VERY LOW OVEN FOR SEVERAL HOURS.
A PARCEL OF RICE IS OFTEN ADDED TO THE BROTH PART-WAY THROUGH COOKING, WHICH PRODUCES A
LIGHTLY PRESSED RICE WITH A SLIGHTLY CHEWY TEXTURE.

SERVES EIGHT

INGREDIENTS

250g/9oz/1 cup chickpeas,
  soaked overnight
45ml/3 tbsp olive oil
1 onion, chopped
10 garlic cloves, chopped
1 parsnip, sliced
3 carrots, sliced
5–10ml/1–2 tsp ground cumin
2.5ml/½ tsp ground turmeric
15ml/1 tbsp chopped fresh root ginger
2 litres/3½ pints/8 cups beef stock
1 potato, peeled and cut into chunks
½ marrow (large zucchini), sliced or
  cut into chunks
400g/14oz fresh or canned
  tomatoes, diced
45–60ml/3–4 tbsp brown or
  green lentils
2 bay leaves
250g/9oz salted meat such as
  salt (corned) beef (or double the
  quantity of lamb)
250g/9oz piece of lamb
½ large bunch fresh coriander
  (cilantro), chopped
200g/7oz/1 cup long grain rice
1 lemon, cut into wedges and a spicy
  sauce or fresh chillies, finely
  chopped, to serve

1 Preheat the oven to 120°C/250°F/
Gas ½. Drain the chickpeas.

2 Heat the oil in a large flameproof
casserole, add the onion, garlic,
parsnip, carrots, cumin, turmeric and
ginger and cook for 2–3 minutes. Add
the chickpeas, stock, potato, marrow,
tomatoes, lentils, bay leaves, salted
meat, lamb and coriander. Cover and
cook in the oven for about 3 hours.

COOK'S TIP
Add 1–2 pinches of bicarbonate of soda
(baking soda) to the soaking chickpeas
to make them tender, but do not add too
much as it can make them mushy.

3 Put the rice on a double thickness of
muslin (cheesecloth) and tie together
at the corners, leaving enough room for
the rice to expand while it is cooking.

4 Two hours before the end of cooking,
remove the casserole from the oven.
Place the rice parcel in the casserole,
anchoring the edge of the muslin parcel
under the lid so that the parcel is held
above the soup and allowed to steam.
Return the casserole to the oven and
continue cooking for a further 2 hours.

5 Carefully remove the lid and the rice.
Skim any fat off the top of the soup
and ladle the soup into warm bowls with
a scoop of the rice and one or two
pieces of meat. Serve with lemon
wedges and a spoonful of hot sauce or
chopped fresh chillies.

Per portion: Energy 384Kcal/1619kJ; Protein 22.1g; Carbohydrate 46.8g, of which sugars 5.6g; Fat 13.4g, of which saturates 3.9g; Cholesterol 43mg; Calcium 95mg; Fibre 5.4g; Sodium 88mg.

FRAGRANT BEETROOT AND VEGETABLE SOUP WITH SPICED LAMB KUBBEH

THE JEWISH COMMUNITY FROM COCHIN IN INDIA IS SCATTERED NOW BUT IT IS STILL FAMOUS FOR ITS CUISINE. THIS TANGY SOUP IS SERVED WITH DUMPLINGS MADE OF BRIGHT YELLOW PASTA WRAPPED AROUND A SPICY LAMB FILLING AND A SPOONFUL OF FRAGRANT GREEN HERB PASTE.

SERVES SIX TO EIGHT

INGREDIENTS
    15ml/1 tbsp vegetable oil
    ½ onion, finely chopped
    6 garlic cloves
    1 carrot, diced
    1 courgette (zucchini), diced
    ½ celery stick, diced (optional)
    4–5 cardamom pods
    2.5ml/½ tsp curry powder
    4 vacuum-packed beetroot (beets)
      (cooked not pickled), finely diced
      and juice reserved
    1 litre/1¾ pints/4 cups
      vegetable stock
    400g/14oz can chopped tomatoes
    45–60ml/3–4 tbsp chopped fresh
      coriander (cilantro) leaves
    2 bay leaves
    15ml/1 tbsp sugar
    salt and ground black pepper
    15–30ml/1–2 tbsp white wine
      vinegar, to serve
For the kubbeh
    2 large pinches of saffron threads
    15ml/1 tbsp hot water
    15ml/1 tbsp vegetable oil
    1 large onion, chopped
    250g/9oz lean minced (ground) lamb
    5ml/1 tsp vinegar
    ½ bunch fresh mint, chopped
    115g/4oz/1 cup plain (all-purpose) flour
    2–3 pinches of salt
    2.5–5ml/½–1 tsp ground turmeric
    45–60ml/3–4 tbsp cold water
For the ginger and coriander paste
    4 garlic cloves, chopped
    15–25ml/1–1½ tbsp chopped
      fresh root ginger
    ½–4 fresh mild chillies
    ½ large bunch of fresh
      coriander (cilantro)
    30ml/2 tbsp white wine vinegar
    extra virgin olive oil

COOK'S TIP
Serve any leftover paste with meatballs or spread on sandwiches.

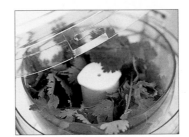

1 To make the paste, put the garlic, ginger and chillies in a food processor and process. Add the coriander, vinegar, oil and salt and process to a purée. Set aside.

2 To make the kubbeh filling, place the saffron and hot water in a small bowl and leave to infuse (steep). Meanwhile, heat the oil in a pan and cook the onion until softened. Put the onion and saffron water in a food processor and blend. Add the lamb, season and blend. Add the vinegar and mint, then chill.

3 To make the kubbeh dough, put the flour, salt and ground turmeric in a food processor, then gradually add the water, processing until it forms a sticky dough. Knead on a floured surface for 5 minutes, wrap in a plastic bag and leave to stand for 30 minutes.

4 Divide the dough into 10–15 pieces. Roll each into a ball, then, using a pasta machine, roll into very thin rounds.

5 Lay the rounds on a well-floured surface. Place a spoonful of filling in the middle of each. Dampen the edges of the dough, then bring them together and seal. Set aside on a floured surface.

6 To make the soup, heat the oil in a pan, add the onion and cook for about 10 minutes, or until softened but not browned. Add half the garlic, the carrot, courgette, celery, if using, cardamom pods and curry powder and cook for 2–3 minutes.

7 Add three of the diced beetroot, the stock, tomatoes, coriander, bay leaves and sugar to the pan. Bring to the boil, then reduce the heat and simmer for about 20 minutes.

8 Add the remaining beetroot, beetroot juice and garlic to the soup. Season with salt and pepper to taste and set aside until ready to serve.

9 To serve, reheat the soup and poach the dumplings in a large pan of salted boiling water for about 4 minutes. Using a slotted spoon, remove the dumplings from the water as they are cooked and place on a plate to keep warm.

10 Ladle the soup into bowls, adding a dash of vinegar to each bowl, then add two or three dumplings and a small spoonful of the ginger and coriander paste to each. Serve immediately.

Per portion: Energy 253Kcal/1061kJ; Protein 12.2g; Carbohydrate 26.6g, of which sugars 10.8g; Fat 11.6g, of which saturates 3.4g; Cholesterol 32mg; Calcium 73mg; Fibre 2.8g; Sodium 90mg.

EGG AND CHEESE DISHES

Although eggs and cheese feature in every one of the recipes that follow, they are not always principal ingredients. In this eclectic collection, Sea Trout Mousse rubs shoulders with Classic Cheese Soufflé and a very up-market omelette that was invented in honour of the novelist Arnold Bennett. Roulades make very good main courses, and this chapter includes a delectable combination of leek roulade with cheese walnut and sweet pepper filling. Many recipes are ideal for vegetarians — if cheese is included, choose a variety made without rennet.

POTATO AND RED PEPPER FRITTATA

A FRITTATA IS LIKE A LARGE OMELETTE. THIS TASTY VERSION IS FILLED WITH POTATOES AND PLENTY OF HERBS. DO USE FRESH MINT IN PREFERENCE TO DRIED IF YOU CAN FIND IT.

2 Whisk together the eggs, mint and seasoning in a bowl, then set aside. Heat the oil in a large frying pan.

3 Add the onion, garlic, peppers and potatoes to the pan and cook, stirring occasionally, for 5 minutes.

4 Pour the egg mixture over the vegetables in the frying pan and stir gently over a low heat.

5 Push the mixture towards the centre of the pan as it cooks to allow the liquid egg to run on to the base. Meanwhile preheat the grill (broiler).

6 When the frittata is lightly set, place the pan under the hot grill for 2–3 minutes until the top is a light golden brown colour.

7 Serve hot or cold, cut into wedges piled high on a serving dish and garnished with sprigs of mint.

SERVES THREE TO FOUR

INGREDIENTS
    450g/1lb small new or
     salad potatoes
    6 eggs
    30ml/2 tbsp chopped
     fresh mint
    30ml/2 tbsp olive oil
    1 onion, chopped
    2 garlic cloves, crushed
    2 red (bell) peppers, seeded and
     coarsely chopped
    salt and ground black pepper
    fresh mint sprigs,
     to garnish

1 Cook the potatoes in their skins in lightly salted, boiling water until just tender. Drain and leave to cool slightly, then cut into thick slices.

Per portion: Energy 374Kcal/1563kJ; Protein 16.7g; Carbohydrate 34.9g, of which sugars 11.3g; Fat 19.4g, of which saturates 4.5g; Cholesterol 381mg; Calcium 87mg; Fibre 3.9g; Sodium 162mg.

FRITTATA WITH LEEK, RED PEPPER AND SPINACH

ALTHOUGH ITALIAN FRITTATA IS GENERALLY SLIGHTLY SOFTER IN TEXTURE, IT IS NOT HUGELY DIFFERENT FROM SPANISH TORTILLA. THIS COMBINATION OF SWEET LEEK, RED PEPPER AND SPINACH IS WONDERFULLY DELICIOUS WITH THE EGG.

SERVES THREE TO FOUR

INGREDIENTS

30ml/2 tbsp olive oil
1 red (bell) pepper, seeded and diced
2.5–5ml/½–1 tsp ground
   toasted cumin
3 leeks (about 450g/1lb),
   thinly sliced
150g/5oz small spinach leaves
45ml/3 tbsp pine nuts, toasted
5 large (US extra large) eggs
15ml/1 tbsp chopped fresh basil
15ml/1 tbsp chopped fresh flat
   leaf parsley
salt and ground black pepper
watercress, to garnish
50g/2oz/⅔ cup grated Parmesan
   cheese, to serve (optional)

1 Heat a frying pan and add the oil. Add the red pepper and cook over a medium heat, stirring occasionally, for 6–8 minutes, until soft and beginning to brown. Add 2.5ml/½ tsp of the cumin and cook for another 1–2 minutes.

2 Stir in the leeks, then part-cover the pan and cook gently for about 5 minutes, until the leeks have softened and collapsed. Season with salt and ground black pepper.

3 Add the spinach and cover. Leave the spinach to wilt in the steam for 3–4 minutes, then stir to mix it into the vegetables, adding the pine nuts.

4 Beat the eggs with salt, pepper, the remaining cumin, basil and parsley. Add to the pan and cook over a gentle heat until the bottom of the omelette sets and turns golden brown. Pull the edges of the omelette away from the sides of the pan as it cooks and tilt the pan so that the uncooked egg runs underneath.

5 Preheat the grill (broiler). Flash the frittata under the hot grill to set the egg on top, but do not let it become too brown. Cut the frittata into wedges and serve warm, garnished with watercress and sprinkled with Parmesan, if using.

VARIATION
A delicious way to serve frittata is to pack it into a slightly hollowed-out crusty loaf and then drizzle it with a little extra virgin olive oil. Wrap tightly in clear film (plastic wrap) and leave to stand for 1–2 hours before cutting into thick slices. It is ideal picnic fare.

Per portion: Energy 268Kcal/1115kJ; Protein 15.5g; Carbohydrate 9.3g, of which sugars 8g; Fat 19g, of which saturates 2g; Cholesterol 0mg; Calcium 132mg; Fibre 5.5g; Sodium 265mg.

LEEK ROULADE WITH CHEESE, WALNUT AND SWEET PEPPER FILLING

THIS ROULADE IS SURPRISINGLY EASY TO PREPARE, AND IT MAKES A GOOD MAIN COURSE WHEN SERVED WITH HOME-MADE TOMATO SAUCE. IT IS ALSO EXCELLENT AS PART OF A BUFFET.

SERVES FOUR TO SIX

INGREDIENTS
   butter or oil, for greasing
   30ml/2 tbsp fine dry
     white breadcrumbs
   75g/3oz/1 cup finely grated
     Parmesan cheese
   50g/2oz/¼ cup butter
   2 leeks, thinly sliced
   40g/1½oz/⅓ cup plain (all-
     purpose) flour
   250ml/8fl oz/1 cup milk
   5ml/1 tsp Dijon mustard
   1.5ml/¼ tsp freshly grated nutmeg
   2 large (US extra large) eggs,
     separated, plus 1 egg white
   2.5ml/½ tsp cream of tartar
   salt and ground black pepper
   rocket (arugula) and balsamic
     dressing, to serve
For the filling
   2 large red (bell) peppers
   350g/12oz/1½ cups ricotta cheese,
   90g/3½oz/scant 1 cup
     chopped walnuts
   4 spring onions (scallions), chopped
   15g/½oz/½ cup fresh basil leaves

1 Grease and line a 30 × 23cm/ 12 × 9in Swiss roll tin (jelly roll pan) with baking parchment, then sprinkle with the breadcrumbs and 30ml/2 tbsp of the grated Parmesan. Preheat the oven to 190°C/375°F/Gas 5.

2 Melt the butter in a pan and cook the leeks for 5 minutes, until softened.

3 Stir in the flour and cook over a low heat, stirring constantly, for 2 minutes, then gradually stir in the milk. Cook for 3–4 minutes, stirring constantly to make a thick sauce.

4 Stir in the mustard and nutmeg and season with salt and plenty of pepper. Reserve 30–45ml/2–3 tbsp of the remaining Parmesan, then stir the rest into the sauce. Cool slightly.

5 Beat the egg yolks into the sauce. In a scrupulously clean bowl, whisk the egg whites and cream of tartar until stiff. Stir 2–3 spoonfuls of the egg white into the leek mixture, then carefully fold in the remaining egg white.

6 Pour the mixture into the tin and gently level it out using a spatula. Bake for 15–18 minutes, until risen and just firm to a light touch in the centre. If the roulade is to be served hot, increase the oven temperature to 200°C/400°F/Gas 6 after removing the roulade.

7 Meanwhile, heat the grill (broiler). Halve and seed the peppers, then grill (broil) them, skin sides uppermost, until black. Place in a bowl, cover and leave for 10 minutes. Peel and cut into strips.

8 Beat the cheese with the walnuts and spring onions. Chop half the basil and beat it into the mixture. Season to taste.

9 Place a large sheet of baking parchment on the work surface and sprinkle with the remaining Parmesan. Turn out the roulade on to it. Strip off the lining paper and allow the roulade to cool slightly. Spread the cheese mixture over it and top with the red pepper strips. Tear the remaining basil leaves and sprinkle them over the top.

10 Using the parchment as a guide, roll up the roulade and roll it on to a serving platter. If serving hot, roll the roulade on to a baking sheet, cover with a tent of foil and bake for 15–20 minutes. Serve with rocket and drizzle with dressing.

Per portion: Energy 602Kcal/2500kJ; Protein 32.9g; Carbohydrate 22.3g, of which sugars 13.7g; Fat 44.1g, of which saturates 18g; Cholesterol 184mg; Calcium 486mg; Fibre 4.3g; Sodium 740mg.

SOFT TACOS WITH SPICED OMELETTE

SERVED HOT, WARM OR COLD, THESE TACOS MAKE EASY FOOD ON THE MOVE FOR YOUNGER MEMBERS OF THE FAMILY, WHEN THEY NEED SOMETHING NOURISHING TO TAKE ON A PICNIC, HIKE OR CYCLE RIDE.

SERVES FOUR

INGREDIENTS
    30ml/2 tbsp sunflower oil
    50g/2oz/1 cup beansprouts
    50g/2oz carrots, cut into
        thin sticks
    25g/1oz Chinese cabbage, chopped
    15ml/1 tbsp light soy sauce
    4 eggs
    1 small spring onion (scallion),
        thinly sliced
    5ml/1 tsp Cajun seasoning
    25g/1oz/2 tbsp butter
    4 soft flour tortillas, warmed in
        the oven or microwave
    salt and ground black pepper

1 Heat the oil in a small frying pan and stir-fry the beansprouts, carrot sticks and chopped cabbage until they begin to soften. Add the soy sauce, stir to combine and set aside.

2 Place the eggs, sliced spring onion, Cajun seasoning, salt and ground black pepper in a bowl, and beat together. Melt the butter in a small pan until it sizzles. Add the beaten eggs and cook over a gentle heat, stirring constantly, until almost firm.

3 Divide the vegetables and scrambled egg evenly among the tortillas, fold up into cones or parcels and serve. For travelling, the tacos can be wrapped in kitchen paper and foil.

VARIATION
Fill warm pitta breads with this spicy omelette mixture. Mini pitta breads are perfect for younger children who may find the folded tacos difficult to handle.

COOK'S TIP
You can buy fresh soft tortillas in large supermarkets. They freeze well, so keep a packet or two in the freezer.

FRENCH COUNTRY-STYLE EGGS

THIS VARIATION ON AN OMELETTE COOKS THE "FILLING" IN THE OMELETTE MIXTURE ITSELF. YOU CAN INCORPORATE LOTS OF DIFFERENT INGREDIENTS, SUCH AS LEFTOVER VEGETABLES.

SERVES TWO

INGREDIENTS
    45–75ml/3–5 tbsp sunflower oil
    50g/2oz thick bacon rashers (strips)
        or pieces, rinds removed
        and chopped
    2 thick slices of bread,
        cut into small cubes
    1 small onion, chopped
    1–2 celery sticks, thinly sliced
    115g/4oz cooked potato, diced
    5 eggs, beaten
    2 garlic cloves, crushed
    handful of young spinach or sorrel
        leaves, stalks removed,
        torn into pieces
    few fresh parsley sprigs, chopped
    salt and ground black pepper

1 Heat the oil in a large heavy frying pan, and cook the bacon and bread cubes until they are crisp and turning golden. Add the chopped onion, celery and diced potato, and continue cooking over a low heat, stirring frequently until all the vegetables have softened and are beginning to turn golden brown.

2 Beat the eggs with the garlic and seasoning, and pour over the vegetables. When the underside is beginning to set, add the spinach or sorrel. Cook until they have wilted and the omelette is only just soft in the middle. Fold the omelette in half and slide it out of the pan. Serve topped with the parsley, if you like.

Top per portion: Energy 280Kcal/1168kJ; Protein 9.5g; Carbohydrate 24.2g, of which sugars 2g; Fat 16.7g, of which saturates 5.5g; Cholesterol 204mg; Calcium 80mg; Fibre 1.5g; Sodium 217mg.
Below per portion: Energy 488Kcal/2034kJ; Protein 23.7g; Carbohydrate 26.2g, of which sugars 3.4g; Fat 32.7g, of which saturates 6.7g; Cholesterol 483mg; Calcium 130mg; Fibre 2.1g; Sodium 649mg.

CLASSIC CHEESE SOUFFLÉ

A LIGHT, DELICATE, MELT-IN-THE-MOUTH CHEESE SOUFFLÉ MAKES ONE OF THE MOST DELIGHTFUL BRUNCHES IMAGINABLE. ALL YOU NEED TO GO WITH IT IS SALAD, A GLASS OF GOOD WINE AND PLENTY OF TIME TO RELAX AND ENJOY A LAZY WEEKEND.

SERVES TWO TO THREE

INGREDIENTS
    50g/2oz/¼ cup butter
    30–45ml/2–3 tbsp dried breadcrumbs
    200ml/7fl oz/scant 1 cup milk
    30g/1¼oz/3 tbsp plain (all-
        purpose) flour
    pinch of cayenne pepper
    2.5ml/½ tsp mustard powder
    50g/2oz/½ cup mature (sharp) grated
        Cheddar cheese
    25g/1oz/⅓ cup freshly grated
        Parmesan cheese
    4 eggs, separated, plus 1 egg white
    salt and ground black pepper

2 Heat the milk in a large pan. Add the remaining butter, flour and cayenne, with the mustard powder. Bring to the boil over a low heat, whisking steadily until the mixture thickens to a smooth sauce.

5 Add a few spoonfuls of the beaten egg whites to the sauce to lighten it. Beat well, then tip the rest of the whites into the pan and, with a large metal spoon, gently fold in the egg whites, using a figure-of-eight movement to combine the mixtures.

1 Preheat the oven to 190°C/375°F/Gas 5. Melt 15ml/1 tbsp of the butter and use to grease a 1.2 litre/2 pint/5 cup soufflé dish thoroughly. Coat the inside of the dish with breadcrumbs. Shake out any excess.

3 Simmer the sauce for a minute or two, then turn off the heat and whisk in all the Cheddar and half the Parmesan. Cool a little, then beat in the egg yolks. Check the seasoning; the mixture should be well seasoned. Set aside.

6 Pour the mixture into the prepared soufflé dish, level the top and, to help the soufflé rise evenly, run your finger around the inside rim of the dish.

7 Place the dish on a baking sheet. Sprinkle the remaining Parmesan over the top of the soufflé mixture and bake for about 25 minutes, until risen and golden brown. Serve immediately.

VARIATIONS
• Crumbled blue cheese, such as Stilton, Shropshire Blue or Fourme d'Ambert, will produce a soufflé with a much stronger, sharper flavour.
• This soufflé can also be served as a more substantial main meal by adding a few extra ingredients. Try putting a layer of chopped vegetables, such as ratatouille or sautéed mushrooms, at the base of the dish before adding the cheese mixture. Bake as above.

4 Whisk the egg whites in a large grease-free bowl until they form soft, glossy peaks. Do not overbeat or the whites will become grainy and difficult to fold in.

COOK'S TIP
It is important to serve soufflé the moment it is cooked and taken from the oven. Otherwise, the wonderful puffed top may sink before it reaches the expectantly waiting diners.

Per portion: Energy 654Kcal/2721kJ; Protein 31.9g; Carbohydrate 28.2g, of which sugars 5.5g; Fat 46.1g, of which saturates 25.3g; Cholesterol 476mg; Calcium 558mg; Fibre 0.8g; Sodium 797mg.

SOUFFLÉ OMELETTE WITH MUSHROOMS

A LIGHT-AS-AIR OMELETTE MAKES AN IDEAL MEAL FOR ONE, ESPECIALLY WITH THIS DELICIOUS FILLING. USE A COMBINATION OF DIFFERENT MUSHROOMS IF YOU LIKE.

SERVES ONE

INGREDIENTS
2 eggs, separated
15g/½oz/1 tbsp butter
flat leaf parsley or coriander
  (cilantro) leaves, to garnish
For the mushroom sauce
15g/½oz/1 tbsp butter
75g/3oz/generous 1 cup button
  (white) mushrooms, thinly sliced
15ml/1 tbsp plain (all-purpose) flour
85–120ml/3–4fl oz/⅓–½ cup milk
5ml/1 tsp chopped fresh
  parsley (optional)
salt and ground black pepper

1 To make the mushroom sauce, melt the butter in a pan or frying pan and add the sliced mushrooms. Cook gently for 4–5 minutes, stirring occasionally, until tender and golden.

2 Stir in the flour, then gradually add the milk, stirring constantly. Cook until boiling and thickened. Add the parsley, if using, and season to taste with salt and pepper. Keep warm.

3 Beat the egg yolks with 15ml/1 tbsp water and season with a little salt and pepper. Whisk the egg whites until stiff, then fold into the egg yolks using a metal spoon. Preheat the grill (broiler).

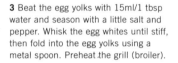

4 Melt the butter in a large frying pan and pour the egg mixture into the pan. Cook over a gentle heat for 2–4 minutes. Place the frying pan under the grill and cook for a further 3–4 minutes until the top is golden brown.

5 Slide the omelette on to a warmed serving plate, pour the mushroom sauce over the top and fold the omelette in half. Serve, garnished with parsley or coriander leaves.

COOK'S TIP
For extra flavour, add a few drops of Worcestershire sauce to the mushrooms as they are cooking.

Per portion: Energy 566Kcal/2348kJ; Protein 18.9g; Carbohydrate 20.1g, of which sugars 4.7g; Fat 46.1g, of which saturates 25g; Cholesterol 471mg; Calcium 199mg; Fibre 1.4g; Sodium 423mg.

OMELETTE ARNOLD BENNETT

CREATED FOR THE AUTHOR ARNOLD BENNETT, WHO FREQUENTLY DINED AT THE SAVOY HOTEL IN LONDON, THIS CREAMY, SMOKED HADDOCK SOUFFLÉ OMELETTE IS NOW SERVED ALL OVER THE WORLD.

SERVES TWO

INGREDIENTS

175g/6oz smoked haddock fillet,
   poached and drained
50g/2oz/4 tbsp butter, diced
175ml/6fl oz/¾ cup whipping or
   double (heavy) cream
4 eggs, separated
40g/1½oz/⅓ cup grated mature
   (sharp) Cheddar cheese
ground black pepper
watercress, to garnish

COOK'S TIP

Try to buy traditional cold-smoked haddock that does not contain artificial colouring for this recipe. Besides being better for you, it gives the omelette a lighter, more attractive colour.

1 Remove the skin and any bones from the haddock fillet and discard. Carefully flake the flesh using a fork.

2 Melt half the butter with 60ml/4 tbsp of the cream in a fairly small non-stick pan, then add the flaked fish and stir together gently. Cover the pan with a lid, remove it from the heat and set aside to cool completely.

3 Mix the egg yolks with 15ml/1 tbsp cream. Add pepper, then stir into the fish. In a separate bowl, mix the cheese and the remaining cream. Stiffly whisk the egg whites, then fold into the fish mixture. Heat the remaining butter in an omelette pan, add the fish mixture and cook until browned underneath. Pour the cheese mixture over and grill (broil) until bubbling. Garnish and serve.

Per portion: Energy 821Kcal/3396kJ; Protein 36.1g; Carbohydrate 2.6g, of which sugars 2.6g; Fat 74g, of which saturates 42.6g; Cholesterol 577mg; Calcium 280mg; Fibre 0g; Sodium 1123mg.

PRAWN, EGG AND AVOCADO MOUSSES

*LIGHT AND CREAMY, WITH LOTS OF TEXTURE AND A DELICIOUS COMBINATION OF FLAVOURS,
THESE LITTLE MOUSSES ARE BEST SERVED AS A LIGHT LUNCH ON THE DAY YOU MAKE THEM.*

SERVES SIX

INGREDIENTS
olive oil, for greasing
11g/¼oz sachet (envelope) gelatine
juice and rind of 1 lemon
60ml/4 tbsp good mayonnaise
60ml/4 tbsp chopped fresh dill
5ml/1 tsp anchovy essence (extract)
5ml/1 tsp Worcestershire sauce
4 eggs, hard-boiled, shelled
    and chopped
175g/6oz/1 cup cooked, peeled
    prawns (shrimp), chopped if large
1 large ripe but just firm avocado,
    peeled, stoned (pitted) and diced
250ml/8fl oz/1 cup double (heavy) or
    whipping cream, lightly whipped
2 egg whites
salt and ground black pepper
fresh dill sprigs, to garnish
hot bread or toast, to serve

1 Lightly grease six small ramekins, then
wrap a piece of greaseproof (waxed)
paper tightly around each of the dishes
to form a collar. Make sure that the paper
comes well above the top of the dish,
allowing plenty of room for the mousse
to stand above the top of the dish.
Secure firmly with tape so that the
paper will support the mousse as it sets.
If you prefer, prepare one small soufflé
dish rather than individual ramekins.

2 Place the gelatine, lemon juice and
15ml/1 tbsp hot water in a small bowl,
and place over a pan of hot water. Stir
until the mixture becomes clear. Cool
slightly, then blend in the lemon rind,
mayonnaise, dill and sauces.

3 Mix the chopped hard-boiled eggs,
prawns and avocado in a medium bowl.
Stir in the gelatine mixture, then fold in
the whipped cream. Whisk the egg
whites until holding soft peaks and fold
into the mixture with seasoning to taste.
Spoon into the ramekins and chill for
about 4 hours. Garnish with dill and
serve with hot bread or toast.

COOK'S TIP
Other fish or shellfish can make a good
alternative to prawns. Try substituting
the same quantity of smoked trout or
cooked crab meat.

Per portion: Energy 431Kcal/1778kJ; Protein 7.5g; Carbohydrate 1.7g, of which sugars 1.2g; Fat 43.9g, of which saturates 17.5g; Cholesterol 131mg; Calcium 50mg; Fibre 0.8g; Sodium 195mg.

SMOKED FISH AND ASPARAGUS MOUSSE

THIS ELEGANT MOUSSE LOOKS VERY SPECIAL WITH ITS STUDDING OF ASPARAGUS AND SMOKED SALMON.
SERVE A MUSTARD AND DILL DRESSING SEPARATELY IF YOU LIKE.

SERVES EIGHT

INGREDIENTS

15ml/1 tbsp powdered gelatine
juice of 1 lemon
105ml/7 tbsp fish stock
50g/2oz/¼ cup butter, plus extra
   for greasing
2 shallots, finely chopped
225g/8oz smoked trout fillets
105ml/7 tbsp sour cream
225g/8oz/1 cup low-fat cream cheese
   or cottage cheese
1 egg white
12 spinach leaves, blanched
12 fresh asparagus spears,
   lightly cooked
115g/4oz smoked salmon, cut into
   long strips
salt
shredded beetroot (beet) and leaves,
   to garnish

4 Grease a 1 litre/1¾ pint/4 cup loaf tin (pan) or terrine with butter, then line it with the spinach leaves. Carefully spread half the trout mousse over the spinach-covered base, arrange the asparagus spears on top, then cover with the remaining trout mousse.

5 Arrange the smoked salmon strips lengthways on the mousse and fold over the overhanging spinach leaves. Cover with clear film (plastic wrap) and chill for 4 hours, until set. To serve, remove the clear film, turn out on to a serving dish and garnish.

1 Sprinkle the gelatine over the lemon juice and leave until spongy. In a small pan, heat the fish stock, then add the soaked gelatine and stir to dissolve completely. Set aside. Melt the butter in a small pan, add the shallots and cook gently until softened but not coloured.

2 Break up the smoked trout fillets and put them in a food processor with the shallots, sour cream, stock mixture and cream or cottage cheese. Process until smooth, then spoon into a bowl.

3 In a clean bowl, beat the egg white with a pinch of salt to soft peaks. Fold into the fish. Cover the bowl and chill for 30 minutes, or until starting to set.

Per portion: Energy 174Kcal/723kJ; Protein 15.8g; Carbohydrate 2.8g, of which sugars 2.6g; Fat 11g, of which saturates 6g; Cholesterol 58mg; Calcium 75mg; Fibre 0.8g; Sodium 432mg.

STRIPED FISH TERRINE

SERVE THIS ATTRACTIVE TERRINE COLD OR JUST WARM, WITH A HOLLANDAISE SAUCE IF YOU LIKE.
IT IS IDEAL FOR A SUMMER LUNCHEON OR BUFFET.

SERVES EIGHT

INGREDIENTS

  15ml/1 tbsp sunflower oil
  450g/1lb salmon fillet, skinned
  450g/1lb sole fillets, skinned
  3 egg whites
  105ml/7 tbsp double (heavy) cream
  15ml/1 tbsp finely chopped
    fresh chives
  juice of 1 lemon
  115g/4oz/1 cup fresh or frozen
    peas, cooked
  5ml/1 tsp chopped fresh mint leaves
  salt, ground white pepper and
    grated nutmeg
  thinly sliced cucumber, salad cress
    and chives, to garnish

1 Grease a 1 litre/1¾ pint/4 cup loaf tin (pan) or terrine with the oil. Slice the salmon thinly, then cut it and the sole into long strips, 2.5cm/1in wide. Preheat the oven to 200°C/400°F/Gas 6.

3 In a grease-free bowl, beat the egg whites with a pinch of salt until they form soft peaks. Purée the remaining sole in a food processor. Spoon into a mixing bowl, season, then fold in two-thirds of the egg whites, followed by two-thirds of the cream. Put half the mixture into a second bowl; stir in the chives. Add nutmeg to the first bowl.

6 Add the salmon mixture, then finish with the plain sole mixture. Cover with the overhanging fish fillets and make a lid of oiled foil. Stand the terrine in a roasting pan and pour in enough boiling water to come halfway up the sides.

7 Bake for 15–20 minutes, until the top fillets are just cooked and the mousse feels springy. Remove the foil, lay a wire rack over the top of the terrine and invert both rack and terrine on to a lipped baking sheet to catch the cooking juices that drain out. Keep these to make fish stock or soup.

8 Leaving the tin in place, let the terrine stand for about 15 minutes, then turn the terrine over again. Invert it on to a serving dish and lift off the tin carefully. Serve warm, or chill in the refrigerator first and serve cold. Garnish with thinly sliced cucumber, salad cress and chives before serving.

4 Purée the remaining salmon, scrape it into a bowl; add the lemon juice. Fold in the remaining whites, then the cream.

2 Line the terrine neatly with alternate slices of salmon and sole, leaving the ends overhanging the edge. You should be left with about a third of the salmon and half the sole.

5 Process the peas and mint. Season the mixture and spread it over the base of the terrine, smoothing the surface with a spatula. Spoon over the sole with chives mixture and spread evenly.

COOK'S TIPS
• Pop the salmon into the freezer about an hour before slicing it. If it is almost frozen, it will be much easier to slice.
• You can line the tin or terrine with oven-safe clear film (plastic wrap) after greasing and before adding the salmon and sole strips. This makes it a little easier to turn out the terrine but is not strictly necessary.

Per portion: Energy 245Kcal/1019kJ; Protein 23.8g; Carbohydrate 1.9g, of which sugars 0.6g; Fat 15.8g, of which saturates 5.7g; Cholesterol 74mg; Calcium 38mg; Fibre 0.7g; Sodium 107mg.

QUENELLES OF SOLE

TRADITIONALLY, THESE LIGHT FISH "DUMPLINGS" ARE MADE WITH PIKE, BUT THEY ARE EVEN BETTER MADE WITH SOLE OR OTHER WHITE FISH. IF YOU ARE FEELING EXTRAVAGANT, SERVE THEM WITH A CREAMY SHELLFISH SAUCE STUDDED WITH CRAYFISH TAILS OR PRAWNS.

SERVES SIX

INGREDIENTS
450g/1lb sole fillets, skinned and cut
   into large pieces
4 egg whites
600ml/1 pint/2½ cups double
   (heavy) cream
salt, ground white pepper and
   grated nutmeg
For the sauce
1 small shallot, finely chopped
60ml/4 tbsp dry vermouth
120ml/4fl oz/½ cup fish stock
150ml/¼ pint/⅔ cup double
   (heavy) cream
50g/2oz/¼ cup butter, diced
chopped fresh parsley, to garnish

1 Check the sole for stray bones, then put the pieces in a blender or food processor. Add a generous pinch of salt and a grinding of pepper. Switch on and, with the motor running, add the egg whites one at a time through the feeder tube to make a smooth purée. Press the purée through a metal sieve placed over a bowl. Stand the bowl of purée in a larger bowl and surround it with plenty of crushed ice or ice cubes.

2 Whip the cream until very thick and floppy, but not stiff. Gradually fold it into the fish mousse, making sure each spoonful has been absorbed completely before adding the next. Season with salt and pepper, then stir in nutmeg to taste. Cover the bowl of mousse and transfer it, still in its bowl of ice, to the refrigerator. Chill for several hours.

3 To make the sauce, combine the shallot, vermouth and fish stock in a small pan. Bring to the boil and cook until reduced by half. Add the cream and boil again until the sauce has the consistency of single (light) cream. Strain, return to the pan and whisk in the butter, one piece at a time, until the sauce is very creamy. Season and keep hot, but do not let it boil.

4 Bring a wide shallow pan of lightly salted water to the boil, then reduce the heat so that the water surface barely trembles. Using two tablespoons dipped in hot water, shape the fish mousse into ovals. As each quenelle is shaped, slip it into the simmering water.

5 Poach the quenelles, in batches, for 8–10 minutes, until they feel just firm to the touch, but are still slightly creamy inside. As each is cooked, lift it out on a slotted spoon, drain on kitchen paper and keep hot. When all the quenelles are cooked, arrange them on heated plates. Pour the sauce around. Serve garnished with parsley.

COOK'S TIP
Keep the heat low when poaching, as quenelles disintegrate in boiling water.

Per portion: Energy 767Kcal/3165kJ; Protein 17.6g; Carbohydrate 2.5g, of which sugars 2.5g; Fat 75.3g, of which saturates 46.1g; Cholesterol 227mg; Calcium 86mg; Fibre 0g; Sodium 195mg.

SEA TROUT MOUSSE

THIS DELICIOUSLY CREAMY MOUSSE MAKES A LITTLE SEA TROUT GO A LONG WAY. IT IS EQUALLY GOOD MADE WITH FRESH SALMON FILLETS IF SEA TROUT IS UNAVAILABLE.

SERVES SIX

INGREDIENTS

250g/9oz sea trout fillet
120ml/4fl oz/½ cup fish stock
2 gelatine leaves, or 15ml/1 tbsp
   powdered gelatine
juice of ½ lemon
30ml/2 tbsp dry sherry or
   dry vermouth
30ml/2 tbsp freshly grated Parmesan
300ml/½ pint/1¼ cups
   whipping cream
2 egg whites
15ml/1 tbsp sunflower oil
salt and ground white pepper
For the garnish
5cm/2in piece of cucumber, with
   peel, thinly sliced and halved
fresh dill or chervil

3 When the trout is cool enough to handle, remove the skin and flake the flesh. Pour the stock into a food processor or blender. Process briefly, then gradually add the flaked trout, lemon juice, sherry or vermouth and Parmesan through the feeder tube, continuing to process the mixture until it is smooth. Scrape into a large bowl and leave to cool completely.

4 Lightly whip the cream in a bowl; fold it into the cold trout mixture. Season to taste, then cover with clear film (plastic wrap) and chill until the mousse is just beginning to set. It should have the consistency of mayonnaise.

5 In a grease-free bowl, beat the egg whites with a pinch of salt until softly peaking. Using a large metal spoon, stir one-third into the trout mixture to slacken it, then fold in the rest.

6 Lightly grease six ramekins with the sunflower oil. Divide the mousse among the ramekins and level the surface. Place in the refrigerator for 2–3 hours, until set. Just before serving, arrange a few slices of cucumber and a small herb sprig on each mousse and add a little chopped dill or chervil.

1 Put the sea trout in a shallow pan. Pour in the fish stock and heat to simmering point. Poach the fish for 3–4 minutes, until it is lightly cooked. Strain the stock into a jug (pitcher) and leave the trout to cool slightly.

2 Add the gelatine to the hot stock and stir until it has dissolved completely. Set aside until required.

COOK'S TIP
Serve the mousse with Melba toast, if you like. Toast thin slices of bread on both sides under the grill (broiler), then cut off the crusts and carefully slice each piece of toast in half horizontally. Return to the grill pan, untoasted sides up, and grill (broil) again. The thin slices will swiftly brown and curl.

Per portion: Energy 286Kcal/1181kJ; Protein 12g; Carbohydrate 1.5g, of which sugars 1.5g; Fat 25.2g, of which saturates 13.9g; Cholesterol 58mg; Calcium 94mg; Fibre 0g; Sodium 111mg.

SALADS

These are salads in a starring role — main course dishes that can be served solo or used as the main attractions on a buffet table. For a summer lunch, Chicken and Mango Salad would be an excellent choice, or you might like to celebrate a special occasion with a magnificent Insalata di Mare. As the weather cools, introduce a hint of warmth with a Warm Dressed Salad with Poached Eggs or Seared Swordfish with Citrus Dressing. For a picnic or packed lunch, Bean Salad with Tuna and Red Onion would be the ideal choice. Pack the dressing separately and add it about half an hour before serving.

PERUVIAN SALAD

THIS REALLY IS A SPECTACULAR-LOOKING SALAD. IT COULD BE SERVED AS A SIDE DISH OR WOULD MAKE A DELICIOUS LIGHT LUNCH. IN PERU, WHITE RICE WOULD BE USED, BUT BROWN RICE ADDS AN INTERESTING TEXTURE AND FLAVOUR.

SERVES FOUR

INGREDIENTS
225g/8oz/2 cups cooked long grain
    brown or white rice
15ml/1 tbsp chopped fresh parsley
1 red (bell) pepper
1 small onion, sliced
olive oil, for sprinkling
115g/4oz green beans, halved
50g/2oz/½ cup baby corn
4 quail's eggs, hard-boiled
25–50g/1–2oz Spanish ham, cut into
    thin slices (optional)
1 small avocado
lemon juice, for sprinkling
75g/3oz mixed salad leaves
15ml/1 tbsp capers
about 10 stuffed olives, halved
For the dressing
1 garlic clove, crushed
60ml/4 tbsp olive oil
45ml/3 tbsp sunflower oil
30ml/2 tbsp lemon juice
45ml/3 tbsp natural (plain) yogurt
2.5ml/½ tsp mustard
2.5ml/½ tsp sugar
salt and freshly ground black pepper

1 Make the dressing by placing all the ingredients in a bowl and whisking with a fork until smooth. Alternatively, shake the ingredients together in a jam jar.

2 Put the cooked rice into a large, glass salad bowl and spoon in about half the dressing. Add the chopped parsley, stir well to mix and set aside in a cool place.

3 Cut the pepper in half, remove the seeds and pith, then place the halves, cut side down, in a small roasting pan. Add the onion rings. Sprinkle the onion with a little olive oil, place the pan under a hot grill (broiler) and cook for 5–6 minutes, until the pepper blackens and blisters and the onion turns golden. You may need to stir the onion once or twice so that it grills (broils) evenly.

4 Stir the onion in with the rice. Put the pepper in a plastic bag and knot the bag. When the steam has loosened the skin on the pepper halves and they are cool enough to handle, peel them and cut the flesh into thin strips.

COOK'S TIP
This dish looks particularly attractive if served in a deep, glass salad bowl. Guests can then see the various layers, starting with the white rice, then the green salad leaves, topped by the bright colours of peppers, corn, eggs and olives.

5 Cook the green beans in boiling water for 2 minutes, then add the corn and cook for 1–2 minutes more, until tender. Drain both vegetables, refresh them under cold water, then drain again. Place in a large mixing bowl and add the red pepper strips, quails' eggs and ham, if using.

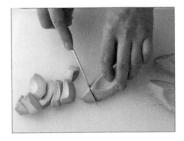

6 Peel the avocado, remove the stone (pit), and cut the flesh into slices or chunks. Sprinkle with the lemon juice to prevent discoloration. Put the salad leaves in a separate mixing bowl, add the avocado and mix lightly. Arrange the salad on top of the rice.

7 Stir about 45ml/3 tbsp of the remaining dressing into the green bean and pepper mixture. Pile this on top of the salad.

8 Sprinkle the capers and stuffed olives on top and serve the salad with the remaining dressing.

Per portion: Energy 404Kcal/1675kJ; Protein 6.3g; Carbohydrate 25.6g, of which sugars 6.9g; Fat 31.3g, of which saturates 5.2g; Cholesterol 58mg; Calcium 75mg; Fibre 3.7g; Sodium 598mg.

CAESAR SALAD

THIS MUCH-ENJOYED SALAD WAS CREATED BY CAESAR CORDONI IN TIJUANA IN 1924. BE SURE TO USE CRISP LETTUCE AND ADD THE SOFT EGGS AND GARLIC CROÛTONS AT THE LAST MINUTE.

3 Add the remaining olive oil to the salad leaves and season with salt and pepper. Toss to coat well.

4 Break the soft-boiled eggs on top. Sprinkle with the lemon juice and toss to combine the ingredients.

5 Add the grated Parmesan cheese and anchovies, if using, then toss again.

6 Sprinkle the croûtons on top of the salad and serve immediately.

COOK'S TIPS
To make a tangier dressing, mix the olive oil with 30ml/2 tbsp white wine vinegar, 2.5ml/½ tsp mustard, 5ml/1 tsp sugar, and salt and pepper.

SERVES SIX

INGREDIENTS

175ml/6fl oz/¾ cup salad oil, preferably olive oil
115g/4oz/2 cups French or Italian bread, cut in 2.5cm/1in cubes
1 large garlic clove, crushed with the flat side of a knife
1 cos or romaine lettuce
2 eggs, boiled for 1 minute
120ml/4fl oz/½ cup lemon juice
50g/2oz/⅔ cup freshly grated Parmesan cheese
6 anchovy fillets, drained and finely chopped (optional)
salt and ground black pepper

1 Heat 50ml/2fl oz/¼ cup of the oil in a frying pan. Add the bread and garlic and cook, stirring constantly, until the cubes are golden brown. Drain on kitchen paper and discard the garlic.

2 Tear large lettuce leaves into smaller pieces. Put all the lettuce in a bowl.

Per portion: Energy 307Kcal/1272kJ; Protein 8g; Carbohydrate 11.7g, of which sugars 1.4g; Fat 25.7g, of which saturates 5.4g; Cholesterol 84mg; Calcium 149mg; Fibre 0.7g; Sodium 230mg.

WARM DRESSED SALAD <u>WITH</u> POACHED EGGS

SOFT POACHED EGGS, CHILLI, HOT CROÛTONS AND COOL, CRISP SALAD LEAVES MAKE A LIVELY AND UNUSUAL COMBINATION. THIS DELICIOUS SALAD IS PERFECT FOR A SUMMER LUNCH.

SERVES TWO

INGREDIENTS
  ½ small loaf Granary (whole-
    wheat) bread
  45ml/3 tbsp chilli oil
  2 eggs
  115g/4oz mixed salad leaves
  45ml/3 tbsp extra virgin olive oil
  2 garlic cloves, crushed
  15ml/1 tbsp balsamic vinegar
  50g/2oz Parmesan cheese, shaved
  ground black pepper (optional)

1 Carefully cut the crust from the Granary loaf and discard. Cut the bread into 2.5cm/1in cubes.

2 Heat the chilli oil in a large frying pan. Add the bread cubes and cook for about 5 minutes, tossing the cubes occasionally, until they are crisp and golden brown all over.

COOK'S TIP
If you are very sensitive to spicy flavours, cook the croûtons in olive oil or a nut oil, such as walnut or hazelnut, rather than using chilli oil.

3 Meanwhile, bring a pan of water to the boil. Break each egg into a jug (pitcher) and carefully slide into the water, one at a time. Gently poach the eggs for about 4 minutes until cooked.

4 Divide the salad leaves between two plates. Remove the croûtons from the pan and arrange them over the leaves.

5 Wipe the pan clean with kitchen paper. Then heat the olive oil in the pan, add the garlic and vinegar and cook over high heat for 1 minute. Pour the warm dressing over the salads.

6 Place a poached egg on each salad. Top with thin Parmesan shavings and a little ground black pepper, if you like.

Per portion: Energy 730Kcal/3042kJ; Protein 26.2g; Carbohydrate 48.4g, of which sugars 3.9g; Fat 49.3g, of which saturates 12.1g; Cholesterol 215mg; Calcium 556mg; Fibre 3.8g; Sodium 890mg.

THAI PRAWN SALAD <u>WITH</u> GARLIC DRESSING <u>AND</u> FRIZZLED SHALLOTS

IN THIS INTENSELY FLAVOURED SALAD, PRAWNS AND MANGO ARE PARTNERED WITH A SWEET-SOUR GARLIC DRESSING HEIGHTENED WITH THE HOT TASTE OF CHILLI. THE CRISP FRIZZLED SHALLOTS ARE A TRADITIONAL ADDITION TO THAI SALADS.

SERVES FOUR TO SIX

INGREDIENTS
  675g/1½lb raw prawns (shrimp),
    peeled and deveined with tails on
  finely shredded rind of 1 lime
  ½ fresh red chilli, seeded and
    finely chopped
  30ml/2 tbsp olive oil, plus extra
    for brushing
  1 ripe but firm mango
  2 carrots, cut into long thin shreds
  10cm/4in piece cucumber, sliced
  1 small red onion, halved and
    thinly sliced
  a few fresh coriander (cilantro) sprigs
  a few fresh mint sprigs
  45ml/3 tbsp roasted peanuts,
    coarsely chopped
  4 large shallots, thinly sliced and
    fried until crisp in 30ml/2 tbsp
    groundnut (peanut) oil
  salt and ground black pepper
For the dressing
  1 large garlic clove, chopped
  10–15ml/2–3 tsp caster
    (superfine) sugar
  juice of 2 limes
  15–30ml/1–2 tbsp Thai fish sauce
  1 fresh red chilli, seeded
  5–10ml/1–2 tsp light rice vinegar

1 Place the prawns in a glass or china dish and add the lime rind and chilli. Season with salt and pepper and spoon the oil over them. Toss to mix and leave to marinate for 30–40 minutes.

2 For the dressing, place the garlic in a mortar with 10ml/2 tsp caster sugar and pound until smooth, then work in the juice of 1½ limes and 15ml/1 tbsp of the Thai fish sauce.

3 Transfer the dressing to a jug (pitcher). Finely chop half the chilli. and add it to the dressing. Taste and add more sugar, lime juice, fish sauce and the rice vinegar to taste.

COOK'S TIP
To devein prawns, make a shallow cut down the back of the prawn using a small, sharp knife. Using the tip of the knife, lift out the thin, black vein, then rinse the prawn thoroughly under cold, running water.

4 Peel and stone (pit) the mango, then cut it into very fine strips.

5 Toss together the mango, carrots, cucumber and onion, and half the dressing. Arrange the salad on individual plates or in bowls.

6 Heat a ridged, cast-iron griddle pan or heavy frying pan until very hot. Brush with a little olive oil, then sear the prawns for 2–3 minutes on each side, until they turn pink and are patched with brown on the outside. Arrange the prawns on the salads.

7 Sprinkle the remaining dressing over the salads and top with the sprigs of coriander and mint. Finely shred the remaining chilli and sprinkle it over the salads with the peanuts and crisp-fried shallots. Serve immediately.

PRAWN SALAD

IN MEXICO, THIS SALAD WOULD FORM THE FISH COURSE IN A FORMAL MEAL, BUT IT IS SO GOOD THAT YOU'LL WANT TO SERVE IT ON ALL SORTS OF OCCASIONS. IT IS PERFECT FOR A BUFFET LUNCH.

SERVES FOUR

INGREDIENTS

   450g/1lb cooked peeled
     prawns (shrimp)
   juice of 1 lime
   3 tomatoes
   1 ripe but firm avocado
   30ml/2 tbsp hot chilli sauce
   5ml/1 tsp sugar
   150ml/¼ pint/⅔ cup sour cream
   2 Little Gem (Bibb) lettuces
   salt and ground black pepper
   fresh basil leaves and strips of green
     (bell) pepper to garnish

1 Put the prawns in a large bowl, add the lime juice and salt and pepper. Toss lightly, then leave to marinate.

2 Cut a cross in the base of each tomato. Place them in a heatproof bowl and pour over boiling water to cover.

3 After 3 minutes, lift the tomatoes out on a slotted spoon and plunge them into a bowl of cold water. Drain. The skins will have begun to peel back easily from the crosses.

4 Peel the tomatoes completely, then cut them in half and squeeze out the seeds. Chop the flesh into 1cm/½in cubes and add it to the prawns.

5 Cut the avocado in half, remove the skin and stone (pit), then slice the flesh into 1cm/½in chunks. Add it to the prawn and tomato mixture.

6 Mix the hot chilli sauce, sugar and sour cream in a bowl. Fold into the prawn mixture. Line a bowl with the lettuce leaves, then top with the prawn mixture. Cover and chill for at least 1 hour, then garnish with fresh basil and strips of green pepper. Crusty bread makes a perfect accompaniment.

Per portion: Energy 284Kcal/1185kJ; Protein 28.1g; Carbohydrate 5g, of which sugars 4.4g; Fat 16.9g, of which saturates 6.7g; Cholesterol 114mg; Calcium 226mg; Fibre 2.3g; Sodium 1814mg.

INSALATA DI MARE

YOU CAN VARY THE SEAFOOD IN THIS ITALIAN SALAD ACCORDING TO WHAT IS AVAILABLE, BUT TRY TO INCLUDE AT LEAST TWO KINDS OF SHELLFISH AND SOME SQUID. THE SALAD IS GOOD WARM OR COLD.

SERVES FOUR

INGREDIENTS
450g/1lb live mussels, scrubbed
    and bearded
450g/1lb small clams, scrubbed
105ml/7 tbsp dry white wine
225g/8oz squid, cleaned
4 large scallops, with their corals
30ml/2 tbsp olive oil
2 garlic cloves, finely chopped
1 small dried red chilli, crumbled
225g/8oz whole cooked prawns
    (shrimp), in the shell
6–8 large chicory (Belgian
    endive) leaves
6–8 radicchio leaves
15ml/1 tbsp chopped fresh flat leaf
    parsley, to garnish
For the dressing
5ml/1 tsp Dijon mustard
30ml/2 tbsp white
    wine vinegar
5ml/1 tsp lemon juice
120ml/4fl oz/½ cup extra virgin
    olive oil
salt and ground black pepper

1 Put the mussels and clams in a large pan with the white wine. Cover and cook over a high heat, shaking the pan occasionally, for about 4 minutes, until they have opened. Discard any that remain closed. Use a slotted spoon to transfer the shellfish to a bowl, then strain and reserve the cooking liquid and set it aside.

2 Cut the squid into thin rings; chop the tentacles. Leave small squid whole. Halve the scallops horizontally.

3 Heat the oil in a frying pan, add the garlic, chilli, squid, scallops and corals, and sauté for about 2 minutes, until just cooked and tender. Lift the squid and scallops out of the pan; reserve the oil.

4 When the shellfish are cool enough to handle, shell them, keeping a dozen of each in the shell. Peel all but 6–8 of the prawns. Pour the shellfish cooking liquid into a small pan, set over a high heat and reduce by half. Mix all the shelled and unshelled mussels and clams with the squid and scallops, then add the prawns.

5 To make the dressing, whisk the mustard with the vinegar and lemon juice together and season to taste. Add the olive oil, whisk vigorously, then whisk in the reserved cooking liquid and the oil from the frying pan. Pour the dressing over the seafood mixture and toss lightly to coat well.

6 Arrange the chicory and radicchio leaves around the edge of a large serving dish and pile the mixed seafood salad into the centre. Sprinkle with the chopped flat leaf parsley and serve immediately or chill first.

Per portion: Energy 445Kcal/1861kJ; Protein 41.1g; Carbohydrate 3.8g, of which sugars 1g; Fat 27.9g, of which saturates 4.3g; Cholesterol 241mg; Calcium 219mg; Fibre 0.5g; Sodium 585mg.

WHITEFISH SALAD

SMOKED WHITEFISH IS ONE OF THE GLORIES OF DELI FOOD AND, MADE INTO A SALAD WITH MAYONNAISE AND SOUR CREAM, IT BECOMES INDISPENSABLE AS A BRUNCH DISH. EAT IT WITH A STACK OF BAGELS, PUMPERNICKEL OR RYE BREAD. IF YOU CAN'T FIND SMOKED WHITEFISH, USE ANY OTHER SMOKED FIRM WHITE FISH, SUCH AS HALIBUT OR COD.

SERVES FOUR TO SIX

INGREDIENTS

1 smoked whitefish, skinned
  and boned
2 celery sticks, chopped
½ red, white or yellow onion
  or 3–5 spring onions
  (scallions), chopped
45ml/3 tbsp mayonnaise
45ml/3 tbsp sour cream or Greek
  (US strained plain) yogurt
juice of ½–1 lemon
1 round lettuce
ground black pepper
5–10ml/1–2 tsp chopped fresh
  parsley, to garnish

1 Break the smoked fish into bitesize pieces. In a bowl, combine the chopped celery, onion or spring onion, mayonnaise, and sour cream or yogurt, and add lemon juice to taste.

2 Fold the fish into the mixture and season with pepper. Arrange the lettuce leaves on serving plates, then spoon the whitefish salad on top. Serve chilled, sprinkled with parsley.

Per portion: Energy 172Kcal/719kJ; Protein 16g; Carbohydrate 4.3g, of which sugars 3.4g; Fat 10.4g, of which saturates 2g; Cholesterol 35mg; Calcium 62mg; Fibre 1.1g; Sodium 640mg.

SALAD NIÇOISE

MADE WITH THE FRESHEST OF INGREDIENTS, THIS CLASSIC PROVENÇAL SALAD MAKES A SIMPLE YET UNBEATABLE SUMMER DISH. SERVE WITH COUNTRY-STYLE BREAD AND CHILLED WHITE WINE.

SERVES FOUR

INGREDIENTS
    115g/4oz green beans, trimmed
      and cut in half
    115g/4oz mixed salad leaves
    ½ small cucumber, thinly sliced
    4 ripe tomatoes, quartered
    50g/2oz can anchovies, drained
    4 eggs, hard-boiled
    1 tuna steak, about 175g/6oz
    olive oil, for brushing
    ½ bunch of small radishes, trimmed
    50g/2oz/½ cup small
      black olives
    salt and ground black pepper
For the dressing
    90ml/6 tbsp extra virgin olive oil
    2 garlic cloves, crushed
    15ml/1 tbsp white wine vinegar

4 Preheat the grill (broiler). Brush the tuna with olive oil and sprinkle with salt and black pepper. Grill (broil) for 3–4 minutes on each side until cooked through. Cool, then flake with a fork.

5 Sprinkle the flaked tuna, sliced anchovies, quartered eggs, radishes and olives over the salad. Pour over the dressing and toss together lightly to combine. Serve immediately.

1 To make the dressing, whisk together the oil, garlic and vinegar in a bowl and season to taste with salt and pepper. Alternatively, shake together in a screw-top jar. Set aside.

2 Cook the green beans in a pan of boiling water for 2 minutes, until just tender, then drain.

3 Mix together the salad leaves, sliced cucumber, tomatoes and green beans in a large, shallow bowl. Halve the anchovies lengthways and shell and quarter the eggs.

VARIATION
Opinions vary on whether Salad Niçoise should include potatoes but, if you like, include a few small cooked new potatoes.

Per portion: Energy 378Kcal/1569kJ; Protein 23g; Carbohydrate 5.1g, of which sugars 4.7g; Fat 29.6g, of which saturates 5.2g; Cholesterol 241mg; Calcium 122mg; Fibre 2.5g; Sodium 889mg.

BEAN SALAD WITH TUNA AND RED ONION

THIS MAKES A GREAT, SUMMERY MAIN MEAL IF SERVED WITH A GREEN SALAD, SOME GARLIC MAYONNAISE AND PLENTY OF WARM, CRUSTY BREAD.

SERVES FOUR

INGREDIENTS

250g/9oz/1⅓ cups dried haricot
   (navy) or cannellini beans, soaked
   overnight in cold water
1 bay leaf
200–250g/7–9oz fine green
   beans, trimmed
1 large red onion, very thinly sliced
45ml/3 tbsp chopped fresh flat
   leaf parsley
200–250g/7–9oz good-quality canned
   tuna in olive oil, drained
200g/7oz cherry tomatoes, halved
salt and ground black pepper
a few onion rings, to garnish

For the dressing

90ml/6 tbsp extra virgin olive oil
15ml/1 tbsp tarragon vinegar
5ml/1 tsp tarragon mustard
1 garlic clove, finely chopped
5ml/1 tsp grated lemon rind
a little lemon juice
pinch of caster (superfine)
   sugar (optional)

1 Drain the beans and bring them to the boil in fresh water with the bay leaf added. Boil rapidly for 10 minutes, then reduce the heat and boil steadily for 1–1½ hours, until tender. Drain well. Discard the bay leaf.

2 Meanwhile, place all the dressing ingredients apart from the lemon juice and sugar in a jug (pitcher) and whisk until mixed. Season to taste with salt, pepper, lemon juice and a pinch of caster sugar, if you like. Leave to stand.

3 Blanch the green beans in plenty of boiling water for 3–4 minutes. Drain, refresh under cold water and drain thoroughly again.

4 Place both types of beans in a bowl. Add half the dressing and toss to mix. Stir in the onion and half the chopped parsley, then season to taste with salt and pepper.

5 Flake the tuna into large chunks with a knife and toss it into the beans with the tomato halves.

6 Arrange the salad on four individual plates. Drizzle the remaining dressing over the salad and sprinkle the remaining chopped parsley on top. Garnish with a few onion rings and serve immediately, at room temperature.

Per portion: Energy 443Kcal/1857kJ; Protein 29.1g; Carbohydrate 33.7g, of which sugars 6.4g; Fat 22.3g, of which saturates 3.3g; Cholesterol 25mg; Calcium 100mg; Fibre 12g; Sodium 162mg.

SEARED SWORDFISH <u>WITH</u> CITRUS DRESSING

THIS CONTEMPORARY JAPANESE DISH TAKES CONVENTIONAL SALAD INGREDIENTS AND MIXES THEM WITH SHOYU, DASHI AND SESAME OIL FOR A BRIGHT, NEW TASTE. FRESH FISH IS SLICED THINLY AND SEARED OR MARINATED, THEN SERVED WITH SALAD LEAVES AND VEGETABLES.

SERVES FOUR

INGREDIENTS

75g/3oz mooli (daikon), peeled
50g/2oz carrot, peeled
1 Japanese or salad cucumber
10ml/2 tsp vegetable oil
300g/11oz skinned fresh swordfish
   steak, cut against the grain
2 cartons salad cress
15ml/1 tbsp toasted
   sesame seeds
For the dressing
105ml/7 tbsp shoyu
105ml/7 tbsp second dashi stock,
   or the same amount of water and
   5ml/1 tsp dashi-no-moto
30ml/2 tbsp toasted sesame oil
juice of ½ lime
rind of ½ lime, shredded into
   thin strips

4 Cut the swordfish steak in half lengthways before slicing it into 5mm/¼in thick pieces in the other direction, against the grain.

5 Arrange the fish slices in a ring on individual plates. Mix the vegetable strands, salad cress and sesame seeds. Fluff up with your hands, then shape them into a sphere. Gently place it in the centre of the plate, on the swordfish. Pour the dressing around the plate's edge and serve immediately.

COOK'S TIP
This dish is traditionally made with fillet cut with the grain. To prepare, cut it in half lengthways, then slice against the grain by holding a knife horizontally to the chopping board.

1 Make the vegetable garnishes first. Use a very sharp knife, mandolin or vegetable slicer with a julienne blade to make very thin (about 4cm/1½in long) strands of mooli, carrot and cucumber. Soak the mooli and carrot in ice-cold water for 5 minutes, then drain well and keep in the refrigerator.

2 Mix together all the ingredients for the dressing and stir well, then chill.

3 Heat the oil in a small frying pan until smoking hot. Sear the fish for 30 seconds on all sides. Plunge it into cold water in a bowl to stop the cooking. Dry on kitchen paper and wipe off as much oil as possible.

Per portion: Energy 192Kcal/799kJ; Protein 15.6g; Carbohydrate 4.1g, of which sugars 3.7g; Fat 12.7g, of which saturates 2g; Cholesterol 31mg; Calcium 53mg; Fibre 1.1g; Sodium 1887mg.

WARM CHICKEN AND TOMATO SALAD WITH HAZELNUT DRESSING

THIS SIMPLE, WARM SALAD COMBINES PAN-FRIED CHICKEN AND SPINACH WITH A LIGHT, NUTTY DRESSING. SERVE IT FOR LUNCH ON AN AUTUMN DAY.

SERVES FOUR

INGREDIENTS
  45ml/3 tbsp olive oil
  30ml/2 tbsp hazelnut oil
  15ml/1 tbsp white wine vinegar
  1 garlic clove, crushed
  15ml/1 tbsp chopped fresh mixed herbs
  225g/8oz baby spinach leaves
  250g/9oz cherry tomatoes, halved
  1 bunch of spring onions
    (scallions), chopped
  2 skinless, chicken breast fillets, cut
    into thin strips
  salt and ground black pepper

VARIATIONS
• Use other meat or fish, such as steak, pork fillet (tenderloin) or salmon fillet, in place of the chicken.
• Any salad leaves can be used instead of the baby spinach.

1 First make the dressing: place 30ml/ 2 tbsp of the olive oil, the hazelnut oil, vinegar, garlic and chopped herbs in a small bowl or jug (pitcher) and whisk together until mixed. Set aside.

2 Trim any long stalks from the spinach leaves, then place in a large serving bowl with the tomatoes and spring onions, and toss together to mix.

3 Heat the remaining olive oil in a frying pan, and stir-fry the chicken over a high heat for 7–10 minutes, until it is cooked, tender and lightly browned.

4 Arrange the cooked chicken pieces over the salad. Give the dressing a quick whisk to blend, then drizzle it over the salad. Add salt and pepper to taste, toss lightly and serve immediately.

Per portion: Energy 234Kcal/973kJ; Protein 20.5g; Carbohydrate 3.6g, of which sugars 3.5g; Fat 15.3g, of which saturates 2.4g; Cholesterol 53mg; Calcium 114mg; Fibre 2.2g; Sodium 131mg.

CHICKEN AND MANGO SALAD
WITH ORANGE RICE

THIS FRESH AND DELICIOUS RECIPE DRAWS ITS INSPIRATION FROM ALL OVER THE WORLD.

SERVES FOUR

INGREDIENTS

15ml/1 tbsp sunflower oil
1 onion, chopped
1 garlic clove, crushed
30ml/2 tbsp red curry paste
10ml/2 tsp apricot jam
30ml/2 tbsp chicken stock
about 450g/1lb cooked chicken, cut
    into small pieces
150ml/¼ pint/⅔ cup natural
    (plain) yogurt
60–75ml/4–5 tbsp mayonnaise
1 large mango, peeled, stoned
    (pitted) and cut into 1cm/½in dice
fresh flat leaf parsley sprigs,
    to garnish
poppadums, to serve
For the orange rice
175g/6oz/scant 1 cup white long
    grain rice
225g/8oz carrots, grated
    (about 1⅓ cups)
1 large orange, cut
    into segments
40g/1½oz/⅓ cup roasted flaked
    (sliced) almonds
For the dressing
45ml/3 tbsp olive oil
60ml/4 tbsp sunflower oil
45ml/3 tbsp lemon juice
1 garlic clove, crushed
15ml/1 tbsp chopped mixed fresh
    herbs, such as tarragon, parsley,
    chives
salt and freshly ground black pepper

1 Heat the oil in a frying pan. Add the onion and garlic and cook over a medium heat, stirring occasionally, for 3–4 minutes, until soft.

2 Stir in the curry paste and cook for about 1 minute, stirring constantly, then lower the heat and stir in the apricot jam and chicken stock. Mix well, then add the chopped chicken and stir until it is thoroughly coated in the paste. Spoon into a bowl, cover with clear film (plastic wrap) and leave to cool.

3 Meanwhile, boil the rice in plenty of lightly salted water until just tender. Drain, rinse under cold water and drain again. When cool, stir into the grated carrots and add the orange segments and flaked almonds.

4 Make the dressing by whisking all the ingredients together in a bowl.

5 When the chicken mixture is cool, stir in the yogurt and mayonnaise, then add the mango, stirring it in carefully so as not to break the flesh. Chill for about 30 minutes.

6 When ready to serve, pour the dressing into the rice salad and mix well. Spoon on to a platter and mound the cold curried chicken on top. Garnish with flat leaf parsley and serve with poppadums.

COOK'S TIP

A simple way of dicing a mango is to take two thick slices from either side of the large flat stone (pit) without peeling the fruit. Make criss-cross cuts in the flesh on each slice and then turn inside out. The cubes of flesh will stand proud of the skin and can be easily cut off.

Per portion: Energy 776Kcal/3245kJ; Protein 35.9g; Carbohydrate 60.2g, of which sugars 21.1g; Fat 45.3g, of which saturates 6.4g; Cholesterol 93mg; Calcium 172mg; Fibre 4.5g; Sodium 206mg.

WARM SALAD ᵒᶠ BAYONNE HAM ᴬᴺᴰ NEW POTATOES

WITH A LIGHTLY SPICED NUTTY DRESSING, THIS WARM SALAD IS AS DELICIOUS AS IT IS FASHIONABLE, AND AN EXCELLENT CHOICE FOR INFORMAL ENTERTAINING.

SERVES FOUR

INGREDIENTS
    225g/8oz new potatoes, halved
       if large
    50g/2oz green beans
    115g/4oz young spinach leaves
    2 spring onions (scallions), sliced
    4 eggs, hard-boiled and quartered
    50g/2oz Bayonne ham, cut
       into strips
    juice of ½ lemon
    salt and ground black pepper
For the dressing
    60ml/4 tbsp olive oil
    5ml/1 tsp ground turmeric
    5ml/1 tsp ground cumin
    50g/2oz/½ cup shelled hazelnuts

1 Cook the potatoes in salted, boiling water for 10–15 minutes, or until tender, then drain. Cook the beans in salted, boiling water for 2 minutes, then drain.

2 Toss the potatoes and beans with the spinach and spring onions in a bowl.

3 Arrange the hard-boiled egg quarters on the salad and sprinkle the strips of ham over the top. Sprinkle with the lemon juice and season with plenty of salt and pepper.

4 Heat the dressing ingredients in a large frying pan and continue to cook, stirring frequently, until the nuts turn golden. Pour the hot, nutty dressing over the salad and serve immediately.

VARIATION
Replace the potatoes with a 400g/14oz can mixed beans and pulses. Drain and rinse the beans and pulses, then drain again. Toss lightly with the green beans and spring onions.

Per portion: Energy 323Kcal/1341kJ; Protein 12.4g; Carbohydrate 10.9g, of which sugars 2.2g; Fat 25.8g, of which saturates 4.2g; Cholesterol 199mg; Calcium 105mg; Fibre 2.3g; Sodium 270mg.

WARM SALAD WITH HAM, EGG AND ASPARAGUS

WHEN YOU THINK IT'S TOO HOT FOR PASTA, TRY SERVING IT IN A WARM SALAD. HERE IT IS COMBINED WITH HAM, EGGS AND ASPARAGUS. A MUSTARD DRESSING MADE FROM THE ASPARAGUS STEMS CREATES A RICH AND TANGY ACCOMPANIMENT.

SERVES FOUR

INGREDIENTS
    450g/1lb asparagus
    450g/1lb dried tagliatelle
    225g/8oz cooked ham, in 5mm/¼in
       thick slices, cut into sticks
    2 eggs, hard-boiled and sliced
    50g/2oz Parmesan cheese, shaved
    salt and ground black pepper
For the dressing
    50g/2oz cooked potato
    75ml/5 tbsp olive oil, preferably Sicilian
    15ml/1 tbsp lemon juice
    10ml/2 tsp Dijon mustard
    120ml/4fl oz/½ cup vegetable stock

VARIATIONS
Use sliced chicken instead of the ham or thin slices of softer Italian cheese, such as Fontina or asiago.

1 Trim and discard the tough woody part of the asparagus. Cut the spears in half and cook the thicker halves in boiling salted water for 12 minutes. After 6 minutes add the tips. Drain, then refresh under cold water until warm.

2 Finely chop 150g/5oz of the thick asparagus pieces. Place in a food processor with the dressing ingredients and process until smooth.

3 Cook the pasta in a large pan of salted water according to the packet instructions, until tender. Refresh under cold water until warm, and drain.

4 To serve, toss the pasta with the asparagus sauce and divide among four plates. Top with the ham, hard-boiled eggs and asparagus tips. Serve immediately with a sprinkling of Parmesan cheese shavings.

Per portion: Energy 707Kcal/2975kJ; Protein 36g; Carbohydrate 88.4g, of which sugars 6.6g; Fat 25.8g, of which saturates 6.4g; Cholesterol 159mg; Calcium 230mg; Fibre 5.3g; Sodium 859mg.

BEEF AND GRILLED SWEET POTATO SALAD WITH SHALLOT AND HERB DRESSING

THIS SALAD MAKES A GOOD MAIN DISH FOR A SUMMER BUFFET, ESPECIALLY IF THE BEEF HAS BEEN CUT INTO FORK-SIZE STRIPS. IT IS ABSOLUTELY DELICIOUS WITH A SIMPLE POTATO SALAD AND SOME PEPPERY LEAVES, SUCH AS WATERCRESS, MIZUNA OR ROCKET.

SERVES SIX TO EIGHT

INGREDIENTS
800g/1¾lb fillet (tenderloin) of beef
5ml/1 tsp black peppercorns, crushed
10ml/2 tsp chopped fresh thyme
60ml/4 tbsp olive oil
450g/1lb orange-fleshed sweet
  potato, peeled
salt and ground black pepper
For the dressing
1 garlic clove, chopped
15g/½oz/½ cup flat leaf parsley
30ml/2 tbsp chopped fresh
  coriander (cilantro)
15ml/1 tbsp salted capers, rinsed
½–1 fresh green chilli, seeded
  and chopped
10ml/2 tsp Dijon mustard
10–15ml/2–3 tsp white wine vinegar
75ml/5 tbsp extra virgin olive oil
2 shallots, finely chopped

1 Roll the beef fillet in the crushed peppercorns and thyme, then set aside to marinate for a few hours. Preheat the oven to 200°C/400°F/Gas 6.

2 Heat half the olive oil in a heavy frying pan. Add the beef and brown it all over, turning frequently, to seal it. Place on a baking tray and cook in the oven for 10–15 minutes.

3 Remove the beef from the oven, and cover with foil, then leave to rest for 10–15 minutes.

4 Meanwhile, preheat the grill (broiler). Cut the sweet potatoes into 1cm/½in slices. Brush with the remaining olive oil, season to taste with salt and pepper, and grill (broil) for about 5–6 minutes on each side, until tender and browned. Cut the sweet potato slices into strips and place them in a bowl.

5 Cut the beef into slices or strips and toss with the sweet potato, then set the bowl aside.

6 For the dressing, process the garlic, parsley, coriander, capers, chilli, mustard and 10ml/2 tsp of the vinegar in a food processor or blender until chopped. With the motor still running, gradually pour in the oil to make a smooth dressing. Season the dressing with salt and pepper and add more vinegar, to taste. Stir in the shallots.

7 Toss the dressing into the sweet potatoes and beef and leave to stand for up to 2 hours before serving.

COOK'S TIP
Not only do orange-fleshed sweet potatoes look more appetizing than white ones, but they are also better for you, as they contain antioxidant vitamins that help protect against disease.

Per portion: Energy 400Kcal/1670kJ; Protein 29.2g; Carbohydrate 16g, of which sugars 4.3g; Fat 24.9g, of which saturates 6.2g; Cholesterol 81mg; Calcium 23mg; Fibre 1.8g; Sodium 89mg.

THAI BEEF SALAD

ALL THE INGREDIENTS FOR THIS TRADITIONAL THAI DISH – KNOWN AS YAM NUA YANG *– ARE WIDELY AVAILABLE IN LARGER SUPERMARKETS.*

SERVES FOUR

INGREDIENTS
675g/1½lb fillet steak
  (beef tenderloin)
30ml/2 tbsp olive oil
2 small mild red chillies, seeded
  and sliced
225g/8oz/3¼ cups shiitake
  mushrooms, sliced
For the dressing
3 spring onions (scallions), chopped
2 garlic cloves, finely chopped
juice of 1 lime
15–30ml/1–2 tbsp fish or oyster
  sauce, to taste
5ml/1 tsp soft light brown sugar
30ml/2 tbsp chopped fresh
  coriander (cilantro)
To serve
1 cos or romaine lettuce, torn
  into strips
175g/6oz cherry tomatoes, halved
5cm/2in piece cucumber, peeled,
  halved and thinly sliced
45ml/3 tbsp toasted sesame seeds

1 Preheat the grill (broiler), then cook the steak for 2–4 minutes on each side depending on how well done you like steak. Leave to cool for at least 15 minutes.

2 Use a very sharp knife to slice the meat as thinly as possible and place the slices in a bowl.

VARIATION
If you can find them, yellow chillies make a colourful addition to this dish. Substitute one for one of the red chillies.

3 Heat the olive oil in a small frying pan. Add the seeded and sliced red chillies and the sliced mushrooms and cook for 5 minutes, stirring occasionally. Turn off the heat and add the grilled (broiled) steak slices to the pan, then stir well to coat the slices in the chilli and mushroom mixture.

4 Stir all the ingredients for the dressing together, then pour it over the meat mixture and toss gently.

5 Arrange the salad ingredients on a serving plate. Spoon the warm steak mixture into the centre and sprinkle the sesame seeds over, then serve.

Per portion: Energy 381Kcal/1591kJ; Protein 39.8g; Carbohydrate 4.1g, of which sugars 3.8g; Fat 23g, of which saturates 6.6g; Cholesterol 103mg; Calcium 105mg; Fibre 2.5g; Sodium 352mg.

RICE AND RISOTTO

If you're the sort of person who finds cooking relaxing and loves chatting to friends while preparing a meal, rustle up a tasty risotto. You need to stand at the stove and stir the rice for twenty minutes just before serving, but the action is both soothing and satisfying and the results are inevitably delicious. Chicken and Prawn Jambalaya is another wonderful dish for entertaining. Like Seafood Paella, it is full of flavour and the combination of ingredients means that every mouthful brings a taste of the delightfully unexpected.

STUFFED VEGETABLES

COLOURFUL, EASY TO PREPARE AND UTTERLY DELICIOUS, THIS MAKES A POPULAR SUPPER DISH, AND WITH A CHOICE OF VEGETABLES INCLUDED IN THE RECIPE, THERE'S BOUND TO BE SOMETHING TO APPEAL TO EVERY MEMBER OF THE FAMILY.

SERVES FOUR

INGREDIENTS

  1 aubergine (eggplant)
  1 green (bell) pepper
  2 beefsteak tomatoes
  45ml/3 tbsp olive oil
  1 onion, chopped
  2 garlic cloves, crushed
  115g/4oz/1–1½ cups button (white)
    mushrooms, chopped
  1 carrot, grated
  225g/8oz/2 cups cooked white long
    grain rice
  15ml/1 tbsp chopped fresh dill
  90g/3½oz/scant ½ cup crumbled feta
    cheese
  75g/3oz/¾ cup pine nuts,
    lightly toasted
  30ml/2 tbsp currants
  salt and ground black pepper

1 Preheat the oven to 190°C/375°F/ Gas 5. Lightly grease a shallow ovenproof dish. Cut the aubergine in half, through the stalk, and scoop out the flesh from each half, taking care not to pierce the skin, to leave two hollow "boats". Dice the aubergine flesh. Cut the pepper in half lengthways and remove the cores and seeds.

2 Cut off the tops from the tomatoes and hollow out the centres with a spoon. Chop the flesh and add it to the diced aubergine. Place the tomatoes upside down on kitchen paper to drain.

3 Bring a pan of water to the boil, add the aubergine halves and blanch for 3 minutes. Add the pepper halves to the boiling water and blanch for 3 minutes more. Drain the vegetables, then place, hollow side up, in the baking dish.

4 Heat 30ml/2 tbsp oil in a pan and cook the onion and garlic for about 5 minutes. Stir in the diced aubergine and tomato mixture with the mushrooms and carrot. Cover, cook for 5 minutes until softened, then mix in the rice, dill, feta, pine nuts and currants. Season to taste.

5 Divide the mixture among the vegetable shells, sprinkle with the remaining olive oil and bake for 20 minutes, until the topping has browned. Serve hot or cold.

Per portion: Energy 544Kcal/2265kJ; Protein 12.9g; Carbohydrate 63.3g, of which sugars 17.2g; Fat 26.8g, of which saturates 5.3g; Cholesterol 16mg; Calcium 134mg; Fibre 4.1g; Sodium 343mg.

ROASTED SQUASH

GEM SQUASH HAS A SWEET, SUBTLE FLAVOUR THAT CONTRASTS WELL WITH OLIVES AND SUN-DRIED TOMATOES IN THIS RECIPE. THE RICE ADDS SUBSTANCE WITHOUT CHANGING ANY OF THE FLAVOURS.

2 Mix the rice, tomatoes, olives, cheese, half the olive oil and basil in a bowl.

3 Oil a shallow ovenproof dish with the remaining oil, just large enough to hold the squash side by side. Divide the rice mixture among the squash and place them in the dish.

SERVES FOUR

INGREDIENTS
    4 whole gem squashes
    225g/8oz/2 cups cooked white
        long grain rice
    75g/3oz/1½ cups sun-dried
        tomatoes in oil, drained
        and chopped
    50g/2oz/½ cup pitted black
        olives, chopped
    60ml/4 tbsp soft goat's cheese
    30ml/2 tbsp olive oil
    15ml/1 tbsp chopped fresh basil
        leaves, plus fresh basil sprigs,
        to serve
    yogurt and mint dressing
        or green salad,
        to serve (optional)

1 Preheat the oven to 180°C/350°F/ Gas 4. Using a sharp knife, trim away the base of each gem squash and then slice off the tops. Using a spoon, scoop out and discard the seeds.

4 Cover with foil and bake for about 45–50 minutes, until the squash is tender when pierced with the point of a sharp knife or skewer. Garnish with basil sprigs and serve with a yogurt and mint dressing or with a green salad if you like.

Per portion: Energy 280Kcal/1170kJ; Protein 8.7g; Carbohydrate 23.6g, of which sugars 5g; Fat 17.4g, of which saturates 6.3g; Cholesterol 23mg; Calcium 125mg; Fibre 3.1g; Sodium 434mg.

BASMATI AND NUT PILAFF

VEGETARIANS WILL LOVE THIS SIMPLE PILAFF. ADD WILD OR CULTIVATED MUSHROOMS, IF YOU LIKE.

SERVES FOUR

INGREDIENTS

  15–30ml/1–2 tbsp sunflower oil
  1 onion, chopped
  1 garlic clove, crushed
  1 large carrot, coarsely grated
  225g/8oz/generous 1 cup basmati
    rice, soaked
  5ml/1 tsp cumin seeds
  10ml/2 tsp ground coriander
  10ml/2 tsp black mustard
    seeds (optional)
  4 green cardamom pods
  450ml/¾ pint/scant 2 cups vegetable
    stock or water
  1 bay leaf
  75g/3oz/¾ cup unsalted walnuts and
    cashew nuts
  salt and ground black pepper
  fresh parsley or coriander (cilantro)
    sprigs, to garnish

1 Heat the oil in a large, shallow frying pan. Add the onion, garlic and carrot and cook over a low heat, stirring occasionally, for 3–4 minutes, until softened. Thoroughly drain the rice and then add to the pan with the cumin seeds, ground coriander, black mustard seeds and cardamom pods. Cook for 1–2 minutes more, stirring constantly to coat the grains in oil.

2 Pour in the stock or water, add the bay leaf and season well. Bring to the boil, lower the heat, cover and simmer very gently for 10–12 minutes.

3 Remove the pan from the heat without lifting the lid. Leave to stand for about 5 minutes, then check the rice. If it is cooked, there will be small steam holes on the surface of the rice. Remove and discard the bay leaf and the cardamom pods.

4 Stir in the nuts, taste and adjust the seasoning if necessary. Spoon on to a warm platter, garnish with the parsley or coriander and serve.

COOK'S TIP
Use whichever nuts you prefer in this dish – even unsalted peanuts taste good, although almonds, cashew nuts or pistachios are more exotic.

Per portion: Energy 376Kcal/1562kJ; Protein 7.5g; Carbohydrate 50g, of which sugars 4g; Fat 16g, of which saturates 1.4g; Cholesterol 0mg; Calcium 43mg; Fibre 1.6g; Sodium 7mg.

Mushroom Pilaff

THIS DISH IS SIMPLICITY ITSELF, YET IT IS FULL OF DELICIOUS INDIAN FLAVOURS.

SERVES FOUR

INGREDIENTS

30ml/2 tbsp vegetable oil
2 shallots, finely chopped
1 garlic clove, crushed
3 green cardamom pods
25g/1oz/2 tbsp ghee or butter
175g/6oz/2½ cups button (white)
  mushrooms, sliced
225g/8oz/generous 1 cup basmati
  rice, soaked
5ml/1 tsp grated fresh root ginger
good pinch of garam masala
15ml/1 tbsp chopped fresh
  coriander (cilantro)
salt

1 Heat the oil in a flameproof casserole and cook the shallots, garlic and cardamom pods over a medium heat for 3–4 minutes, until the shallots have softened and are beginning to brown.

2 Add the ghee or butter. When it has melted, add the mushrooms and cook for 2–3 minutes more.

3 Add the rice, ginger and garam masala. Stir-fry over a low heat for 2–3 minutes, then stir in 450ml/¾ pint/ scant 2 cups water and a little salt. Bring to the boil, then cover tightly and simmer over a low heat for 10 minutes.

4 Remove the casserole from the heat. Leave to stand, still covered, for 5 minutes. Add the chopped coriander and gently fork it through the rice. Spoon into a warm serving bowl and serve immediately.

Per portion: Energy 309Kcal/1286kJ; Protein 5.2g; Carbohydrate 46.3g, of which sugars 1g; Fat 11.2g, of which saturates 4g; Cholesterol 13mg; Calcium 18mg; Fibre 0.7g; Sodium 41mg.

ROASTED PEPPER RISOTTO

THIS MAKES AN EXCELLENT AND COLOURFUL VEGETARIAN LUNCH OR SUPPER DISH.

SERVES THREE TO FOUR

INGREDIENTS
  1 red (bell) pepper
  1 yellow (bell) pepper
  15ml/1 tbsp olive oil
  25g/1oz/2 tbsp butter
  1 onion, chopped
  2 garlic cloves, crushed
  275g/10oz/1½ cups risotto rice
  1 litre/1¾ pints/4 cups simmering
    vegetable stock
  50g/2oz/⅔ cup freshly grated
    Parmesan cheese
  salt and ground black pepper
  freshly grated Parmesan cheese, to
    serve (optional)

1 Preheat the grill (broiler). Cut the peppers in half, remove the seeds and pith and arrange, cut side down, on a baking sheet. Place under the grill for 5–6 minutes until the skin is charred. Put the peppers in a plastic bag, tie the ends and leave for 4–5 minutes.

2 Peel the peppers when they are cool enough to handle and the steam has loosened the skin. Cut into thin strips.

3 Heat the oil and butter in a pan and cook the onion and garlic for 4–5 minutes over a low heat until the onion begins to soften. Add the peppers and cook the mixture for 3–4 minutes more, stirring occasionally.

4 Stir in the rice. Cook over a medium heat for 3–4 minutes, stirring all the time, until the rice is evenly coated in oil and the outer part of each grain has become translucent.

5 Add a ladleful of stock. Cook, stirring, until all the liquid has been absorbed. Continue to add the stock, a ladleful at a time, making sure each quantity has been absorbed before adding the next.

6 When the rice is tender but retains a little "bite", stir in the Parmesan, and add seasoning to taste. Cover and leave to stand for 3–4 minutes, then serve, with extra Parmesan, if using.

Per portion: Energy 555Kcal/2312kJ; Protein 16.1g; Carbohydrate 80.1g, of which sugars 10g; Fat 18g, of which saturates 8.4g; Cholesterol 34mg; Calcium 238mg; Fibre 2.6g; Sodium 241mg.

RISOTTO WITH FOUR VEGETABLES

THIS IS ONE OF THE PRETTIEST RISOTTOS, ESPECIALLY WHEN MADE WITH ACORN SQUASH.

SERVES THREE TO FOUR

INGREDIENTS

115g/4oz/1 cup shelled fresh peas
115g/4oz/1 cup green beans, cut
  into short lengths
30ml/2 tbsp olive oil
75g/3oz/6 tbsp butter
1 acorn squash, skin and seeds
  removed, flesh cut into batons
1 onion, finely chopped
275g/10oz/1½ cups risotto rice
120ml/4fl oz/½ cup Italian dry
  white vermouth
1 litre/1¾ pints/4 cups boiling
  chicken stock
75g/3oz/1 cup freshly grated
  Parmesan cheese
salt and ground black pepper

1 Bring a pan of lightly salted water to the boil, add the peas and beans and cook for 2–3 minutes, until the vegetables are just tender. Drain, refresh under cold running water, drain again and set aside.

2 Heat the oil with 25g/1oz/2 tbsp of the butter in a medium pan until foaming. Add the squash and cook gently for 2–3 minutes, or until just softened. Remove with a slotted spoon and set aside. Add the onion to the pan and cook gently for about 3 minutes, stirring frequently, until softened.

3 Stir in the rice until the grains start to swell and burst, then add the vermouth. Stir until the vermouth stops sizzling and most of it has been absorbed by the rice, then add a few ladlefuls of the stock, with salt and pepper to taste. Stir over a low heat until the stock has been absorbed.

4 Gradually add the remaining stock, a few ladlefuls at a time, allowing the rice to absorb the liquid before adding more, and stirring all the time.

VARIATIONS

Shelled broad (fava) beans can be used instead of the peas, and asparagus tips instead of the green beans. Use courgettes (zucchini) if acorn squash is not available.

5 After about 20 minutes, when all the stock has been absorbed and the rice is cooked and creamy but still has a "bite", gently stir in the vegetables, the remaining butter and about half the grated Parmesan. Heat through, then taste and adjust the seasoning and serve with the remaining grated Parmesan handed around separately.

Per portion: Energy 836Kcal/3472kJ; Protein 22.1g; Carbohydrate 79.4g, of which sugars 6g; Fat 42.6g, of which saturates 22.1g; Cholesterol 89mg; Calcium 379mg; Fibre 3.9g; Sodium 462mg.

RISOTTO WITH FOUR CHEESES

THIS IS A VERY RICH DISH. IT IS THE PERFECT CHOICE FOR A DINNER PARTY WITH AN ITALIAN
THEME, SERVED WITH A LIGHT, DRY SPARKLING WHITE WINE.

SERVES FOUR

INGREDIENTS
40g/1½oz/3 tbsp butter
1 small onion, finely chopped
1.2 litres/2 pints/5 cups chicken
  stock, preferably home-made
350g/12oz/1¾ cups risotto rice
200ml/7fl oz/scant 1 cup dry
  white wine
50g/2oz/½ cup grated Gruyère cheese
50g/2oz/½ cup diced taleggio cheese
50g/2oz/½ cup diced
  Gorgonzola cheese
50g/2oz/⅔ cup freshly grated
  Parmesan cheese
salt and ground black pepper
chopped fresh flat leaf parsley,
  to garnish

1 Melt the butter in a large, heavy pan or deep frying pan and cook the onion over a low heat, stirring frequently, for about 4–5 minutes, until softened and lightly browned. Meanwhile, pour the chicken stock into another pan and heat it to simmering point.

2 Add the rice to the onion mixture, stir until the grains start to swell and burst, then add the wine. Stir until it stops sizzling and most of it has been absorbed by the rice, then pour in a little of the hot stock. Add salt and pepper to taste. Stir over a low heat until the stock has been absorbed.

3 Gradually add the remaining stock, a little at a time, allowing the rice to absorb the liquid before adding more, and stirring constantly. After about 20–25 minutes the rice will be *al dente* and the risotto creamy.

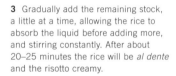

4 Turn off the heat under the pan, then add the Gruyère, taleggio, Gorgonzola and 30ml/2 tbsp of the Parmesan cheese. Stir gently until the cheeses have melted, then taste and adjust the seasoning, if necessary. Spoon the risotto into a warm serving bowl and garnish with parsley. Serve immediately, handing the remaining grated Parmesan separately.

Per portion: Energy 640Kcal/2662kJ; Protein 22.1g; Carbohydrate 67.1g, of which sugars 1.2g; Fat 26g, of which saturates 15.9g; Cholesterol 70mg; Calcium 451mg; Fibre 0.2g; Sodium 473mg.

RISOTTO WITH RICOTTA AND BASIL

THIS IS A WELL-FLAVOURED RISOTTO, WHICH BENEFITS FROM THE DISTINCTIVE PUNGENCY OF BASIL, MELLOWED WITH SMOOTH RICOTTA.

SERVES THREE TO FOUR

INGREDIENTS

45ml/3 tbsp olive oil
1 onion, finely chopped
275g/10oz/1½ cups risotto rice
1 litre/1¾ pints/4 cups hot chicken
 or vegetable stock
175g/6oz/¾ cup ricotta cheese
50g/2oz/2 cups fresh basil leaves,
 finely chopped, plus extra
 to garnish
75g/3oz/1 cup freshly grated
 Parmesan cheese
salt and ground black pepper

1 Heat the oil in a large pan or flameproof casserole and cook the onion over a low heat until soft.

2 Tip in the rice. Cook for a few minutes, stirring constantly, until the rice grains are well coated with oil and are slightly translucent.

3 Pour in about a quarter of the stock. Cook, stirring, until all the stock has been absorbed, then add another ladleful. Continue in this manner, adding more stock when the previous ladleful has been absorbed, until the risotto has been cooking for about 20 minutes and the rice is just tender.

4 Spoon the ricotta into a bowl and break it up a little with a fork. Gently stir it into the risotto along with the chopped basil and grated Parmesan. Taste and adjust the seasoning, if necessary, then cover and leave to stand for 2–3 minutes before serving, garnished with basil leaves.

Per portion: Energy 715Kcal/2975kJ; Protein 22.4g; Carbohydrate 72.6g, of which sugars 2.8g; Fat 36.2g, of which saturates 16.4g; Cholesterol 70mg; Calcium 382mg; Fibre 0.7g; Sodium 442mg.

SEARED SCALLOPS WITH CHIVE SAUCE ON LEEK AND CARROT RICE

SCALLOPS ARE ONE OF THE MOST DELICIOUS SHELLFISH. HERE THEY ARE PARTNERED WITH A DELICATE CHIVE SAUCE AND A PILAFF OF WILD AND WHITE RICE WITH SWEET LEEKS AND CARROTS.

SERVES FOUR

INGREDIENTS
- 12–16 shelled scallops
- 45ml/3 tbsp olive oil
- 50g/2oz/⅓ cup wild rice
- 65g/2½ oz/5 tbsp butter
- 4 carrots, cut into long thin strips
- 2 leeks, cut into thick, diagonal slices
- 1 small onion, finely chopped
- 115g/4oz/⅔ cup long grain rice
- 1 fresh bay leaf
- 200ml/7fl oz/scant 1 cup white wine
- 450ml/¾ pint/scant 2 cups fish stock
- 60ml/4 tbsp double (heavy) cream
- a little lemon juice
- 25ml/5 tsp chopped fresh chives
- 30ml/2 tbsp fresh chervil sprigs
- salt and ground black pepper

1 Lightly season the scallops, brush with 15ml/1 tbsp of the olive oil and set aside.

2 Cook the wild rice in plenty of boiling water for about 30 minutes, until tender, then drain well.

3 Melt half the butter in a small frying pan and cook the carrots over a low heat for 4–5 minutes. Add the leeks and cook for a further 2 minutes. Season with salt and pepper and add 30–45ml/ 2–3 tbsp water, then cover and cook for a few minutes more. Uncover and cook until the liquid has reduced. Remove from the heat and set aside.

4 Melt half the rest of the butter with 15ml/1 tbsp of the remaining oil in a heavy pan. Add the onion and cook over a low heat for 3–4 minutes, until softened but not browned.

5 Add the long grain rice and bay leaf and cook, stirring constantly, until the rice looks translucent and the grains are coated with oil.

6 Pour in half the wine and half the stock. Season with 2.5ml/½ tsp salt and bring to the boil. Stir, then cover and cook very gently for 15 minutes, or until the liquid is absorbed and the rice is cooked and tender.

7 Reheat the carrots and leeks gently, then stir them into the long grain rice with the wild rice. Add seasoning to taste, if necessary.

8 Meanwhile, pour the remaining wine and stock into a small pan and boil rapidly until reduced by half.

COOK'S TIP
Choose fresh, rather than frozen, scallops as the frozen ones tend to exude water on cooking. Scallops need only the briefest cooking at high heat, just until they turn opaque and brown on each side, so have the pan very hot. Although some people avoid eating the orange-coloured coral, it is delicious and many people consider it to be the best part.

9 Heat a heavy frying pan over a high heat. Add the remaining butter and oil. Sear the scallops for 1–2 minutes on each side. Set aside and keep warm.

10 Pour the reduced stock into the pan and heat until bubbling, then add the cream and boil until thickened. Season with lemon juice, salt and pepper. Stir in the chives and scallops.

11 Stir the chervil into the rice and pile it on to plates. Arrange the scallops on top and spoon the sauce over the rice.

Per portion: Energy 482Kcal/2014kJ; Protein 28.1g; Carbohydrate 42.7g, of which sugars 6g; Fat 18.6g, of which saturates 6.7g; Cholesterol 68mg; Calcium 80mg; Fibre 3g; Sodium 200mg.

SEAFOOD PAELLA

*THERE ARE AS MANY VERSIONS OF PAELLA AS THERE ARE REGIONS OF SPAIN. THOSE FROM NEAR THE
COAST CONTAIN A LOT OF SEAFOOD, WHILE INLAND VERSIONS ADD CHICKEN OR PORK. HERE THE
ONLY MEAT IS THE CHORIZO, ESSENTIAL FOR AN AUTHENTIC FLAVOUR.*

SERVES FOUR

INGREDIENTS

45ml/3 tbsp olive oil
1 Spanish (Bermuda) onion, chopped
2 fat garlic cloves, chopped
150g/5oz chorizo sausage, sliced
300g/11oz small squid, cleaned
1 red (bell) pepper, cut into strips
4 tomatoes, peeled, seeded and
   diced, or 200g/7oz can tomatoes
500ml/17fl oz/generous 2 cups
   chicken stock
105ml/7 tbsp dry white wine
200g/7oz/1 cup short grain Spanish
   rice or risotto rice
a large pinch of saffron threads
150g/5oz/1 cup fresh or frozen peas
12 large cooked prawns (shrimp), in
   the shell, or 8 langoustines
450g/1lb fresh mussels, scrubbed
450g/1lb medium clams, scrubbed
salt and ground black pepper

1 Heat the olive oil in a paella pan or
wok, add the onion and garlic and cook
until translucent. Add the chorizo and
cook until lightly golden.

2 If the squid are very small, leave them
whole, otherwise cut the bodies into
rings and the tentacles into pieces. Add
the squid to the pan and sauté over a
high heat for 2 minutes.

3 Stir in the pepper strips and tomatoes
and simmer gently for 5 minutes, until
the pepper strips are tender. Pour in the
stock and white wine, stir well and bring
to the boil.

4 Stir in the rice and saffron threads
and season well with salt and pepper.
Spread the contents of the pan evenly.
Bring the liquid back to the boil, then
lower the heat and simmer gently for
about 10 minutes.

5 Add the peas, prawns or langoustines,
mussels and clams, stirring them gently
into the rice.

6 Cook the paella over a low heat for a
further 15–20 minutes, until the rice is
tender and all the mussels and clams
have opened. If any remain closed,
discard them. If the paella seems dry,
add a little more hot chicken stock.
Gently stir everything together and serve
while piping hot.

Per portion: Energy 618Kcal/2600kJ; Protein 41.4g; Carbohydrate 63.8g, of which sugars 10.3g; Fat 21.9g, of which saturates 5.4g; Cholesterol 290mg; Calcium 179mg; Fibre 4.6g; Sodium 1117mg.

KEDGEREE

THIS CLASSIC DISH ORIGINATED IN INDIA. IT IS BEST MADE WITH BASMATI RICE, WHICH GOES WELL WITH THE MILD CURRY FLAVOUR, BUT LONG GRAIN RICE WILL DO. FOR A COLOURFUL GARNISH, ADD SOME FINELY SLICED RED ONION AND A LITTLE RED ONION MARMALADE.

SERVES FOUR

INGREDIENTS
450g/1lb undyed smoked
  haddock fillet
750ml/1¼ pints/3 cups milk
2 bay leaves
½ lemon, sliced
50g/2oz/¼ cup butter
1 onion, chopped
2.5ml/½ tsp ground turmeric
5ml/1 tsp mild Madras curry powder
2 green cardamom pods
350g/12oz/1¾ cups basmati or long
  grain rice, washed and drained
4 hard-boiled eggs (not *too* hard),
  coarsely chopped
150ml/¼ pint/⅔ cup single (light)
  cream (optional)
30ml/2 tbsp chopped fresh parsley
salt and ground black pepper

1 Put the haddock in a shallow pan and add the milk, bay leaves and lemon slices. Poach gently for 8–10 minutes, until the haddock flakes easily when tested with the tip of a sharp knife. Strain the milk into a jug (pitcher), discarding the bay leaves and lemon slices. Remove the skin from the haddock and flake the flesh into large pieces. Keep hot until required.

2 Melt the butter in the pan, add the onion and cook over a low heat for about 3 minutes, until softened. Stir in the turmeric, the curry powder and cardamom pods and cook for 1 minute.

3 Add the rice, stirring to coat it well with the butter. Pour in the reserved milk, stir and bring to the boil. Lower the heat and simmer the rice for 10–12 minutes, until all the milk has been absorbed and the rice is tender. Season to taste, going easy on the salt.

4 Gently stir in the fish and hard-boiled eggs, with the cream, if using. Sprinkle with the parsley and serve.

VARIATION
Use smoked or poached fresh salmon for a delicious change from haddock.

Per portion: Energy 579Kcal/2421kJ; Protein 34.4g; Carbohydrate 71.1g, of which sugars 0.9g; Fat 17g, of which saturates 8.2g; Cholesterol 257mg; Calcium 76mg; Fibre 0.2g; Sodium 1001mg.

CHICKEN AND PRAWN JAMBALAYA

THE MIXTURE OF CHICKEN, SEAFOOD AND RICE SUGGESTS A CLOSE RELATIONSHIP TO THE SPANISH PAELLA, BUT THE CREOLE NAME IS MORE LIKELY TO HAVE DERIVED FROM JAMBON (THE FRENCH FOR HAM), AND À LA YA (CREOLE FOR RICE). JAMBALAYAS ARE A COLOURFUL MIXTURE OF HIGHLY FLAVOURED INGREDIENTS, AND ARE MADE IN LARGE QUANTITIES FOR FEASTS AND CELEBRATION MEALS.

SERVES TEN

INGREDIENTS

2 chickens, each about 1.5kg/3–3½lb
450g/1lb piece raw smoked gammon (cured ham)
50g/2oz/4 tbsp lard or bacon fat
50g/2oz/½ cup plain (all-purpose) flour
3 onions, finely sliced
2 green (bell) peppers, seeded and sliced
675g/1½lb tomatoes, peeled and chopped
2–3 garlic cloves, crushed
10ml/2 tsp chopped fresh thyme
24 large raw prawns (shrimp), peeled and deveined
500g/1¼lb/3 cups white long grain rice
2–3 dashes Tabasco sauce
45ml/3 tbsp chopped fresh flat leaf parsley, plus sprigs, to garnish
salt and ground black pepper

1 Cut each chicken into 10 pieces and season with salt and pepper. Dice the gammon, discarding the rind and fat.

2 Melt the lard or bacon fat in a large, heavy frying pan. Add the chicken pieces, in batches, brown them all over, then lift them out with a slotted spoon and set them aside.

3 Reduce the heat. Sprinkle the flour into the fat in the pan and stir until the roux turns golden brown. Return the chicken pieces to the pan.

4 Add the diced gammon, onions, green peppers, tomatoes, garlic and thyme. Cook, stirring regularly, for 10 minutes, then add the prawns and mix lightly.

5 Stir the rice into the pan and pour in 1.2 litres/2 pints/5 cups water. Season to taste with salt, pepper and Tabasco sauce. Bring to the boil over a medium heat, then lower the heat, cover and cook gently until the rice is tender and all the liquid has been absorbed. Add a little extra boiling water if the rice looks as if it might be drying out before it is cooked.

6 Add the chopped flat leaf parsley and gently stir it into the finished dish, garnish with tiny sprigs of flat leaf parsley and serve immediately while piping hot.

Per portion: Energy 748Kcal/3117kJ; Protein 54.9g; Carbohydrate 50.3g, of which sugars 5.5g; Fat 36.2g, of which saturates 10.8g; Cholesterol 262mg; Calcium 70mg; Fibre 2g; Sodium 588mg.

CARIBBEAN PEANUT CHICKEN

PEANUT BUTTER IS USED A LOT IN MANY CARIBBEAN DISHES. IT ADDS A RICHNESS TO THE DISH,
AS WELL AS A DELICIOUS DEPTH OF FLAVOUR ALL OF ITS OWN.

SERVES FOUR

INGREDIENTS

    4 skinless, boneless chicken breast
      portions, cut into thin strips
    225g/8oz/generous 1 cup white long
      grain rice
    30ml/2 tbsp groundnut (peanut) oil
    15g/½oz/1 tbsp butter, plus extra
      for greasing
    1 onion, finely chopped
    2 tomatoes, peeled, seeded
      and chopped
    1 fresh green chilli, seeded
      and sliced
    60ml/4 tbsp smooth peanut butter
    450ml/¾ pint/scant 2 cups
      chicken stock
    lemon juice, to taste
    salt and ground black pepper
    lime wedges and fresh flat leaf
      parsley sprigs, to garnish
For the marinade
    15ml/1 tbsp sunflower oil
    1–2 garlic cloves, crushed
    5ml/1 tsp chopped fresh thyme
    25ml/1½ tbsp medium curry powder
    juice of half a lemon

1 Mix all the marinade ingredients in a large bowl and stir in the chicken. Cover loosely with clear film (plastic wrap) and set aside in a cool place for 2–3 hours.

2 Meanwhile, cook the rice in plenty of lightly salted, boiling water until tender. Drain well and turn into a generously buttered casserole.

3 Preheat the oven to 180°C/350°F/Gas 4. Heat 15ml/1 tbsp of the oil and butter in a flameproof casserole and cook the chicken pieces for 4–5 minutes, until evenly brown. Add more oil if necessary.

4 Transfer the chicken to a plate. Add the onion to the casserole and cook for 5–6 minutes until lightly browned. Stir in the tomatoes and chilli. Cook over a low heat for 3–4 minutes, stirring occasionally. Remove from the heat.

5 Mix the peanut butter with the chicken stock. Stir into the tomato and onion mixture, then add the chicken. Stir in the lemon juice, season to taste, then spoon the mixture over the rice in the casserole.

6 Cover the casserole, transfer it to the oven and cook for 15–20 minutes, or until piping hot. Use a large spoon to toss the rice with the chicken mixture. Serve immediately, garnished with the lime wedges and parsley sprigs.

COOK'S TIP
If the casserole is not large enough to let you toss the rice with the chicken mixture before serving, invert a large, deep plate over the casserole, turn both over and toss the mixture on the plate.

Per portion: Energy 606Kcal/2532kJ; Protein 46.4g; Carbohydrate 52.6g, of which sugars 5.3g; Fat 23.2g, of which saturates 6.6g; Cholesterol 113mg; Calcium 41mg; Fibre 2.3g; Sodium 202mg.

BURRITOS WITH CHICKEN AND RICE

*IN MEXICO, BURRITOS ARE A POPULAR STREET FOOD, EATEN ON THE HOOF. THE SECRET OF A
SUCCESSFUL BURRITO IS TO HAVE ALL THE FILLING NEATLY PACKAGED INSIDE THE TORTILLA FOR EASY
EATING, SO THESE SNACKS ARE SELDOM SERVED WITH A POUR-OVER SAUCE.*

SERVES FOUR

INGREDIENTS
   90g/3½oz/½ cup long grain rice
   15ml/1 tbsp vegetable oil
   1 onion, chopped
   2.5ml/½ tsp ground cloves
   5ml/1 tsp dried, or fresh oregano
   200g/7oz can chopped tomatoes
   2 skinless, boneless chicken
      breast portions
   150g/5oz/1¼ cups grated Monterey
      Jack or mild Cheddar cheese
   60ml/4 tbsp sour cream (optional)
   8 x 20–25cm/8–10in fresh wheat
      flour tortillas
   salt
   fresh oregano, to garnish (optional)

1 Bring a pan of lightly salted water to
the boil. Add the rice, bring back to the
boil and cook for 8 minutes. Drain,
rinse and then drain again.

2 Heat the oil in a large pan. Add the
onion, with the ground cloves and
oregano, and cook, stirring occasionally,
for 2–3 minutes. Stir in the rice and
tomatoes, with their can juice, and cook
over a low heat until all the tomato juice
has been absorbed. Remove the pan
from the heat and set aside.

VARIATION
For an extra touch of spice, you can add
3–4 canned or bottled jalapeño chillies
to the filling, with the chicken, and
substitute fresh coriander (cilantro) for
the oregano. Rinse, seed and finely
chop the chillies first.

3 Put the chicken portions in a large
pan, pour in enough water to cover and
bring to the boil. Lower the heat and
simmer for about 10 minutes, or until
the chicken is cooked through. Lift the
chicken out of the pan, put on a plate
and leave to cool slightly.

4 Preheat the oven to 160°C/325°F/
Gas 3. Shred the chicken by pulling the
flesh apart with two forks, then add
the chicken to the rice mixture, with the
grated cheese. Gently stir in the sour
cream, if using.

COOK'S TIP
If you use very fresh tortillas, you may be
able to dispense with the cocktail sticks.
Secure the tortilla parcels by damping
the final fold with a little water. When
you lay the burritos in the dish, place
them with the folded surfaces down.

5 Wrap the tortillas in foil and place
them on a plate. Stand the plate over
boiling water for about 5 minutes.
Alternatively, wrap in microwave-safe
film and heat in a microwave on full
power for 1 minute.

6 Spoon one-eighth of the filling into the
centre of a tortilla and fold in both
sides. Fold the bottom up and the top
down to form a parcel. Secure with a
cocktail stick (toothpick).

7 Put the filled burrito in a shallow dish
or casserole, cover with foil and keep
warm in the oven while you make seven
more. Remove the cocktail sticks before
serving, sprinkled with fresh oregano.

Per portion: Energy 625Kcal/2628kJ; Protein 37.4g; Carbohydrate 82.2g, of which sugars 4.6g; Fat 17.1g, of which saturates 8.7g; Cholesterol 89mg; Calcium 411mg; Fibre 3.3g; Sodium 617mg.

BEEF BIRYANI

THE MOGULS INTRODUCED THIS DRY, SPICY RICE DISH TO CENTRAL INDIA.

SERVES FOUR

INGREDIENTS

2 large onions
2 garlic cloves, chopped
2.5cm/1in piece of fresh root ginger,
   peeled and coarsely chopped
½–1 fresh green chilli, seeded and
   coarsely chopped
bunch of fresh coriander (cilantro)
60ml/4 tbsp flaked (sliced) almonds
30–45ml/2–3 tbsp water
15ml/1 tbsp ghee or butter, plus
   25g/1oz/2 tbsp butter, for the rice
45ml/3 tbsp sunflower oil
30ml/2 tbsp sultanas (golden raisins)
500g/1¼lb braising or stewing
   steak, cubed
5ml/1 tsp ground coriander
15ml/1 tbsp ground cumin
2.5ml/½ tsp ground turmeric
2.5ml/½ tsp ground fenugreek
good pinch of ground cinnamon
175ml/6fl oz/¾ cup natural
   (plain) yogurt
275g/10oz/1½ cups basmati rice
about 1.2 litres/2 pints/5 cups hot
   chicken stock or water
salt and ground black pepper
2 hard-boiled eggs, quartered,
   to garnish

1 Coarsely chop 1 onion and place it in a food processor or blender. Add the garlic, ginger, chilli, fresh coriander and half the flaked almonds. Pour in the water and process to a smooth paste.

2 Thinly slice the remaining onion into rings or half rings. Heat half the ghee or butter with half the oil in a heavy, flameproof casserole and cook the onion rings over a medium heat for 10–15 minutes, until they are a deep golden brown. Transfer to a plate with a slotted spoon. Cook the remaining flaked almonds briefly until golden and set aside with the onion rings, then quickly cook the sultanas until they swell. Transfer to the plate.

3 Heat the remaining ghee or butter in the casserole with a further 15ml/1 tbsp of the oil. Cook the meat, in batches, until evenly browned. Transfer to a plate and set aside.

4 Wipe the casserole clean with kitchen paper, heat the remaining oil and pour in the onion and ginger paste. Cook over a medium heat, stirring constantly, for 2–3 minutes, until the mixture begins to brown lightly. Stir in the ground coriander, cumin, turmeric, fenugreek and cinnamon, season to taste with salt and pepper and cook for 1 minute more.

5 Lower the heat, then gradually stir in the yogurt, a little at a time. When all of it has been incorporated into the spice mixture, return the meat to the casserole. Stir to coat, cover tightly and simmer over a gentle heat for about 40–45 minutes, until the meat is tender.

6 Meanwhile, place the rice in a large bowl, pour in cold water to cover and leave to soak for 15–20 minutes.

7 Preheat the oven to 160°C/325°F/ Gas 3. Drain the rice, place it in a pan and add the hot chicken stock or water, together with a little salt. Bring back to the boil, cover, lower the heat and cook for 5–6 minutes.

8 Drain the rice and pile it in a mound on top of the meat in the casserole. Using the handle of a spoon, make a hole through the rice and meat mixture, to the base of the pan. Sprinkle the onion rings, almonds and sultanas over the top and dot with butter. Cover the casserole tightly with a double layer of foil and secure with a lid.

9 Cook the biryani in the oven for 30–40 minutes. To serve, spoon the mixture on to a warmed serving plate and garnish with the quartered hard-boiled eggs. Serve with parathas, naan bread or chapatis, if you like.

COOK'S TIP
When you are cooking the onion and ginger paste and the ground spices, reduce the heat to very low and stir constantly to avoid scorching them.

Per portion: Energy 778Kcal/3240kJ; Protein 40g; Carbohydrate 70.4g, of which sugars 13.4g; Fat 37.4g, of which saturates 11.8g; Cholesterol 94mg; Calcium 164mg; Fibre 2.3g; Sodium 183mg.

PASTA, GNOCCHI AND NOODLES

For sheer all-round popularity, pasta dishes top the bill.

Pasta cooks quickly and looks as good as it tastes. It is easy

to digest and gives slow-release energy. This chapter includes

dishes suitable for vegetarians and vegans, as well as such

classics as Clams with Neapolitan Tomato Sauce, which

features vermicelli. Asian noodles are well represented, too.

For a special treat, try Thai Crispy Noodles with Beef, or

give your tastebuds a treat with Potato Gnocchi with

Simple Tomato and Butter Sauce.

PASTA WITH GARLIC AND CHILLI

THIS IS THE SIMPLEST OF PASTA DISHES AND ONE OF THE BEST. MINT AND OREGANO GIVE VERY DIFFERENT RESULTS, BOTH GOOD. THERE IS NO NEED TO SERVE GRATED PARMESAN WITH THIS DISH – INSTEAD, LET THE CLEAR FLAVOUR OF THE GARLIC AND OLIVE OIL SING OUT.

SERVES THREE TO FOUR

INGREDIENTS
400g/14oz dried spaghetti
105ml/7 tbsp extra virgin olive oil,
  plus extra to taste
1.5ml/¼ tsp dried red chilli flakes or
  2 small whole dried red chillies
6 large garlic cloves, finely chopped
15ml/1 tbsp chopped fresh mint
  or oregano
15g/½ oz chopped fresh flat
  leaf parsley
salt and ground black pepper

1 Cook the spaghetti in lightly salted, boiling water for 9–11 minutes, or according to the packet instructions, until just tender.

2 Meanwhile, heat the oil in a large frying pan or pan over a very gentle heat. Add the chilli flakes or whole chillies and cook very gently for 2–3 minutes.

COOK'S TIP
If you use fresh spaghetti, cook for only 2–3 minutes in salted, boiling water.

3 Add the garlic to the pan. Keep the heat very low, so that the garlic barely bubbles and does not brown, then cook, shaking the pan occasionally, for about 2 minutes. Remove the pan from the heat and cool a little, then add the fresh mint or oregano.

4 Drain the pasta, then immediately add it to the oil and garlic mixture, with the parsley. Toss thoroughly. Season with freshly ground black pepper and transfer to warmed serving bowls. Serve immediately, offering more olive oil for drizzling at the table.

VARIATION
Cook 250g/9oz broccoli florets in salted, boiling water for 4 minutes. Add to the chilli oil and cook for 5–8 minutes.

Per portion: Energy 688Kcal/2897kJ; Protein 16.2g; Carbohydrate 98.9g, of which sugars 4.5g; Fat 28.1g, of which saturates 3.9g; Cholesterol 0mg; Calcium 43mg; Fibre 4.1g; Sodium 6mg.

RIGATONI WITH TOMATOES AND FRESH HERBS

THIS PRETTY AND COLOURFUL PASTA DISH RELIES FOR ITS SUCCESS ON THE BEST ITALIAN CANNED TOMATOES AND TENDER YOUNG HERBS, FRESHLY PICKED. FOR A REAL TREAT, USE FRESH TOMATOES, PEELED AND PURÉED. ADD A LITTLE SUGAR IF THE TOMATOES ARE NOT AT THE PEAK OF RIPENESS.

SERVES SIX TO EIGHT

INGREDIENTS
    1 onion
    1 carrot
    1 celery stick
    60ml/4 tbsp olive oil
    1 garlic clove, thinly sliced
    a few leaves each of fresh basil,
        thyme and oregano or marjoram
    2 x 400g/14oz cans chopped Italian
        plum tomatoes
    15ml/1 tbsp sun-dried tomato paste
    5ml/1 tsp granulated sugar
    about 90ml/6 tbsp dry red or white
        wine (optional)
    350g/12oz/3 cups dried rigatoni
    salt and ground black pepper
    coarsely shaved Parmesan cheese,
        to serve

COOK'S TIP
Large pasta tubes are best for this recipe, as they capture the wonderful tomato and herb sauce. If you can't get rigatoni, try penne or penne rigate (ridged penne).

1 Chop the onion, carrot and celery stick finely, either in a food processor or by hand, with a sharp knife.

2 Heat the olive oil in a medium pan, add the garlic slices and stir over a very low heat for 1–2 minutes. Do not let the garlic burn or it will taste bitter.

3 Add the chopped vegetables and the fresh herbs, reserving a few to garnish. Cook over a low heat, stirring frequently, for 5–7 minutes, until the vegetables have softened and are lightly coloured.

4 Add the canned tomatoes, tomato paste and sugar, then stir in the wine, if using. Add salt and pepper to taste. Bring to the boil, stirring, then lower the heat to a gentle simmer. Cook, stirring frequently, for about 45 minutes.

5 Cook the pasta in lightly salted, boiling water for 10–12 minutes, drain and tip into a warmed bowl. Pour the sauce over the pasta and toss well. Garnish with the reserved herbs. Serve immediately, with shavings of Parmesan handed separately.

Per portion: Energy 313Kcal/1323kJ; Protein 8.8g; Carbohydrate 51g, of which sugars 8.8g; Fat 8.6g, of which saturates 1.2g; Cholesterol 0mg; Calcium 43mg; Fibre 3.3g; Sodium 62mg.

CLAMS WITH NEAPOLITAN TOMATO SAUCE

THIS RECIPE TAKES ITS NAME FROM THE CITY OF NAPLES, WHERE BOTH FRESH TOMATO SAUCE AND SHELLFISH ARE TRADITIONALLY SERVED WITH VERMICELLI. HERE THE TWO ARE COMBINED TO MAKE A VERY TASTY DISH THAT IS PERFECT FOR A COLD WINTER'S EVENING.

SERVES FOUR

INGREDIENTS

1kg/2¼lb fresh clams
250ml/8fl oz/1 cup dry white wine,
    or vegetable stock
2 garlic cloves, bruised
1 large handful fresh flat leaf parsley
30ml/2 tbsp extra virgin olive oil or
    sunflower oil
1 small onion, finely chopped
8 ripe plum tomatoes, peeled, seeded
    and finely chopped
½–1 fresh red chilli, seeded and
    finely chopped
350g/12oz dried vermicelli
salt and ground black pepper

1 Scrub the clams thoroughly with a brush under cold running water and discard any that are open or do not close their shells when sharply tapped against the work surface.

2 Pour the white wine or vegetable stock into a large, heavy pan and add the bruised garlic cloves. Shred half the parsley finely, add to the wine or stock, then add the clams.

3 Cover the pan tightly with the lid and bring to the boil over a high heat. Cook for about 5 minutes, shaking the pan frequently, until the clams have opened.

4 Tip the clams into a large colander set over a bowl and let the liquid drain through. Leave the clams until cool enough to handle, then remove about two-thirds of them from their shells, tipping the clam liquor into the bowl of cooking liquid. Discard any clams that have failed to open.

5 Set both shelled and unshelled clams aside, keeping the unshelled clams warm in a bowl covered with a lid or thick cloth.

6 Heat the oil in a pan, add the onion and cook gently, stirring frequently, for about 5 minutes, until softened and lightly coloured. Add the tomatoes, then strain in the clam cooking liquid. Add the chilli, and salt and pepper to taste.

7 Bring to the boil, half cover the pan and simmer gently for 15–20 minutes. Meanwhile, cook the pasta according to the packet instructions. Chop the remaining parsley finely.

8 Add the shelled clams to the tomato sauce, stir well and heat through very gently for 2–3 minutes.

9 Drain the cooked pasta well and tip it into a warmed bowl. Taste the sauce for seasoning, then pour the sauce over the pasta and toss everything together well. Garnish with the reserved clams, sprinkle the parsley over the pasta and serve immediately.

Per portion: Energy 500Kcal/2091kJ; Protein 21.6g; Carbohydrate 77.3g, of which sugars 6.9g; Fat 7.1g, of which saturates 1.1g; Cholesterol 50mg; Calcium 134mg; Fibre 2.9g; Sodium 932mg.

PASTA WITH TOMATOES AND SHELLFISH

COLOURFUL AND DELICIOUS, THIS TYPICAL GENOESE DISH IS IDEAL FOR A DINNER PARTY. THE TOMATO SAUCE IS QUITE RUNNY, SO SERVE IT WITH CRUSTY BREAD AND SPOONS AS WELL AS FORKS. FOR A REAL TASTE OF ITALY, CHOOSE A DRY WHITE ITALIAN WINE TO SERVE WITH THE MEAL.

SERVES FOUR

INGREDIENTS
45ml/3 tbsp olive oil
1 small onion, chopped
1 garlic clove, crushed
½ fresh red chilli, seeded
and chopped
200g/7oz can chopped
plum tomatoes
30ml/2 tbsp chopped fresh flat
leaf parsley
400g/14oz fresh clams
400g/14oz fresh mussels
60ml/4 tbsp dry white wine
400g/14oz/3½ cups dried trenette
or spaghetti
a few fresh basil leaves
90g/3½oz/⅔ cup cooked, peeled
prawns (shrimp), thawed and
thoroughly dried if frozen
salt and ground black pepper
lemon wedges and chopped fresh herbs,
such as parsley or thyme, to garnish

1 Heat 30ml/2tbsp of the oil in a frying pan or medium pan. Add the onion, garlic and chilli and cook over a medium heat for 1–2 minutes, stirring constantly. Stir in the tomatoes, half the parsley and pepper to taste. Bring to the boil, lower the heat, cover and simmer for 15 minutes.

2 Meanwhile, scrub the clams and mussels under cold running water. Discard any that are open and that do not close when sharply tapped against the work surface.

3 In a large pan, heat the remaining oil. Add the clams and mussels, with the rest of the parsley and toss over a high heat for a few seconds. Pour in the wine, then cover tightly. Cook for about 5 minutes, shaking the pan frequently, until the clams and mussels have opened.

4 Transfer the clams and mussels to a bowl, discarding any shellfish that have failed to open. Strain the cooking liquid and set aside. Reserve eight clams and four mussels for the garnish, then remove the rest from their shells.

5 Cook the pasta according to the instructions on the packet. Meanwhile, add 120ml/4fl oz/½ cup of the reserved shellfish liquid to the tomato sauce. Add the basil, prawns, shelled clams and mussels to the sauce. Season.

6 Drain the pasta and tip it into a warmed bowl. Add the sauce and toss well to combine. Serve in individual bowls. Sprinkle with herbs and garnish each portion with lemon, two clams and one mussel in their shells.

Per portion: Energy 510Kcal/2160kJ; Protein 27.2g; Carbohydrate 77.1g, of which sugars 5.6g; Fat 11.5g, of which saturates 1.6g; Cholesterol 68mg; Calcium 180mg; Fibre 3.5g; Sodium 193mg.

LOBSTER RAVIOLI

*IT IS ESSENTIAL TO USE HOME-MADE PASTA TO OBTAIN THE DELICACY AND THINNESS THAT THIS
SUPERB FILLING DESERVES. BEFORE YOU START THE RECIPE, MAKE A WELL-FLAVOURED FISH STOCK,
USING THE LOBSTER SHELL AND HEAD.*

SERVES FOUR

INGREDIENTS

   1 lobster, about 450g/1lb, cooked
     and taken out of the shell
   2 soft white bread slices, about
     50g/2oz, crusts removed
   200ml/7fl oz/scant 1 cup fish stock
   1 egg
   250ml/8fl oz/1 cup double
     (heavy) cream
   15ml/1 tbsp chopped fresh chives,
     plus extra to garnish
   15ml/1 tbsp finely chopped
     fresh chervil
   salt and ground white pepper
   fresh chives, to garnish
For the pasta dough
   225g/8oz/2 cups strong plain (all-
     purpose) flour
   2 eggs, plus 2 egg yolks
For the mushroom sauce
   a large pinch of saffron threads
   25g/1oz/2 tbsp butter
   2 shallots, finely chopped
   200g/7oz/3 cups button (white)
     mushrooms, finely chopped
   juice of ½ lemon
   200ml/7fl oz/scant 1 cup
     double (heavy) cream

1 Make the pasta dough. Sift the flour
with a pinch of salt. Put into a food
processor with the eggs and yolks and
process until the mixture resembles
breadcrumbs. Turn out on to a floured
surface; knead to a smooth dough. Wrap
in clear film (plastic wrap) and leave to
rest in the refrigerator for 1 hour.

2 Meanwhile, make the lobster filling.
Cut the lobster meat into large chunks
and place in a bowl. Tear the white
bread into small pieces and soak them
in 45ml/3 tbsp of the fish stock. Place in
a food processor with half the egg and
30–45ml/2–3 tbsp of the double cream
and process until smooth. Stir the
mixture into the lobster meat, then add
the chives and chervil and season to
taste with salt and white pepper.

3 Roll the ravioli dough to a thickness of
3mm/⅛in, preferably using a pasta
machine. The process can be done by
hand with a rolling pin but is quite
hard work. Divide the dough into four
rectangles and dust each rectangle
lightly with flour.

4 Spoon six equal heaps of filling on to
one sheet of pasta, leaving about
3cm/1¼in between each pile of filling.
Lightly beat the remaining egg with a
tablespoon of water and brush it over
the pasta between the piles of filling.
Cover with a second sheet of pasta.
Repeat with the other two sheets of
pasta and remaining filling.

5 Using your fingertips, press the top
layer of dough down well between the
piles of filling, making sure each is well
sealed. Cut between the heaps with a
7.5cm/3in fluted pastry cutter or a
pasta wheel to make twelve ravioli.

6 Place the ravioli in a single layer on a
baking sheet, cover with clear film or a
damp cloth, and put in the refrigerator
while you make the sauces.

7 Make the mushroom sauce. Soak the
saffron in 15ml/1 tbsp warm water. Melt
the butter in a pan and cook the
shallots over a low heat until they are
soft but not coloured.

8 Add the chopped mushrooms and
lemon juice and continue to cook over a
low heat until almost all the liquid has
evaporated. Stir in the saffron, with its
soaking water, and the cream, then
cook gently, stirring occasionally, until
the sauce has thickened. Keep warm
while you cook the ravioli.

9 In another pan, bring the remaining fish stock to the boil, stir in the rest of the cream and bubble to make a slightly thickened sauce. Season to taste with salt and pepper and keep warm. Bring a large pan of lightly salted water to a rolling boil. Gently drop in the ravioli (left) and cook for 3–4 minutes, until the pasta is just tender.

10 Place three ravioli on to the centre of each of four individual warmed plates, spoon over a little of the mushroom sauce and pour a ribbon of fish sauce around the edge. Serve immediately, garnished with chopped and whole fresh chives.

SEAFOOD LASAGNE

THIS DISH CAN BE AS SIMPLE OR AS ELEGANT AS YOU LIKE. FOR A DINNER PARTY, DRESS IT UP WITH SCALLOPS, MUSSELS OR PRAWNS AND A REALLY GENEROUS PINCH OF SAFFRON IN THE SAUCE; FOR A FAMILY SUPPER, USE SIMPLE FISH, SUCH AS COD AND SMOKED HADDOCK. THE LASAGNE CAN BE PREPARED IN ADVANCE AND BAKED AT THE LAST MOMENT.

SERVES EIGHT

INGREDIENTS
   350g/12oz monkfish
   350g/12oz salmon fillet
   350g/12oz undyed smoked haddock
   1 litre/1¾ pints/4 cups milk
   500ml/17fl oz/generous 2 cups
      fish stock
   2 bay leaves or a good pinch of
      saffron threads
   1 small onion, peeled and halved
   75g/3oz/6 tbsp butter, plus extra
      for greasing
   45ml/3 tbsp plain (all-purpose) flour
   150g/5oz/2 cups mushrooms, sliced
   225–300g/8–11oz no-precook or
      fresh lasagne
   60ml/4 tbsp freshly grated
      Parmesan cheese
   salt, ground black pepper, grated
      nutmeg and paprika
   rocket (arugula) leaves, to garnish
For the tomato sauce
   30ml/2 tbsp olive oil
   1 red onion, finely chopped
   1 garlic clove, finely chopped
   400g/14oz can chopped tomatoes
   15ml/1 tbsp tomato purée (paste)
   15ml/1 tbsp torn fresh basil leaves

1 Make the tomato sauce. Heat the oil in a pan and cook the onion and garlic over a low heat for 5 minutes, until softened and golden. Stir in the tomatoes and tomato purée and simmer for 20–30 minutes, stirring occasionally. Season to taste with salt and pepper and stir in the basil.

COOK'S TIP
It is preferable to use fresh lasagne, if available, as it has a better flavour and texture. Cook the sheets, in batches if necessary, in a large pan of lightly salted, boiling water for 3 minutes. Do not overcrowd the pan or the sheets will stick together.

2 Put all the fish in a shallow flameproof dish or pan with the milk, stock, bay leaves or saffron and onion. Bring to the boil over a medium heat. Poach for 5 minutes, until almost cooked. Leave to cool.

3 When the fish is almost cold, strain it, reserving the liquid. Remove the skin and any bones and flake the flesh.

4 Preheat the oven to 180°C/350°F/ Gas 4. Melt the butter in a pan, stir in the flour; cook for 2 minutes, stirring. Gradually add the poaching liquid and bring to the boil, stirring. Add the mushrooms, cook for 2–3 minutes; season with salt, pepper and nutmeg.

5 Lightly grease a shallow ovenproof dish. Spoon a thin layer of the mushroom sauce over the base of the dish and spread it with a spatula. Stir the fish into the remaining mushroom sauce in the pan.

6 Make a layer of lasagne, then a layer of fish and sauce. Add another layer of lasagne, then spread over all the tomato sauce. Continue to layer the lasagne and fish, finish with a layer of lasagne.

7 Sprinkle over the grated Parmesan cheese. Bake for 30–45 minutes, until bubbling and golden. Before serving, sprinkle with paprika and garnish with rocket leaves.

Per portion: Energy 411Kcal/1724kJ; Protein 32.2g; Carbohydrate 29.8g, of which sugars 3.6g; Fat 18.9g, of which saturates 7.8g; Cholesterol 71mg; Calcium 143mg; Fibre 1.9g; Sodium 525mg.

SPAGHETTI WITH EGGS, BACON AND CREAM

THIS ITALIAN CLASSIC, FLAVOURED WITH PANCETTA AND A GARLIC AND EGG SAUCE THAT COOKS AROUND THE HOT SPAGHETTI, IS POPULAR WORLDWIDE. IT MAKES A GREAT LAST-MINUTE SUPPER.

3 Meanwhile, cook the spaghetti in a large pan of salted, boiling water according to the instructions on the packet until *al dente*.

4 Put the eggs, crème fraîche and grated Parmesan in a bowl. Stir in plenty of black pepper, then beat together well.

5 Drain the pasta thoroughly, tip it into the pan with the pancetta or bacon and toss well to mix.

6 Turn off the heat under the pan, then immediately add the egg mixture and toss thoroughly so that it cooks lightly and coats the pasta.

7 Season to taste, then divide the spaghetti among four warmed bowls and sprinkle with freshly ground black pepper. Serve immediately, with extra grated Parmesan handed separately.

COOK'S TIP
You can replace the crème fraîche with either double (heavy) cream or sour cream, if you like.

SERVES FOUR

INGREDIENTS
30ml/2 tbsp olive oil
1 small onion, finely chopped
1 large garlic clove, crushed
8 pancetta or rindless smoked streaky (fatty) bacon rashers (strips), cut into 1cm/½in strips
350g/12oz fresh or dried spaghetti
4 eggs
90–120ml/6–8 tbsp/½ cup crème fraîche
60ml/4 tbsp freshly grated Parmesan cheese, plus extra to serve
salt and ground black pepper

1 Heat the oil in a large pan, add the onion and garlic and cook gently for about 5 minutes, until softened.

2 Add the pancetta or bacon to the pan and cook for 10 minutes, stirring.

Per portion: Energy 686Kcal/2873kJ; Protein 31.1g; Carbohydrate 66.6g, of which sugars 4.2g; Fat 34.5g, of which saturates 14.8g; Cholesterol 213mg; Calcium 243mg; Fibre 2.8g; Sodium 1098mg.

TURKEY LASAGNE

THIS EASY MEAL-IN-ONE BAKED PASTA DISH IS DELICIOUS MADE WITH COOKED TURKEY PIECES AND BROCCOLI IN A RICH, CREAMY PARMESAN SAUCE.

SERVES FOUR

INGREDIENTS

   30ml/2 tbsp light olive oil
   1 onion, chopped
   2 garlic cloves, chopped
   450g/1lb cooked turkey meat,
     finely diced
   225g/8oz/1 cup mascarpone cheese
   30ml/2 tbsp chopped fresh tarragon
   300g/11oz broccoli, broken
     into florets
   salt and ground black pepper
For the sauce
   50g/2oz/¼ cup butter
   30ml/2 tbsp plain (all-purpose) flour
   600ml/1 pint/2½ cups milk
   75g/3oz/1 cup freshly grated
     Parmesan cheese
   115g/4oz no pre-cook lasagne verdi

3 To make the sauce, melt the butter in a pan, stir in the flour and cook for 1 minute, still stirring. Remove from the heat and gradually stir in the milk. Return to the heat and bring the sauce to the boil, stirring constantly. Simmer for 1 minute, then add 50g/2oz/⅔ cup of the Parmesan and plenty of salt and pepper.

4 Spoon a layer of the turkey mixture into a large, shallow ovenproof dish. Add a layer of broccoli and cover with sheets of lasagne. Coat with cheese sauce. Repeat these layers, finishing with a layer of cheese sauce on top. Sprinkle with the remaining Parmesan and bake for 35–40 minutes.

1 Preheat the oven to 180°C/350°F/ Gas 4. Heat the oil in a heavy pan and cook the onion and garlic until softened but not coloured. Remove the pan from the heat and stir in the diced turkey, mascarpone and tarragon and season with salt and pepper to taste.

2 Blanch the broccoli in a large pan of salted, boiling water for 1 minute, then drain and rinse thoroughly under cold water to prevent the broccoli from overcooking. Drain well and set aside.

COOK'S TIP
This is a delicious way of using up any cooked turkey that is left over after Christmas or Thanksgiving celebrations. It is also especially good made with half ham and half turkey.

Per portion: Energy 732Kcal/3072kJ; Protein 61.6g; Carbohydrate 43g, of which sugars 13.1g; Fat 36.2g, of which saturates 19.4g; Cholesterol 138mg; Calcium 539mg; Fibre 3.6g; Sodium 475mg.

POTATO GNOCCHI

GNOCCHI CAN BE MADE EITHER WITH MASHED POTATO AND FLOUR, OR WITH SEMOLINA. TO MAKE SURE THAT THEY ARE LIGHT AND FLUFFY, TAKE CARE NOT TO OVERMIX THE DOUGH.

4 Divide the dough into four pieces. On a lightly floured surface, form each into a roll about 2cm/¾in in diameter. Cut the rolls crossways into pieces about 2cm/¾in long.

5 Hold an ordinary table fork with tines sideways, leaning on the board. Then one by one, press and roll the gnocchi lightly along the tines of the fork towards the points, making ridges on one side, and a depression from your thumb on the other.

6 Bring a large pan of salted water to a fast boil, then drop in about half the prepared gnocchi.

7 When the gnocchi rise to the surface, after 3–4 minutes, they are done. Lift them out with a slotted spoon, drain well, and place in a warmed serving bowl. Dot with butter. Cover to keep warm while cooking the remainder. As soon as they are cooked, toss the gnocchi with the butter, garnish with Parmesan shavings and fresh basil leaves, and serve immediately.

SERVES FOUR TO SIX

INGREDIENTS
  1kg/2¼lb waxy potatoes
  250–300g/9–11oz/2¼–2¾ cups
    plain flour (all-purpose), plus more
    if necessary
  1 egg
  pinch of freshly grated nutmeg
  25g/1oz/2 tbsp butter
  salt
  fresh basil leaves, to garnish
  Parmesan cheese cut in shavings,
    to garnish

COOK'S TIP
Gnocchi are also excellent served with a heated sauce, such as Bolognese or a simple cheese sauce.

1 Cook the potatoes in their skins in a large pan of lightly salted, boiling water until tender but not falling apart. Drain and peel while the potatoes are still hot.

2 Spread a layer of flour on a work surface. Pass the hot potatoes through a food mill, dropping them directly on to the flour. Sprinkle with about half of the remaining flour and mix in very lightly. Break the egg into the mixture.

3 Finally, add the nutmeg to the dough and knead lightly, adding more flour if the mixture is too loose. When the dough is light to the touch and no longer moist, it is ready to be rolled.

Per portion: Energy 454Kcal/1921kJ; Protein 11.7g; Carbohydrate 88.9g, of which sugars 4.2g; Fat 8.1g, of which saturates 4g; Cholesterol 61mg; Calcium 111mg; Fibre 4.5g; Sodium 85mg.

POTATO GNOCCHI <u>WITH</u> SIMPLE TOMATO <u>AND</u> BUTTER SAUCE

GNOCCHI MAKE A SUBSTANTIAL AND TASTY ALTERNATIVE TO PASTA. IN THIS DISH THEY ARE SERVED WITH A VERY SIMPLE, BUT DELICIOUS, FRESH TOMATO SAUCE.

<u>SERVES FOUR</u>

INGREDIENTS

675g/1½lb floury potatoes
2 egg yolks
75g/3oz/¾ cup plain (all-purpose) flour
60ml/4 tbsp finely chopped fresh
    parsley, to garnish
For the sauce
25g/1oz/2 tbsp butter, melted
450g/1lb plum tomatoes, peeled,
    seeded and chopped
salt

1 Preheat the oven to 200°C/400°F/ Gas 6. Scrub the potatoes, then bake them in their skins in the oven for 1 hour, or until the flesh feels soft when pricked with a fork.

2 While the potatoes are still warm, cut them in half and gently squeeze the flesh into a bowl, or use a spoon to scrape the flesh out of the shells. Mash the potato well, then season with a little salt. Add the egg yolks and mix lightly with a fork or spoon.

3 Add the flour and mix to a coarse dough. Place on a floured work surface and knead for 5 minutes, until the dough is smooth and elastic.

4 Shape the dough into thumb-sized shapes by making long rolls and cutting them into segments. Press each of these with the back of a fork. Place the gnocchi on a floured work surface.

5 Preheat the oven to 140°C/275°F/ Gas 1. Cook the gnocchi, in small batches, in barely simmering, slightly salted water for about 10 minutes. Remove with a slotted spoon, drain well and tip into a dish. Cover and keep hot in the oven.

6 To make the sauce, heat the butter in a small pan for 1 minute, then add the tomatoes and cook over a low heat until the juice starts to run. Sprinkle the gnocchi with chopped parsley and serve with the sauce.

Per portion: Energy 278Kcal/1174kJ; Protein 6.9g; Carbohydrate 45.3g, of which sugars 6g; Fat 9g, of which saturates 4.4g; Cholesterol 114mg; Calcium 57mg; Fibre 3.4g; Sodium 72mg.

INDIAN MEE GORENG

THIS IS A TRULY INTERNATIONAL DISH COMBINING INDIAN, CHINESE AND WESTERN INGREDIENTS.
IT IS A DELICIOUS TREAT FOR LUNCH OR SUPPER AND IN SINGAPORE AND MALAYSIA CAN BE
BOUGHT IN MANY STREETS FROM ONE OF THE NUMEROUS HAWKERS' STALLS.

2 If using fried tofu, cut each cube in half, refresh it in a pan of boiling water, then drain well. Heat 30ml/2 tbsp of the oil in a large frying pan. If using plain tofu, cut it into cubes and cook until brown, then lift it out with a slotted spoon and set aside.

3 Beat the eggs with the water and seasoning. Add to the oil in the frying pan and cook without stirring until set. Flip over, cook the other side, then slide it out of the pan, roll up and slice thinly.

SERVES FOUR TO SIX

INGREDIENTS
    450g/1lb fresh yellow egg noodles
    60–90ml/4–6 tbsp vegetable oil
    115g/4oz fried tofu or 150g/5oz
      firm tofu
    2 eggs
    30ml/2 tbsp water
    1 onion, sliced
    1 garlic clove, crushed
    15ml/1 tbsp light soy sauce
    30–45ml/2–3 tbsp tomato ketchup
    15ml/1 tbsp chilli sauce (or to taste)
    1 large cooked potato, diced
    4 spring onions (scallions), shredded
    1–2 fresh green chillies, seeded
      and thinly sliced (optional)

1 Bring a large pan of water to the boil, add the fresh egg noodles and cook for just 2 minutes. Drain the noodles and immediately rinse them under cold water to halt cooking. Drain again and set aside.

4 Heat the remaining oil in a wok and cook the onion and garlic for 2–3 minutes. Add the drained noodles, soy sauce, ketchup and chilli sauce. Toss well over medium heat for 2 minutes, then add the diced potato. Reserve a few spring onions for garnish and stir the rest into the noodles with the chilli, if using, and the tofu.

5 When hot, stir in the omelette. Serve on a hot platter, garnished with the remaining spring onion.

Per portion: Energy 662Kcal/2788kJ; Protein 20.7g; Carbohydrate 95.8g, of which sugars 8.8g; Fat 24.5g, of which saturates 4.9g; Cholesterol 129mg; Calcium 210mg; Fibre 4.5g; Sodium 715mg.

SICHUAN NOODLES <u>WITH</u> SESAME SAUCE

THIS TASTY CHINESE VEGETARIAN DISH RESEMBLES THAMIN LETHOK, A BURMESE DISH, WHICH ALSO CONSISTS OF FLAVOURED NOODLES SERVED WITH SEPARATE VEGETABLES THAT ARE TOSSED AT THE TABLE. THIS ILLUSTRATES NEATLY HOW RECIPES MIGRATE FROM ONE COUNTRY TO ANOTHER.

SERVES THREE TO FOUR

INGREDIENTS

450g/1lb fresh or 225g/8oz dried
  egg noodles
1/2 cucumber, sliced lengthways,
  seeded and diced
4–6 spring onions (scallions)
a bunch of radishes, about 115g/4oz
225g/8oz mooli (daikon), peeled
115g/4oz/2 cups beansprouts, rinsed
  then left in iced water and drained
60ml/4 tbsp groundnut (peanut) oil
  or sunflower oil
2 garlic cloves, crushed
45ml/3 tbsp toasted sesame paste
15ml/1 tbsp sesame oil
15ml/1 tbsp light soy sauce
5–10ml/1–2 tsp chilli sauce, to taste
15ml/1 tbsp rice vinegar
120ml/4fl oz/1/2 cup chicken stock
  or water
5ml/1 tsp sugar, or to taste
salt and ground black pepper
roasted peanuts or cashew nuts,
  to garnish

1 If using fresh noodles, cook them in boiling water for 1 minute, then drain well. Rinse the noodles in fresh water and drain again. Cook dried noodles according to the instructions on the packet, draining and rinsing them as for fresh noodles.

2 Sprinkle the cucumber with salt, leave for 15 minutes, rinse well, then drain and pat dry on kitchen paper. Place in a large salad bowl.

3 Cut the spring onions into fine shreds. Cut the radishes in half and slice finely. Coarsely grate the mooli using a mandolin or a food processor. Add all the vegetables to the cucumber and toss gently.

4 Heat half the oil in a wok or frying pan and stir-fry the noodles for about 1 minute. Using a slotted spoon, transfer the noodles to a large serving bowl and keep warm.

5 Add the remaining oil to the wok. When it is hot, cook the garlic to flavour the oil. Remove from the heat and stir in the sesame paste, with the sesame oil, soy and chilli sauces, vinegar and stock or water. Add a little sugar and season to taste. Warm through over a gentle heat. Do not overheat or the sauce will thicken too much. Pour the sauce over the noodles and toss well. Garnish with peanuts or cashew nuts and serve with the vegetables.

Per portion: Energy 383Kcal/1592kJ; Protein 8.7g; Carbohydrate 24.9g, of which sugars 4.8g; Fat 28.3g, of which saturates 3.9g; Cholesterol 9mg; Calcium 153mg; Fibre 4.2g; Sodium 398mg.

FIVE-FLAVOUR NOODLES

THE JAPANESE NAME FOR THIS DISH IS GOMOKU YAKISOBA, *MEANING FIVE DIFFERENT INGREDIENTS; HOWEVER, YOU CAN ADD AS MANY DIFFERENT INGREDIENTS AS YOU WISH TO MAKE AN EXCITING AND TASTY NOODLE STIR-FRY.*

SERVES FOUR

INGREDIENTS
300g/11oz dried Chinese thin egg
  noodles or 500g/1¼lb fresh yakisoba noodles
200g/7oz lean boneless pork,
  thinly sliced
22.5ml/4½ tsp sunflower oil
10g/¼oz grated fresh root ginger
1 garlic clove, crushed
200g/7oz green cabbage,
  coarsely chopped
115g/4oz/2 cups beansprouts
1 green (bell) pepper, seeded and cut
  into fine strips
1 red (bell) pepper, seeded and cut
  into fine strips
salt and ground black pepper
20ml/4 tsp ao-nori seaweed, to
  garnish (optional)

For the seasoning mix
60ml/4 tbsp Worcestershire sauce
15ml/1 tbsp Japanese soy sauce
15ml/1 tbsp oyster sauce
15ml/1 tbsp sugar
2.5ml/½ tsp salt
ground white pepper

1 Cook the noodles according to the instructions on the packet. Drain well and set aside.

2 Cut the pork into 3–4cm/1¼–1½in strips and season with salt and pepper.

3 Heat 7.5ml/1½ tsp of the oil in a large wok or frying pan. Add the pork and stir-fry until it is just cooked, then remove it from the pan.

4 Wipe the wok with kitchen paper, and heat the remaining oil in it. Add the ginger, garlic and cabbage and stir-fry for 1 minute.

5 Add the beansprouts, stir until softened, then add the green and red peppers and stir-fry for 1 minute more.

6 Return the pork to the pan and add the noodles. Stir in all the ingredients for the seasoning mix and stir-fry for 2–3 minutes. Serve immediately, sprinkled with ao-nori seaweed, if using.

Per portion: Energy 437Kcal/1848kJ; Protein 22.7g; Carbohydrate 65.6g, of which sugars 12.4g; Fat 11.2g, of which saturates 2.8g; Cholesterol 54mg; Calcium 64mg; Fibre 5.1g; Sodium 686mg.

RICE NOODLES WITH PORK

ALTHOUGH RICE NOODLES HAVE LITTLE FLAVOUR THEMSELVES, THEY HAVE A WONDERFUL ABILITY TO TAKE ON THE FLAVOUR OF OTHER INGREDIENTS.

SERVES FOUR TO SIX

INGREDIENTS
    450g/1lb pork fillet (tenderloin)
    225g/8oz dried rice noodles
    115g/4oz/1 cup broccoli florets
    1 red (bell) pepper, quartered
        and seeded
    45ml/3 tbsp groundnut (peanut) oil
    2 garlic cloves, crushed
    10 spring onions (scallions), cut into
        5cm/2in diagonal slices
    1 lemon grass stalk, finely chopped
    1–2 fresh red chillies, seeded and
        finely chopped
    300ml/½ pint/1¼ cups coconut milk
    15ml/1 tbsp tomato purée (paste)
    3 kaffir lime leaves (optional)
For the marinade
    45ml/3 tbsp light soy sauce
    15ml/1 tbsp rice wine
    30ml/2 tbsp groundnut (peanut) oil
    2.5cm/1in piece of fresh root ginger

1 Cut the pork into strips 2.5cm/1in long and 1cm/½in wide. Mix all the marinade ingredients in a bowl, add the pork, stir and marinate for 1 hour.

2 Spread out the rice noodles in a large, shallow dish, pour over enough hot water to cover and leave to soak for 20 minutes, until soft. Drain well and set aside.

3 Meanwhile, blanch the broccoli florets in a small pan of boiling water for 2 minutes, then drain, refresh under cold water and drain well again. Set aside until required.

4 Place the pepper pieces under a hot grill (broiler) for a few minutes until the skin blackens and blisters. Put in a plastic bag for about 10 minutes and then, when cool enough to handle, peel off the skin and slice the flesh thinly.

5 Drain the pork, reserving the marinade. Heat 30ml/2 tbsp of the oil in a large frying pan. Stir-fry the pork, in batches if necessary, for about 3–4 minutes, until the meat is tender. Transfer to a plate and keep warm.

6 Add a little more oil to the pan if necessary and stir-fry the garlic, spring onions, lemon grass and chillies over a low to medium heat for 2–3 minutes. Add the broccoli and pepper slices and stir-fry for a few minutes more.

7 Stir in the reserved marinade, coconut milk and tomato purée, with the kaffir lime leaves, if using. Simmer gently until the broccoli is nearly tender, then add the pork and noodles. Toss over the heat for 3–4 minutes until completely heated through. Transfer to a warm dish and serve immediately.

Per portion: Energy 454Kcal/1901kJ; Protein 30.1g; Carbohydrate 53.2g, of which sugars 7.1g; Fat 12.8g, of which saturates 3.2g; Cholesterol 70mg; Calcium 57mg; Fibre 1.5g; Sodium 428mg.

CANTONESE FRIED NOODLES

CHOW MEIN IS HUGELY POPULAR WITH THE THRIFTY CHINESE WHO BELIEVE IN TURNING LEFTOVERS INTO TASTY DISHES. FOR THIS DELICIOUS DISH, BOILED NOODLES ARE FRIED TO FORM A CRISPY CRUST, WHICH IS TOPPED WITH A SAVOURY SAUCE CONTAINING WHATEVER TASTES GOOD AND NEEDS EATING UP.

SERVES TWO TO THREE

INGREDIENTS

225g/8oz lean beef steak or pork
   fillet (tenderloin)
225g/8oz can bamboo shoots, drained
1 leek, trimmed
25g/1oz Chinese dried mushrooms,
   soaked for 30 minutes in 120ml/
   4fl oz/½ cup warm water
150g/5oz Chinese leaves
   (Chinese cabbage)
450g/1lb cooked egg noodles
   (255g/8oz dried), drained well
90ml/6 tbsp vegetable oil
30ml/2 tbsp dark soy sauce
15ml/1 tbsp cornflour (cornstarch)
15ml/1 tbsp rice wine or dry sherry
5ml/1 tsp sesame oil
5ml/1 tsp caster (superfine) sugar
salt and ground black pepper

1 Slice the beef or pork, bamboo shoots and leek into thin batons. Drain the mushrooms, reserving 90ml/6 tbsp of the soaking water. Cut off and discard the stems, then slice the caps finely. Cut the Chinese leaves into 2.5cm/1in diamond-shaped pieces and sprinkle with salt. Pat the noodles dry with kitchen paper.

2 Heat a third of the oil in a large wok or frying pan and sauté the noodles. After turning them over once, press the noodles evenly against the base of the pan with a wooden spatula until they form a flat, even cake. Cook over a medium heat for about 4 minutes, or until the noodles on the underside have become crisp.

3 Turn the noodle cake over with a spatula or fish slice or invert on to a large plate and slide back into the wok. Cook for 3 minutes more, then slide on to a heated plate. Keep warm.

4 Heat 30ml/2 tbsp of the remaining oil in the wok. Add the strips of leek, then the meat strips and stir-fry for 10–15 seconds. Sprinkle over half the soy sauce and then add the bamboo shoots and mushrooms, with salt and pepper to taste. Toss over the heat for 1 minute, then transfer this mixture to a plate and set aside.

5 Heat the remaining oil in the wok and sauté the Chinese leaves for 1 minute. Return the meat and vegetable mixture to the wok and sauté with the leaves for 30 seconds, stirring constantly.

6 Mix the cornflour with the reserved mushroom water. Stir into the wok along with the rice wine or sherry, sesame oil, sugar and remaining soy sauce. Cook for 15 seconds to thicken. Divide the noodles among serving dishes and pile the meat and vegetables on top.

Per portion· Energy 695Kcal/2895kJ; Protein 35.3g; Carbohydrate 38.8g, of which sugars 7.7g; Fat 45.3g, of which saturates 8.5g; Cholesterol 79mg; Calcium 79mg; Fibre 4.6g; Sodium 1185mg.

THAI CRISPY NOODLES WITH BEEF

RICE VERMICELLI ARE VERY FINE, DRY, WHITE NOODLES BUNDLED IN LARGE FRAGILE LOOPS AND SOLD IN PACKETS. THEY ARE DEEP-FRIED BEFORE BEING ADDED TO THIS DISH, AND IN THE PROCESS THEY EXPAND TO AT LEAST FOUR TIMES THEIR ORIGINAL SIZE.

SERVES FOUR

INGREDIENTS

about 450g/1lb rump (round) or
  sirloin steak
teriyaki sauce, for sprinkling
175g/6oz rice vermicelli
groundnut (peanut) oil for deep-frying
  and stir-frying
8 spring onions (scallions),
  diagonally sliced
2 garlic cloves, crushed
4–5 carrots, cut into julienne strips
1–2 fresh red chillies, seeded and
  finely sliced
2 small courgettes (zucchini),
  diagonally sliced
5ml/1 tsp grated fresh root ginger
60ml/4 tbsp white or yellow
  rice vinegar
90ml/6 tbsp light soy sauce
about 475ml/16fl oz/2 cups
  spicy stock

1 Using a meat mallet or the side of a rolling pin, beat out the steak, if necessary, to about 2.5cm/1in thick. Place in a shallow dish, brush generously with the teriyaki sauce and set aside for 2–4 hours to marinate.

2 Separate the rice vermicelli into manageable loops and spread several layers of kitchen paper on a very large plate. Pour the oil into a large wok to a depth of about 5cm/2in, and heat until a strand of vermicelli cooks as soon as it is lowered into the oil.

3 Carefully add a loop of rice vermicelli to the oil. It should immediately expand and become opaque. Turn the noodles over so that the strands cook on both sides and then transfer the cooked noodles to the prepared plate to drain. Repeat the process until all the noodles have been cooked. Transfer the cooked rice vermicelli to a separate wok or a deep serving bowl and keep them warm while you are cooking the steak and vegetables.

4 Strain the oil from the wok into a heatproof bowl and set it aside. Heat 15ml/1 tbsp groundnut oil in the clean wok. When it sizzles, cook the steak for about 30 seconds on each side until browned. Transfer to a board and cut into thick slices. The meat should be well browned on the outside but still pink inside. Set aside.

5 Add a little extra oil to the wok and stir-fry the spring onions, garlic and carrots over a medium heat for about 5–6 minutes until the carrots are slightly soft and glazed. Add the chillies, courgettes and ginger and stir-fry for 1–2 minutes more.

6 Stir in the rice vinegar, soy sauce and stock. Cook for about 4 minutes, until the sauce has slightly thickened. Add the steak and cook for a further 1–2 minutes (or longer, if you prefer your meat well done).

7 Pour the steak, vegetables and all the mixture over the noodles and toss lightly and carefully to mix, then serve.

COOK'S TIP

As soon as you add the meat mixture to the noodles, they will soften. If you wish to keep a few crispy noodles, stir some to the surface so they do not come into contact with the hot liquid.

Per portion: Energy 510Kcal/2122kJ; Protein 30.7g; Carbohydrate 41.6g, of which sugars 6.8g; Fat 24.5g, of which saturates 5.7g; Cholesterol 66mg; Calcium 51mg; Fibre 2.1g; Sodium 1262mg.

PAN-FRIED
DISHES

Some of the simplest dishes are those that sizzle on top of the stove, leaving the oven free for a baked potato accompaniment, or a hot dessert. With wok or frying pan at the ready, sample such delights as Kofta Kebabs or Salmon with Tequila Cream Sauce. Pan-fried dishes include fritters and fish cakes of various kinds, including completely irresistible Salt Cod Fritters with Aioli. On nights when poultry is on the menu, plump for Stir-fried Chicken with Basil and Chilli for a deliciously spicy stir-fry supper.

CHEESE AND LEEK SAUSAGES
WITH TOMATO, GARLIC AND CHILLI SAUCE

*THESE ARE BASED ON THE WELSH SPECIALITY OF GLAMORGAN SAUSAGES, WHICH ARE TRADITIONALLY
MADE USING WHITE OR WHOLEMEAL BREADCRUMBS ALONE. HOWEVER, ADDING A LITTLE MASHED
POTATO LIGHTENS THE SAUSAGES AND MAKES THEM MUCH EASIER TO HANDLE.*

SERVES FOUR

INGREDIENTS
  25g/1oz/2 tbsp butter
  175g/6oz leeks, finely chopped
  90ml/6 tbsp cold mashed potato
  115g/4oz/2 cups fresh white or
    wholemeal (whole-wheat)
    breadcrumbs
  150g/5oz/1¼ cups grated Caerphilly,
    Lancashire or Cantal cheese
  30ml/2 tbsp chopped fresh parsley
  5ml/1 tsp chopped fresh sage
    or marjoram
  2 large (US extra large) eggs, beaten
  cayenne pepper
  65g/2½oz/1 cup dry
    white breadcrumbs
  oil for shallow frying
For the sauce
  30ml/2 tbsp olive oil
  2 garlic cloves, thinly sliced
  1 fresh red chilli, seeded and finely
    chopped, or a good pinch of dried
    red chilli flakes
  1 small onion, finely chopped
  500g/1¼lb tomatoes, peeled, seeded
    and chopped
  few fresh thyme sprigs
  10ml/2 tsp balsamic vinegar or red
    wine vinegar
  pinch of light muscovado
    (brown) sugar
  15–30ml/1–2 tbsp chopped fresh
    marjoram or oregano
  salt and ground black pepper

1 Melt the butter and cook the leeks for 4–5 minutes, until softened but not browned. Mix with the mashed potato, fresh breadcrumbs, cheese, parsley and sage or marjoram. Add sufficient beaten egg (about two-thirds of the quantity) to bind the mixture. Season well and add a good pinch of cayenne.

COOK'S TIP
These sausages are also delicious served with garlic mayonnaise.

2 Shape the mixture into 12 sausage shapes. Dip in the remaining egg, then coat with the dry breadcrumbs. Chill the coated sausages.

3 To make the sauce, heat the oil over a low heat in a pan, add the garlic, chilli and onion and cook for 3–4 minutes. Add the tomatoes, thyme and vinegar. Season with salt, pepper and sugar.

4 Cook the sauce for 40–50 minutes, until much reduced. Remove the thyme and purée the sauce in a blender. Reheat with the marjoram or oregano, then adjust the seasoning, adding more sugar, if necessary.

5 Cook the sausages in shallow oil until golden brown on all sides. Drain on kitchen paper and serve with the sauce.

Per portion: Energy 580Kcal/2416kJ; Protein 19.2g; Carbohydrate 35.5g, of which sugars 7g; Fat 40.3g, of which saturates 15.2g; Cholesterol 164mg; Calcium 361mg; Fibre 3.5g; Sodium 604mg.

POTATO AND ONION CAKES WITH BEETROOT RELISH

THESE IRRESISTIBLE PANCAKES ARE BASED ON TRADITIONAL EASTERN EUROPEAN LATKE, GRATED POTATO CAKES. THEY ARE DELICIOUS WITH A SWEET-SHARP BEETROOT RELISH AND SOUR CREAM.

SERVES FOUR

INGREDIENTS
500g/1¼lb potatoes
1 small cooking apple, peeled, cored and coarsely grated
1 small onion, finely chopped
50g/2oz/½ cup plain (all-purpose) flour
2 large (US extra large) eggs, beaten
30ml/2 tbsp chopped chives
vegetable oil, for shallow frying
salt and ground black pepper
250ml/8fl oz/1 cup sour cream or crème fraîche
fresh dill sprigs and fresh chives or chive flowers, to garnish
For the beetroot (beet) relish
250g/9oz beetroot (beet), cooked and peeled
1 large eating apple, cored and finely diced
15ml/1 tbsp finely chopped red onion
15–30ml/1–2 tbsp tarragon vinegar
15ml/1 tbsp chopped fresh dill
15–30ml/1–2 tbsp light olive oil
pinch of caster (superfine) sugar

1 To make the relish, finely dice the beetroot, then mix it with the apple and onion. Add 15ml/1 tbsp of the vinegar, the dill and 15ml/1 tbsp of the oil. Season, adding more vinegar and oil, and a pinch of caster sugar to taste.

2 Coarsely grate the potatoes, then rinse in cold water, drain and dry them on a clean dishtowel.

3 Mix the potatoes, apple and onion in a bowl. Stir in the flour, eggs and chives. Season and mix again.

4 Heat about 5mm/¼in depth of oil in a frying pan and cook spoonfuls of the mixture. Flatten them to make pancakes 7.5–10cm/3–4in across and cook for 3–4 minutes on each side, until browned. Drain on kitchen paper and keep warm until the mixture is used up.

5 Serve a stack of pancakes – there should be about 16–20 in total – with spoonfuls of sour cream or crème fraîche, and beetroot relish. Garnish with dill sprigs and chives or chive flowers and grind black pepper on top just before serving.

VARIATION
To make a leek and potato cake, melt 25g/1oz/2 tbsp butter in a pan, add 400g/14oz thinly sliced leeks and cook until tender. Season well. Coarsely grate 500g/1¼lb peeled potatoes, then season. Melt another 25g/1oz/2 tbsp butter in a medium frying pan and add a layer of half the potatoes. Cover with the leeks, then add the remaining potatoes, pressing down with a spatula to form a cake. Cook for 20–25 minutes over a low heat until the potatoes are browned, then turn over and cook for 15–20 minutes to brown the other side.

Per portion: Energy 471Kcal/1964kJ; Protein 10.3g; Carbohydrate 42.1g, of which sugars 13.4g; Fat 30.2g, of which saturates 10.6g; Cholesterol 152mg; Calcium 118mg; Fibre 3.7g; Sodium 125mg.

CRAB CAKES

UNLIKE FISH CAKES, CRAB CAKES ARE BOUND WITH EGG AND MAYONNAISE OR TARTARE SAUCE INSTEAD OF POTATOES, WHICH MAKES THEM LIGHT IN TEXTURE. IF YOU PREFER, THEY CAN BE GRILLED INSTEAD OF FRIED; BRUSH WITH A LITTLE OIL FIRST.

SERVES FOUR

INGREDIENTS

450g/1lb mixed brown and white
   crab meat
30ml/2 tbsp mayonnaise or
   tartare sauce
2.5–5ml/½–1 tsp mustard powder
1 egg, lightly beaten
Tabasco sauce
45ml/3 tbsp chopped
   fresh parsley
4 spring onions (scallions), finely
   chopped (optional)
50–75g/2–3oz/½–¾ cup dried
   breadcrumbs, preferably home-made
sunflower oil, for frying
salt, ground black pepper and
   cayenne pepper
chopped spring onions (scallions),
   to garnish
red onion marmalade, to serve

1 Put the crab meat in a bowl and stir in the mayonnaise or tartare sauce, with the mustard and egg. Season with Tabasco, salt, pepper and cayenne.

2 Stir in the parsley, spring onions, if using, and 50g/2oz/½ cup of the breadcrumbs. The mixture should be just firm enough to hold together; depending on how much brown crab meat there is, you may need to add some more breadcrumbs.

3 Divide the mixture into eight portions, roll each into a ball and flatten slightly to make a thick flat disc. Spread out the crab cakes on a platter and put in the refrigerator for 30 minutes before frying.

4 Pour the oil into a shallow pan to a depth of about 5mm/¼in. Cook the crab cakes, in two batches, until golden brown all over. Drain on kitchen paper and keep hot. Serve with a spring onion garnish and red onion marmalade.

Per portion: Energy 285Kcal/1187kJ; Protein 23.9g; Carbohydrate 10.3g, of which sugars 0.9g; Fat 16.7g, of which saturates 2.4g; Cholesterol 134mg; Calcium 178mg; Fibre 0.8g; Sodium 768mg.

VEGETABLE-STUFFED SQUID

SHIRLEY CONRAN FAMOUSLY SAID THAT LIFE IS TOO SHORT TO STUFF A MUSHROOM. THE SAME MIGHT BE SAID OF SQUID, EXCEPT THAT THE RESULT IS SO DELICIOUS THAT IT MAKES THE EFFORT SEEM WORTHWHILE. SMALL CUTTLEFISH CAN BE PREPARED IN THE SAME WAY. SERVE WITH SAFFRON RICE.

SERVES FOUR

INGREDIENTS

4 medium squid, or 12 small squid, skinned and cleaned
75g/3oz/6 tbsp butter
50g/2oz/1 cup fresh white breadcrumbs
2 shallots, chopped
4 garlic cloves, chopped
1 leek, thinly sliced
2 carrots, finely diced
150ml/¼ pint/⅔ cup fish stock
30ml/2 tbsp olive oil
30ml/2 tbsp chopped fresh parsley
salt and ground black pepper
fresh rosemary sprigs, to garnish
saffron rice, to serve

1 Preheat the oven to 220°C/425°F/ Gas 7. Cut off the tentacles and side flaps from the squid and chop these finely. Set the squid aside. Melt half the butter in a large frying pan that can safely be used in the oven. Add the fresh white breadcrumbs and cook until they are golden brown, stirring to prevent them from burning. Transfer the breadcrumbs to a bowl and set aside until required.

2 Heat the remaining butter in the frying pan and add the chopped and diced vegetables. Cook until softened but not browned, then stir in the fish stock and cook until it has reduced and the vegetables are very soft. Season to taste with salt and ground black pepper and transfer to the bowl with the breadcrumbs. Mix lightly together.

3 Heat half the olive oil in the frying pan, add the chopped squid and cook over a high heat for 1 minute. Remove the squid with a slotted spoon and stir into the vegetables. Stir in the parsley.

4 Put the stuffing mixture into a piping (pastry) bag or use a teaspoon to stuff the squid tubes with the mixture. Do not overfill them, as the stuffing will swell lightly during cooking. Secure the openings with cocktail sticks (toothpicks) or sew up with fine thread.

5 Heat the remaining olive oil in the frying pan, place the stuffed squid in the pan and cook until they are sealed on all sides and golden brown. Transfer the frying pan to the oven and roast the squid for 20 minutes.

6 Unless the squid are very small, carefully cut them into three or four slices and arrange on a bed of saffron rice. Spoon the cooking juices over the squid and serve immediately, garnished with sprigs of rosemary.

Per portion: Energy 356Kcal/1486kJ; Protein 21.8g; Carbohydrate 15.2g, of which sugars 3.6g; Fat 23.6g, of which saturates 11.1g; Cholesterol 321mg; Calcium 55mg; Fibre 1.9g; Sodium 352mg.

SALT COD FRITTERS WITH AIOLI

AIOLI IS A FIERCELY GARLICKY, OLIVE OIL MAYONNAISE FROM PROVENCE IN THE SOUTH OF FRANCE AND IS A TRADITIONAL ACCOMPANIMENT TO SALT COD.

SERVES SIX

INGREDIENTS
    450g/1lb salt cod
    500g/1¼lb floury potatoes
    300ml/½ pint/1¼ cups milk
    6 spring onions (scallions),
       finely chopped
    30ml/2 tbsp extra virgin olive oil
    30ml/2 tbsp chopped fresh parsley
    juice of ½ lemon, to taste
    2 eggs, beaten
    60ml/4 tbsp plain (all-purpose) flour
    90g/3½oz/1⅓ cups dry
       white breadcrumbs
    vegetable oil, for shallow frying
    salt and ground black pepper
    lemon wedges and salad, to serve
For the aioli
    2 large garlic cloves
    2 egg yolks
    300ml/½ pint/1¼ cups olive oil
    lemon juice, to taste

1 Soak the salt cod in cold water for 24–36 hours, changing the water 5–6 times. It swells as it rehydrates and a tiny piece should not taste too salty when tried. Drain well.

2 Cook the potatoes, unpeeled, in a pan of boiling salted water for about 20 minutes, until tender. Drain, then peel and mash the potatoes.

3 Poach the cod very gently in the milk with half the spring onions for 10–15 minutes, or until it flakes easily. Remove the cod and flake it with a fork into a bowl, discarding bones and skin.

4 Add 60ml/4 tbsp mashed potato to the flaked cod and beat with a wooden spoon. Work in the olive oil, then gradually add the remaining potato. Beat in the remaining spring onions and the parsley. Season with lemon juice and pepper to taste – the mixture may need a little salt. Beat in one egg, then chill the mixture until firm.

5 Shape the mixture into 12–18 small round cakes. Coat them in flour, then dip them in the remaining egg and coat with the breadcrumbs. Chill.

COOK'S TIPS
• Try to find a thick, creamy white piece of salt cod, preferably cut from the middle of the fish rather than the tail and fin ends. Avoid thin, yellowish salt cod, as it will be too dry and salty.
• Mash potatoes by hand, never in a food processor, as it makes them gluey.
• Aioli traditionally has a sharp bite from the raw garlic. However, if you prefer a milder flavour, blanch the garlic once or twice in boiling water for about 3 minutes each time before using it.

6 Meanwhile, make the aioli. Place the garlic and a good pinch of salt in a mortar and pound to a paste with a pestle. Transfer to a bowl and using a small whisk or a wooden spoon, gradually work in the egg yolks.

7 Add the olive oil, a drop at a time, until half is incorporated. When the sauce is as thick as soft butter, beat in 5–10ml/ 1–2 tsp lemon juice, then continue adding oil until the aioli is very thick. Adjust the seasoning, adding lemon juice to taste.

8 Heat about 2cm/¾in depth of oil in a large, heavy frying pan. Add the salt cod fritters and cook over a medium-high heat for about 4 minutes. Turn them over and cook for a further 4 minutes on the other side, until crisp and golden. Drain on crumpled kitchen paper, then serve with the aioli, lemon wedges and salad leaves.

Per portion: Energy 718Kcal/2980kJ; Protein 21.1g; Carbohydrate 33.1g, of which sugars 1.9g; Fat 56.5g, of which saturates 8.3g; Cholesterol 165mg; Calcium 67mg; Fibre 1.6g; Sodium 196mg.

FRIED FISH WITH TOMATO SAUCE

THIS SIMPLE DISH IS PERENNIALLY POPULAR WITH CHILDREN. IT WORKS EQUALLY WELL WITH LEMON SOLE OR DABS (THESE DO NOT NEED SKINNING), OR FILLETS OF HADDOCK AND WHITING.

SERVES FOUR

INGREDIENTS
- 60ml/4 tbsp plain (all-purpose) flour
- 2 eggs, beaten
- 75g/3oz/¾ cup dried breadcrumbs
- 4 small plaice or flounder, dark skin removed
- 15g/½oz/1 tbsp butter
- 15ml/1 tbsp sunflower oil
- salt and ground black pepper
- 1 lemon, quartered, to serve
- fresh basil leaves, to garnish

For the tomato sauce
- 30ml/2 tbsp olive oil
- 1 red onion, finely chopped
- 1 garlic clove, finely chopped
- 400g/14oz can chopped tomatoes
- 15ml/1 tbsp tomato purée (paste)
- 15ml/1 tbsp torn fresh basil leaves

1 First make the tomato sauce. Heat the olive oil in a large pan, add the finely chopped onion and garlic and cook gently for about 5 minutes, until softened and pale golden. Stir in the chopped tomatoes and tomato purée and simmer for 20–30 minutes, stirring occasionally. Season with salt and pepper and stir in the basil.

2 Spread out the flour in a shallow dish, pour the beaten eggs into another and spread out the breadcrumbs in a third. Season the fish with salt and pepper.

3 Hold a fish in your left hand and dip it first in flour, then in egg and finally in the breadcrumbs, patting the crumbs on with your dry right hand.

4 Heat the butter and oil in a frying pan until foaming. Cook the fish, one at a time, in the hot fat for about 5 minutes on each side, until golden brown and cooked through, but still juicy in the middle. Drain on kitchen paper and keep hot while you cook the rest. Serve with lemon wedges and the tomato sauce, garnished with basil leaves.

Per portion: Energy 345Kcal/1445kJ; Protein 23g; Carbohydrate 28.3g, of which sugars 5.6g; Fat 16.3g, of which saturates 4.2g; Cholesterol 144mg; Calcium 105mg; Fibre 2g; Sodium 338mg.

TROUT WITH TAMARIND AND CHILLI SAUCE

ALTHOUGH VERY ECONOMICAL, TROUT CAN TASTE RATHER BLAND. THIS SPICY THAI-INSPIRED SAUCE REALLY GIVES IT ZING. IF YOU LIKE YOUR FOOD VERY SPICY, ADD AN EXTRA CHILLI.

SERVES FOUR

INGREDIENTS

    4 trout, 350g/12oz each, cleaned
    6 spring onions (scallions), sliced
    60ml/4 tbsp soy sauce
    15ml/1 tbsp stir-fry oil
    30ml/2 tbsp chopped fresh
        coriander (cilantro)
For the sauce
    50g/2oz tamarind pulp
    105ml/7 tbsp boiling water
    2 shallots, coarsely chopped
    1 fresh red chilli, seeded
        and chopped
    1cm/½in piece fresh root ginger,
        peeled and chopped
    5ml/1 tsp soft brown sugar
    45ml/3 tbsp Thai fish sauce

1 Slash the trout diagonally four or five times on each side with a sharp knife and place in a shallow dish.

2 Fill the cavities with spring onions and douse each fish with soy sauce. Carefully turn the fish over to coat both sides with the sauce. Sprinkle on any remaining spring onions and set aside until required.

3 Make the sauce. Put the tamarind pulp in a small bowl and pour on the boiling water. Mash well with a fork until soft. Tip the mixture into a food processor or blender, add the shallots, fresh chilli, chopped ginger, brown sugar and Thai fish sauce and process to a coarse pulp.

4 Heat the stir-fry oil in a large frying pan or wok and cook the trout, one at a time if necessary, for about 5 minutes on each side, until the skin is crisp and browned and the flesh cooked. Put on warmed plates and spoon over some sauce. Sprinkle with the coriander and serve with the remaining sauce.

Per portion: Energy 352Kcal/1481kJ; Protein 55g; Carbohydrate 3.3g, of which sugars 2.8g; Fat 13.4g, of which saturates 2.8g; Cholesterol 224mg; Calcium 95mg; Fibre 0.4g; Sodium 721mg.

SALMON FISH CAKES

THE SECRET OF A GOOD FISH CAKE IS TO MAKE IT WITH FRESHLY PREPARED FISH AND POTATOES,
HOME-MADE BREADCRUMBS AND PLENTY OF INTERESTING SEASONING.

SERVES FOUR

INGREDIENTS

450g/1lb cooked salmon fillet
450g/1lb cooked potatoes, mashed
25g/1oz/2 tbsp butter, melted
10ml/2 tsp wholegrain mustard
15ml/1 tbsp each chopped fresh dill
  and chopped fresh parsley
grated rind and juice of ½ lemon
15g/½oz/1 tbsp plain (all-
  purpose) flour
1 egg, lightly beaten
150g/5oz/1¼ cups dried breadcrumbs
60ml/4 tbsp sunflower oil
salt and ground black pepper
rocket (arugula) leaves, chives and
  lemon wedges to garnish

1 Flake the cooked salmon, discarding any skin and bones. Put it in a bowl with the mashed potato, melted butter and wholegrain mustard and mix well. Stir in the dill and parsley and lemon rind and juice. Season to taste with salt and pepper.

2 Divide the mixture into eight portions and shape each into a ball, then flatten into a thick disc. Dip the fish cakes first in flour, then in egg and, finally, in breadcrumbs to coat evenly.

3 Heat the oil in a frying pan until it is very hot. Cook the fish cakes, in batches, until golden brown and crisp all over. As each batch is ready, drain on kitchen paper and keep hot. Garnish with rocket leaves and chives and serve with lemon wedges.

COOK'S TIP
Almost any fresh white or hot-smoked fish is suitable; smoked cod and haddock are particularly good.

Per portion: Energy 586Kcal/2453kJ; Protein 29.8g; Carbohydrate 49.9g, of which sugars 3.2g; Fat 31g, of which saturates 7.2g; Cholesterol 117mg; Calcium 79mg; Fibre 1.3g; Sodium 266mg.

SALMON <u>WITH</u> TEQUILA CREAM SAUCE

*USE REPOSADA TEQUILA, WHICH IS LIGHTLY AGED, FOR THIS SAUCE. IT HAS A SMOOTHER, MORE
ROUNDED FLAVOUR, WHICH GOES WELL WITH THE CREAM.*

SERVES FOUR

INGREDIENTS

3 fresh jalapeño chillies
45ml/3 tbsp olive oil
1 small onion, finely chopped
150ml/¼ pint/⅔ cup fish stock
grated rind and juice of 1 lime
120ml/4fl oz/½ cup single
  (light) cream
30ml/2 tbsp reposada tequila
1 firm avocado
4 salmon fillets
salt and ground white pepper
strips of green (bell) pepper

1 Roast the chillies in a frying pan until
the skins are blistered, being careful
not to let the flesh burn. Put them in
a strong plastic bag and tie the top
to keep the steam in. Set aside for
20 minutes.

2 Heat 15ml/1 tbsp of the oil in a pan.
Cook the onion for 3–4 minutes, then
add the stock, lime rind and juice. Cook
for 10 minutes, until the stock starts to
reduce. Remove the chillies from the
bag and peel off the skins, slit them and
scrape out the seeds.

3 Stir the cream into the onion and
stock mixture. Slice the chilli flesh into
strips and add to the pan. Cook over a
gentle heat, stirring constantly, for
2–3 minutes. Season to taste with salt
and white pepper.

4 Stir the tequila into the onion and
chilli mixture. Leave the pan over a very
low heat. Peel the avocado, remove the
stone (pit) and slice the flesh. Brush
the salmon fillets on one side with a
little of the remaining oil.

5 Heat a frying pan or ridged griddle
pan until very hot and add the salmon,
oiled side down. Cook for 2–3 minutes,
until the underside is golden, then
brush the top with oil, turn each fillet
over and cook the other side until the
fish is cooked and flakes easily when
tested with the tip of a sharp knife.

6 Serve the fish on a pool of sauce,
with the avocado slices. Garnish with
strips of green pepper and fresh flat
leaf parsley, if you like.

Per portion: Energy 445Kcal/1846kJ; Protein 27.1g; Carbohydrate 2.5g, of which sugars 1.7g; Fat 34.8g, of which saturates 8.7g; Cholesterol 79mg; Calcium 61mg; Fibre 1.5g; Sodium 68mg.

CHICKEN WITH PEAS

THIS ITALIAN DISH STRONGLY REFLECTS THE TRADITIONS OF BOTH MEDITERRANEAN AND JEWISH COOKING. JEWS FAVOUR THE ENRICHMENT OF MEAT SAUCES WITH EGG BECAUSE OF THE LAWS OF THE KASHRUT, WHICH FORBIDS THE ADDITION OF CREAM TO MEAT DISHES.

SERVES FOUR

INGREDIENTS

4 skinless, boneless chicken
  breast portions
plain (all-purpose) flour, for dusting
30–45ml/2–3 tbsp olive oil
1–2 onions, chopped
¼ fennel bulb, chopped (optional)
15ml/1 tbsp chopped fresh parsley,
  plus extra to garnish
7.5ml/1½ tsp fennel seeds
75ml/5 tbsp dry Marsala
120ml/4fl oz/½ cup chicken stock
300g/11oz/2¼ cups petits pois
  (baby peas)
juice of 1½ lemons
2 egg yolks
salt and ground black pepper

1 Season the chicken with salt and pepper, then dust generously with flour. Shake off the excess flour; set aside.

2 Heat 15ml/1 tbsp oil in a pan, add the onions, fennel, if using, parsley and fennel seeds. Cook for 5 minutes.

3 Add the remaining oil and the chicken to the pan and cook for 2–3 minutes on each side, until lightly browned. Remove the chicken and onion mixture from the pan and set aside.

4 Deglaze the pan by pouring in the Marsala and cooking over a high heat until reduced to about 30ml/2 tbsp, then pour in the stock. Add the peas and return the chicken and onion mixture to the pan. Cook over a very low heat while you prepare the egg mixture.

5 In a bowl, beat the lemon juice and egg yolks together, then gradually add about 120ml/4fl oz/½ cup of the hot liquid from the chicken and peas, stirring well to combine.

6 Return the mixture to the pan and cook over a low heat, stirring, until the mixture thickens slightly. (Do not allow the mixture to boil or the eggs will curdle and spoil the sauce.) Serve the chicken immediately, sprinkled with a little extra chopped fresh parsley.

Per portion: Energy 319Kcal/1338kJ; Protein 42g; Carbohydrate 9.1g, of which sugars 5.9g; Fat 10.7g, of which saturates 2.2g; Cholesterol 206mg; Calcium 67mg; Fibre 4.2g; Sodium 150mg.

STIR-FRIED CHICKEN WITH BASIL AND CHILLI

THIS QUICK AND EASY CHICKEN DISH IS AN EXCELLENT INTRODUCTION TO THAI CUISINE. THAI BASIL, WHICH IS SOMETIMES KNOWN AS HOLY BASIL, HAS A UNIQUE, PUNGENT FLAVOUR THAT IS BOTH SPICY AND SHARP. DEEP-FRYING THE LEAVES ADDS ANOTHER DIMENSION TO THIS DISH.

SERVES FOUR TO SIX

INGREDIENTS

    45ml/3 tbsp vegetable oil
    4 garlic cloves, thinly sliced
    2–4 fresh red chillies, seeded
      and finely chopped
    450g/1lb skinless boneless chicken
      breast portions, diced
    45ml/3 tbsp Thai fish sauce
    10ml/2 tsp dark soy sauce
    5ml/1 tsp sugar
    10–12 Thai basil leaves
    2 fresh red chillies, seeded and
      finely chopped and about 20 deep-
      fried Thai basil leaves, to garnish

1 Heat the oil in a wok or large frying pan. Add the garlic and chillies and stir-fry over a medium heat for 1–2 minutes, until the garlic is golden.

2 Add the pieces of chicken to the wok or pan and stir-fry until the chicken changes colour.

3 Stir in the Thai fish sauce, soy sauce and sugar. Continue to stir-fry the mixture for 3–4 minutes, or until the chicken is fully cooked with the sauce.

4 Stir in the fresh Thai basil leaves. Spoon the entire mixture on to a warm serving platter or individual serving dishes, and garnish with the sliced chillies and deep-fried Thai basil.

COOK'S TIP

To deep-fry Thai basil leaves, first make sure that the leaves are completely dry or they will splutter when added to the oil. Deep-fry the leaves briefly in hot oil until they are crisp and translucent – this will take only about 30–40 seconds. Lift out the leaves using a slotted spoon or wire basket and leave them to drain on kitchen paper.

Per portion: Energy 196Kcal/819kJ; Protein 27.2g; Carbohydrate 0.4g, of which sugars 0.4g; Fat 9.5g, of which saturates 1.3g; Cholesterol 79mg; Calcium 7mg; Fibre 0g; Sodium 424mg.

TURKEY <u>OR</u> CHICKEN SCHNITZEL

*IN AUSTRIA, WHERE THIS DISH ORIGINATED, SCHNITZEL WAS ALWAYS MADE FROM VEAL, POUNDED
FLAT, CRISPLY COATED AND THEN FRIED. NOWADAYS, IT MAY BE MADE FROM STEAK, CHICKEN OR
TURKEY. THIS IS A POPULAR ISRAELI VERSION. SERVE WITH A SELECTION OF VEGETABLES.*

SERVES FOUR

INGREDIENTS

4 boneless turkey or chicken breast
   fillets, each weighing about 175g/6oz
juice of 1 lemon
2 garlic cloves, chopped
plain (all-purpose) flour, for dusting
1–2 eggs
15ml/1 tbsp water
about 50g/2oz/½ cup matzo meal
paprika
a mixture of vegetable and olive oil,
   for shallow frying
salt and ground black pepper
lemon wedges and a selection of
   vegetables, to serve (optional)

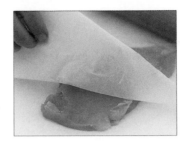

1 Lay each piece of meat between two
sheets of greaseproof (waxed) paper
and pound with a mallet or the end of
a rolling pin until it is about half its
original thickness and fairly even.

2 In a bowl, combine the lemon juice,
garlic, salt and pepper. Coat the meat
in it, then leave to marinate.

3 Meanwhile, arrange three wide plates
or shallow dishes in a row. Fill one
plate or dish with flour, beat the egg
and water together in another and mix
the matzo meal, salt, pepper and
paprika together on the third.

4 Working quickly, dip each fillet into
the flour, then the egg, then the matzo
meal. Pat everything in well, then
arrange the crumbed fillets on a plate
and chill for at least 30 minutes and
up to 2 hours.

5 In a large, heavy frying pan, heat
the oil until it will turn a cube of bread
dropped into the oil golden brown in
30–60 seconds. Carefully add the
crumbed fillets (in batches if necessary)
and cook until golden brown, turning
once. Remove and drain on kitchen
paper. Serve immediately with lemon
wedges and a selection of vegetables.

Per portion: Energy 368Kcal/1546kJ; Protein 45.4g; Carbohydrate 14.7g, of which sugars 0.6g; Fat 14.6g, of which saturates 2.3g; Cholesterol 170mg; Calcium 27mg; Fibre 0.5g; Sodium 125mg.

TURKEY CROQUETTES

IN THESE CRISP PATTIES, SMOKED TURKEY IS MIXED WITH MASHED POTATO AND SPRING ONIONS,
ROLLED IN BREADCRUMBS, AND SERVED WITH A TANGY TOMATO SAUCE.

3 Meanwhile, to make the sauce, heat the oil in a frying pan and fry the onion for 5 minutes until softened. Add the tomatoes and purée, stir and simmer for 10 minutes. Stir in the parsley, season with salt and pepper and keep the sauce warm until needed.

SERVES FOUR

INGREDIENTS
450g/1lb potatoes, diced
3 eggs
30ml/2 tbsp milk
175g/6oz smoked turkey rashers
  (strips), finely chopped
2 spring onions (scallions),
  thinly sliced
115g/4oz/2 cups fresh
  white breadcrumbs
vegetable oil, for deep-frying
For the sauce
15ml/1 tbsp olive oil
1 onion, finely chopped
400g/14oz can tomatoes, drained
30ml/2 tbsp tomato purée (paste)
15ml/1 tbsp chopped
  fresh parsley
salt and ground black pepper

1 Boil the potatoes for 20 minutes, or until tender. Drain and return the pan to a low heat to make sure all the excess water evaporates.

2 Mash the potatoes with two eggs and the milk. Season well with salt and pepper. Stir in the turkey and spring onions. Chill for 1 hour.

4 Remove the potato mixture from the refrigerator and divide into eight pieces. Shape each piece into a sausage shape and dip in the remaining beaten egg and then the breadcrumbs.

5 Heat the vegetable oil in a pan or deep-fryer to 175°C/330°F and deep-fry the croquettes for 5 minutes, or until golden and crisp. Drain and serve immediately with the sauce.

COOK'S TIP
Test the oil is at the correct temperature by dropping a cube of bread on to the surface. If it sinks, rises and sizzles in 10 seconds, the oil is ready to use.

Per portion: Energy 404Kcal/1698kJ; Protein 19.4g; Carbohydrate 47g, of which sugars 7.7g; Fat 16.7g, of which saturates 2.4g; Cholesterol 73mg; Calcium 93mg; Fibre 3.3g; Sodium 315mg.

KOFTA KEBABS

THESE SPICY PATTIES OF MINCED LAMB ARE SPIKED WITH AROMATIC HERBS AND SEASONINGS. THEY ARE VERY POPULAR THROUGHOUT THE MIDDLE EAST RIGHT THROUGH TO THE INDIAN SUBCONTINENT. SERVE WITH FLAT BREAD AND A SELECTION OF REFRESHING AND EXOTIC SALADS, SUCH AS ORANGES SPRINKLED WITH CAYENNE OR PAPRIKA, ONIONS SPRINKLED WITH SUMAC, AND TOMATO WEDGES WITH HERBS AND CHILLIES.

SERVES FOUR

INGREDIENTS

450g/1lb minced (ground) lamb
1–2 large slices of French bread,
  very finely crumbled
½ bunch fresh coriander (cilantro),
  finely chopped
5 garlic cloves, chopped
1 onion, finely chopped
juice of ½ lemon
5ml/1 tsp ground cumin
5ml/1 tsp paprika
15ml/1 tbsp curry powder
pinch each of ground cardamom,
  turmeric and cinnamon
15ml/1 tbsp tomato purée (paste)
cayenne pepper or chopped fresh
  chillies (optional)
1 egg, beaten, if needed
salt and ground black pepper
flat bread and salads, to serve

1 Put the lamb, crumbled bread, coriander, garlic, onion, lemon juice, spices, tomato purée, cayenne pepper or chillies and seasoning in a large bowl. Mix well. If the mixture does not bind together, add the beaten egg and a little more bread.

2 With wet hands, shape the mixture into four large or eight small patties.

3 Heat a heavy, non-stick frying pan, add the patties and cook, taking care that they do not fall apart, and turning once or twice, until browned. Serve hot with flat bread and salads.

VARIATION
Mix a handful of raisins or sultanas (golden raisins) into the meat mixture before shaping it into patties.

Per portion: Energy 414Kcal/1740kJ; Protein 29.3g; Carbohydrate 36.9g, of which sugars 4.1g; Fat 17.7g, of which saturates 7.6g; Cholesterol 134mg; Calcium 131mg; Fibre 2.5g; Sodium 470mg.

LAMB BURGERS WITH RED ONION AND TOMATO RELISH

A SHARP-SWEET RED ONION RELISH WORKS WELL WITH BURGERS BASED ON MIDDLE-EASTERN STYLE LAMB. SERVE WITH PITTA BREAD AND TABBOULEH OR WITH FRIES AND A CRISP GREEN SALAD.

SERVES FOUR

INGREDIENTS
  25g/1oz/3 tbsp bulgur wheat
  500g/1¼lb lean minced
    (ground) lamb
  1 small red onion, finely chopped
  2 garlic cloves, finely chopped
  1 green chilli, seeded and
    finely chopped
  5ml/1 tsp ground toasted cumin seeds
  2.5ml/½ tsp ground sumac
  15g/½oz chopped fresh flat
    leaf parsley
  30ml/2 tbsp chopped fresh mint
  olive oil, for frying
  salt and ground black pepper
For the relish
  2 red (bell) peppers, halved
    and seeded
  2 red onions, cut into 5mm/¼in
    thick slices
  75–90ml/5–6 tbsp extra virgin olive oil
  350g/12oz cherry tomatoes, chopped
  ½–1 fresh red or green chilli, seeded
    and finely chopped (optional)
  30ml/2 tbsp chopped fresh mint
  30ml/2 tbsp chopped fresh parsley
  15ml/1 tbsp chopped fresh oregano
  2.5–5ml/½–1 tsp each ground toasted
    cumin seeds
  2.5–5ml/½–1 tsp sumac
  juice of ½ lemon
  caster (superfine) sugar, to taste

1 Pour 150ml/¼ pint/⅔ cup hot water over the bulgur wheat in a bowl and leave to stand for 15 minutes, then drain in a sieve and squeeze out the excess moisture.

2 Place the bulgur wheat in a bowl and add the minced lamb, onion, garlic, chilli, cumin, sumac, parsley and mint. Mix the ingredients thoroughly together by hand, then season with 5ml/1 tsp salt and plenty of black pepper and mix again. Form the mixture into eight small burgers and set aside in the refrigerator while you make the relish.

3 Grill (broil) the peppers, skin side up, until the skin chars and blisters. Place in a bowl, cover and leave to stand for 10 minutes. Peel off the skin, dice the peppers finely and place in a bowl.

4 Brush the onions with 15ml/1 tbsp oil and grill for 5 minutes on each side, until browned. Cool, then chop.

5 Add the onions, tomatoes, chilli to taste, the mint, parsley, oregano and 2.5ml/½ tsp each of the cumin and sumac to the peppers. Stir in 60ml/4 tbsp of the remaining oil and 15ml/1 tbsp of the lemon juice. Season with salt, pepper and sugar and leave to stand for 20–30 minutes.

6 Heat a heavy frying pan or a ridged, cast-iron griddle pan over a high heat and grease lightly with olive oil. Cook the burgers for about 5–6 minutes on each side, until cooked at the centre.

7 While the burgers are cooking, taste the relish and adjust the seasoning, adding more salt, pepper, sugar, oil, chilli, cumin, sumac and lemon juice to taste. Serve the burgers as soon as they are cooked, with the relish.

Per portion: Energy 537Kcal/2228kJ; Protein 27.2g; Carbohydrate 19g, of which sugars 13.4g; Fat 39.6g, of which saturates 11.1g; Cholesterol 96mg; Calcium 83mg; Fibre 4.2g; Sodium 105mg.

FILLET OF BEEF STROGANOFF

LEGEND HAS IT THAT THIS FAMOUS RUSSIAN RECIPE WAS DEVISED BY COUNT PAUL STROGANOFF'S COOK TO USE BEEF FROZEN BY THE SIBERIAN CLIMATE. THE ONLY WAY IN WHICH IT COULD BE PREPARED WAS CUT INTO VERY THIN STRIPS. THE STRIPS OF LEAN BEEF WERE SERVED IN A SOUR CREAM SAUCE FLAVOURED WITH BRANDY.

3 Add the mushrooms and stir-fry over a high heat. Transfer the vegetables and their juices to a dish and set aside.

4 Wipe the pan, then add and heat the remaining oil. Coat a batch of meat with flour, then stir-fry over a high heat until browned. Remove from the pan, then coat and stir-fry another batch. When the last batch of steak is cooked, replace all the meat and vegetables. Add the brandy and simmer until it has almost evaporated.

5 Stir in the stock or consommé and seasoning and cook for 10–15 minutes, stirring frequently, or until the meat is tender and the sauce is thick and glossy. Add the sour cream and sprinkle with chopped parsley. Serve with rice and a simple salad.

SERVES EIGHT

INGREDIENTS
1.2kg/2½lb fillet (tenderloin) of beef
30ml/2 tbsp plain (all-purpose) flour
large pinch each of cayenne pepper
  and paprika
75ml/5 tbsp sunflower oil
1 large onion, chopped
3 garlic cloves, finely chopped
450g/1lb/6½ cups chestnut
  mushrooms, sliced
75ml/5 tbsp brandy
300ml/½ pint/1¼ cups beef stock
  or consommé
300ml/½ pint/1¼ cups sour cream
45ml/3 tbsp chopped fresh flat
  leaf parsley
salt and ground black pepper

1 Thinly slice the fillet of beef across the grain, then cut it into fine strips. Season the flour with the cayenne pepper and paprika.

2 Heat half the oil in a large frying pan, add the onion and garlic and cook gently until the onion has softened.

COOK'S TIP
If you do not have a very large pan, it may be easier to cook the meat and vegetables in two separate pans. A large flameproof casserole may be used.

Per portion: Energy 407Kcal/1693kJ; Protein 34.9g; Carbohydrate 8.1g, of which sugars 3.4g; Fat 24g, of which saturates 9.8g; Cholesterol 114mg; Calcium 70mg; Fibre 1.5g; Sodium 87mg.

PAN-FRIED CALF'S LIVER
WITH CRISP ONIONS

SAUTÉED OR CREAMY MASHED POTATOES GO WELL WITH FRIED CALF'S LIVER. SERVE A SALAD OF MIXED LEAVES WITH PLENTY OF DELICATE FRESH HERBS, SUCH AS FENNEL, DILL AND PARSLEY, TO COMPLEMENT THE SIMPLE FLAVOURS OF THIS MAIN COURSE.

SERVES FOUR

INGREDIENTS
50g/2oz/¼ cup butter
4 onions, thinly sliced
5ml/1 tsp caster (superfine) sugar
4 slices calf's liver, each weighing
   about 115g/4oz
30ml/2 tbsp plain (all-purpose) flour
30ml/2 tbsp olive oil
salt and ground black pepper
parsley, to garnish

1 Melt the butter in a large, heavy pan with a lid. Add the onions and mix well to coat with butter. Cover the pan with a tight-fitting lid and cook gently for 10 minutes, stirring occasionally.

2 Stir in the sugar and cover the pan. Cook the onions for 10 minutes more, or until they are soft and golden. Increase the heat, remove the lid and stir the onions over a high heat until they are deep gold and crisp. Use a slotted spoon to remove the onions from the pan, draining off the fat.

3 Meanwhile, rinse the calf's liver in cold water and pat it dry on kitchen paper. Season the flour, put it on a plate and turn the slices of liver in it until they are lightly coated in flour.

COOK'S TIP
Take care not to cook the liver for too long as this may cause it to toughen.

4 Heat the oil in a large frying pan, add the liver and cook for about 2 minutes on each side, or until lightly browned and just firm. Arrange the liver on warmed plates, with the crisp onions. Garnish with parsley and serve with sautéed or mashed potatoes.

Per portion: Energy 350Kcal/1458kJ; Protein 23.9g; Carbohydrate 19.7g, of which sugars 8.6g; Fat 20.1g, of which saturates 8.5g; Cholesterol 452mg; Calcium 61mg; Fibre 2.4g; Sodium 162mg.

STEWS,
CASSEROLES
AND CURRIES

After the fast-food revolution, slow food is enjoying a

renaissance as more and more people take time to make — and

enjoy — delectable stews and casseroles. It's almost mystical,

the way disparate ingredients are transformed by slow cooking

into a dish in which all the different flavours blend to create a

harmonious whole. Beef Carbonade and Lamb and New Potato

Curry are especially fine examples of the genre.

ITALIAN FISH STEW

THIS ROBUST FISH AND TOMATO STEW COMES FROM ITALY WHERE IT IS KNOWN AS BRODETTO. THERE ARE MANY VERSIONS, BUT ALL REQUIRE FLAVOURSOME SUN-RIPENED TOMATOES AND A GOOD FISH STOCK. BUY SOME OF THE FISH WHOLE SO THAT YOU CAN SIMPLY SIMMER THEM, REMOVE THE COOKED FLESH AND STRAIN THE DELICIOUSLY FLAVOURED JUICES TO MAKE THE STOCK.

SERVES FOUR TO FIVE

INGREDIENTS
  900g/2lb mixture of fish fillets or
    steaks, such as monkfish, cod,
    haddock or hake
  900g/2lb mixture of conger eel,
    red or grey mullet, snapper or
    small white fish, prepared
    according to type
  1 onion, halved
  1 celery stick, coarsely chopped
  225g/8oz squid
  225g/8oz fresh mussels
  675g/1½lb ripe tomatoes
  60ml/4 tbsp olive oil
  1 large onion, thinly sliced
  3 garlic cloves, crushed
  5ml/1 tsp saffron threads
  150ml/¼ pint/⅔ cup dry white wine
  90ml/6 tbsp chopped fresh parsley
  salt and ground black pepper
  croûtons, to serve

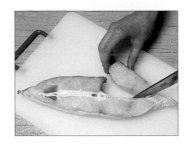

1 Remove any skin and bones from the fish fillets or steaks, cut the fish into large pieces and reserve. Place the bones in a pan with all the remaining fish.

2 Add the halved onion and the celery and just cover with water. Bring almost to the boil, then reduce the heat and simmer gently for about 30 minutes. Lift out the fish and remove the flesh from the bones. Strain the stock.

3 To prepare the squid, twist the head and tentacles away from the body. Cut the head from the tentacles. Discard the body contents and peel away the mottled skin. Wash the tentacles and bodies and dry on kitchen paper.

4 Scrub the mussels, discarding any that are damaged or open ones that do not close when sharply tapped.

5 Plunge the tomatoes into boiling water for 30 seconds, then refresh in cold water. Peel off the skins and chop the flesh coarsely.

6 Heat the oil in a large sauté pan. Add the sliced onion and the garlic, and cook gently for 3 minutes. Add the squid and the uncooked white fish, which you reserved earlier, and cook quickly on all sides. Remove the fish from the pan using a slotted spoon.

7 Add 475ml/16fl oz/2 cups strained reserved fish stock, the saffron and tomatoes to the pan. Pour in the wine. Bring to the boil, then reduce the heat and simmer for about 5 minutes. Add the mussels, cover, and cook for 3–4 minutes, until the mussels have opened. Discard any mussels that remain closed.

8 Season the sauce with salt and pepper and put all the fish in the pan. Cook gently for 5 minutes. Sprinkle with the parsley and serve with the croûtons.

Per portion: Energy 624Kcal/2624kJ; Protein 98.6g; Carbohydrate 12.6g, of which sugars 9.7g; Fat 17.5g, of which saturates 2.9g; Cholesterol 322mg; Calcium 163mg; Fibre 2.8g; Sodium 448mg.

CURRIED PRAWNS IN COCONUT MILK

A WONDERFULLY QUICK AND EASY DISH, THIS FEATURES PRAWNS IN A SPICY YELLOW CURRY GRAVY.

SERVES FOUR TO SIX

INGREDIENTS

600ml/1 pint/2½ cups coconut milk
30ml/2 tbsp yellow curry paste (see
  Cook's Tip)
15ml/1 tbsp Thai fish sauce
2.5ml/½ tsp salt
5ml/1 tsp sugar
450g/1lb raw king prawns (jumbo
  shrimp) peeled, thawed if frozen
225g/8oz cherry tomatoes
yellow and orange (bell) peppers,
  seeded and cut into thin strips,
  chives and juice of ½ lime,
  to garnish

VARIATION

Use cooked prawns (shrimp) for an even
quicker version. Add after the tomatoes
and heat through for 1–2 minutes.

1 Put half the coconut milk in a wok or
pan and bring to the boil. Add the
yellow curry paste, stir until it disperses,
then lower the heat and simmer for
about 10 minutes.

2 Add the Thai fish sauce, salt, sugar
and remaining coconut milk to the
sauce. Simmer for 5 minutes more.

3 Add the prawns and cherry tomatoes.
Simmer very gently for about 5 minutes,
until the prawns are pink and tender.

4 Spoon into a serving dish, sprinkle
with lime juice and garnish with strips
of yellow peppers and chives.

COOK'S TIP

To make yellow curry paste, put into a
food processor or blender 6–8 fresh
yellow chillies, the chopped base of
1 lemon grass stalk, 4 chopped shallots,
4 chopped garlic cloves, 15ml/1 tbsp
chopped peeled fresh root ginger, 5ml/
1 tsp coriander seeds, 5ml/1 tsp mustard
powder, 5ml/1 tsp salt, 2.5ml/½ tsp
ground cinnamon, 15ml/1 tbsp light
brown sugar and 30ml/2 tbsp sunflower
oil. Process to a paste, scrape into a jar,
cover and keep in the refrigerator.

Per portion: Energy 160Kcal/679kJ; Protein 21.5g; Carbohydrate 15.8g, of which sugars 15.5g; Fat 1.7g, of which saturates 0.6g; Cholesterol 219mg; Calcium 144mg; Fibre 2g; Sodium 584mg.

LOUISIANA SEAFOOD GUMBO

GUMBO IS A SOUP, BUT IS SERVED OVER RICE AS A MAIN COURSE. IN LOUISIANA, OYSTERS ARE CHEAP AND PROLIFIC, AND OYSTERS WOULD BE USED THERE INSTEAD OF MUSSELS.

SERVES SIX

INGREDIENTS
    450g/1lb fresh mussels
    450g/1lb raw prawns (shrimp)
    1 cooked crab, about 1kg/2¼lb
    small bunch of fresh parsley, leaves
        chopped and stalks reserved
    150ml/¼ pint/⅔ cup vegetable oil
    115g/4oz/1 cup plain (all-
        purpose) flour
    1 green (bell) pepper, chopped
    1 large onion, chopped
    2 celery sticks, sliced
    3 garlic cloves, finely chopped
    75g/3oz smoked spiced sausage,
        skinned and sliced
    275g/10oz/1½ cups long grain rice
    6 spring onions (scallions), shredded
    cayenne pepper, to taste
    Tabasco sauce, to taste
    salt

1 Wash the mussels in several changes of cold water, pulling away the black beards. Discard any mussels that are broken or do not close when you tap them firmly.

2 Bring 250ml/8fl oz/1 cup water to the boil in a deep pan. Add the mussels, cover the pan tightly and cook over a high heat, shaking frequently, for 3 minutes. As the mussels open, lift them out with tongs into a sieve set over a bowl. Discard any that fail to open. Shell the mussels, discarding the shells. Return the liquid from the bowl to the pan and make the quantity up to 2 litres/3½ pints/8 cups with water.

3 Peel the prawns and set them aside, reserving a few for the garnish. Put the shells and heads into the pan.

4 Remove all the meat from the crab, separating the brown and white meat. Add all the pieces of shell to the pan with 5ml/2 tsp salt.

5 Bring the shellfish stock to the boil, skimming it regularly. When there is no more froth on the surface, add the parsley stalks and simmer for 15 minutes. Cool, then strain it into a measuring jug (cup) and make up to 2 litres/3½ pints/8 cups with water.

6 Heat the oil in a heavy pan and stir in the flour. Stir constantly over a medium heat with a wooden spoon or whisk until the roux reaches a golden-brown colour. Immediately add the pepper, onion, celery and garlic. Continue cooking for about 3 minutes, until the onion is softened. Stir in the sausage. Reheat the stock.

7 Stir the brown crab meat into the roux, then ladle in the hot stock, a little at a time, stirring constantly until it has all been smoothly incorporated. Bring to a low boil, partially cover the pan, then simmer the gumbo for 30 minutes.

8 Meanwhile, cook the rice in plenty of lightly salted, boiling water until the grains are tender.

9 Add the prawns, mussels, white crab meat and spring onions to the gumbo. Return to the boil and season with salt if necessary, cayenne and a dash or two of Tabasco sauce. Simmer for a further minute, then add the chopped parsley leaves. Serve immediately, ladling the soup over the hot rice in soup plates.

COOK'S TIP
It is essential to stir constantly to darken the roux without burning. Should black specks occur at any stage of cooking, discard the roux and start again. Have the onion, green (bell) pepper and celery ready to add to the roux the minute it reaches the correct golden-brown stage, as this arrests its darkening.

Per portion: Energy 559Kcal/2336kJ; Protein 31.1g; Carbohydrate 57.6g, of which sugars 3.7g; Fat 23g, of which saturates 3.4g; Cholesterol 183mg; Calcium 145mg; Fibre 1.9g; Sodium 474mg.

GREEN FISH CURRY

ANY FIRM-FLESHED FISH CAN BE USED FOR THIS DELICIOUS CURRY, WHICH GAINS ITS RICH COLOUR FROM A MIXTURE OF FRESH HERBS; TRY EXOTICS, SUCH AS MAHI-MAHI, HOKI OR SWORDFISH, OR HUMBLER FISH, SUCH AS COLEY. SERVE IT WITH BASMATI OR THAI FRAGRANT RICE AND LIME WEDGES.

SERVES FOUR

INGREDIENTS

4 garlic cloves, coarsely chopped
5cm/2in piece fresh root ginger,
   peeled and coarsely chopped
2 fresh green chillies, seeded and
   coarsely chopped
grated rind and juice of 1 lime
5–10ml/1–2 tsp shrimp paste
5ml/1 tsp coriander seeds
5ml/1 tsp five-spice powder
75ml/5 tbsp sesame oil
2 red onions, finely chopped
900g/2lb hoki fillets, skinned
400ml/14fl oz/1⅔ cups coconut milk
45ml/3 tbsp Thai fish sauce
50g/2oz fresh coriander
   (cilantro) leaves
50g/2oz fresh mint leaves
50g/2oz fresh basil leaves
6 spring onions (scallions), chopped
150ml/¼ pint/⅔ cup sunflower oil
sliced fresh green chilli and finely
   chopped fresh coriander (cilantro),
   to garnish
cooked rice and lime wedges,
   to serve

2 Heat a wok or large shallow pan and pour in the remaining sesame oil. When it is hot, stir-fry the red onions over a high heat for 2 minutes. Add the fish and stir-fry for 1–2 minutes to seal the fillets on all sides.

3 Lift out the red onions and fish and put them on a plate. Add the curry paste to the wok or pan and cook for 1 minute, stirring. Return the fish and red onions to the wok or pan, pour in the coconut milk and bring to the boil. Lower the heat, add the Thai fish sauce and simmer for 5–7 minutes, until the fish is cooked through.

4 Meanwhile, process the herbs, spring onions, lime rind and oil in a food processor to a coarse paste. Stir into the fish curry. Garnish with chilli and coriander and serve with rice and lime wedges.

1 First make the curry paste. Combine the garlic, fresh root ginger, green chillies, the lime juice and shrimp paste in a food processor. Add the coriander seeds and five-spice powder, with half the sesame oil. Process to a fine paste, then set aside until required.

COOK'S TIP
Shrimp paste, also known as blachan or terasi, is available in Asian food stores.

OCTOPUS STEW

THIS RUSTIC STEW IS A PERFECT DISH FOR ENTERTAINING, AS IT TASTES EVEN BETTER IF MADE A DAY IN ADVANCE. SERVE WITH A COLOURFUL SALAD OF BABY CHARD, ROCKET AND RADICCHIO.

SERVES FOUR TO SIX

INGREDIENTS
  1kg/2¼lb octopus, cleaned
  45ml/3 tbsp olive oil
  1 large red onion, chopped
  3 garlic cloves, finely chopped
  30ml/2 tbsp brandy
  300ml/½ pint/1¼ cups dry
    white wine
  800g/1¾lb ripe plum tomatoes,
    peeled and chopped, or 2 × 400g/
    14oz cans chopped tomatoes
  1 fresh red chilli, seeded and
    chopped (optional)
  450g/1lb small new potatoes
  15ml/1 tbsp chopped fresh rosemary
  15ml/1 tbsp fresh thyme leaves
  1.2 litres/2 pints/5 cups fish stock
  30ml/2 tbsp fresh flat leaf
    parsley leaves
  salt and ground black pepper
  fresh rosemary sprigs, to garnish
For the garlic croûtes
  1 fat garlic clove, peeled
  8 thick slices of baguette or ciabatta
  30ml/2 tbsp olive oil

3 Pour the brandy over the octopus and ignite it. When the flames have died down, add the wine, bring to the boil and bubble gently for about 5 minutes. Stir in the tomatoes, with the chilli, if using, then add the potatoes, rosemary and thyme. Simmer for 5 minutes.

4 Pour in the fish stock and season well. Cover the pan and simmer for 20–30 minutes, stirring occasionally. The octopus and potatoes should be very tender and the sauce should have thickened slightly. At this stage, you can leave the stew to cool, then put it in the refrigerator overnight.

5 Preheat the grill (broiler). To make the garlic croûtes, cut the garlic clove in half and rub both sides of the slices of baguette or ciabatta with the cut side. Crush the garlic, stir it into the oil and brush the mixture over both sides of the bread. Grill (broil) on both sides until the croûtes are golden brown and crisp.

6 To serve the stew, reheat it gently if it has been in the refrigerator overnight, check the seasoning and stir in the parsley leaves. Serve piping hot in individual warmed bowls, garnished with rosemary sprigs and accompanied by the warm garlic croûtes.

1 Cut the octopus into large pieces, put these in a pan and pour in cold water to cover. Season with salt, bring to the boil, then lower the heat and simmer for 30 minutes to tenderize. Drain and cut into bitesize pieces.

2 Heat the oil in a large shallow pan. Cook the onion for 2–3 minutes, until lightly coloured, then add the garlic and cook for 1 minute more. Add the octopus and cook for 2–3 minutes, stirring to colour it lightly on all sides.

Per portion: Energy 588Kcal/2477kJ; Protein 51.6g; Carbohydrate 41.6g, of which sugars 11.5g; Fat 18.1g, of which saturates 2.8g; Cholesterol 120mg; Calcium 163mg; Fibre 3.8g; Sodium 225mg.

RED CHICKEN CURRY WITH BAMBOO SHOOTS

BAMBOO SHOOTS HAVE A LOVELY CRUNCHY TEXTURE. IT IS QUITE ACCEPTABLE TO USE CANNED ONES, AS FRESH BAMBOO IS NOT READILY AVAILABLE IN THE WEST. BUY CANNED WHOLE BAMBOO SHOOTS, WHICH ARE CRISPER AND OF BETTER QUALITY THAN SLICED SHOOTS. RINSE BEFORE USING.

SERVES FOUR TO SIX

INGREDIENTS
   1 litre/1³/₄ pints/4 cups coconut milk
   450g/1lb skinless, boneless chicken
     breast portions, cut into
     bitesize pieces
   30ml/2 tbsp Thai fish sauce
   15ml/1 tbsp sugar
   225g/8oz drained canned bamboo
     shoots, rinsed and sliced
   5 kaffir lime leaves, torn
   salt and ground black pepper
   chopped fresh red chillies and kaffir
     lime leaves, to garnish
For the red curry paste
   5ml/1 tsp coriander seeds
   2.5ml/¹/₂ tsp cumin seeds
   12–15 fresh red chillies, seeded and
     coarsely chopped
   4 shallots, thinly sliced
   2 garlic cloves, chopped
   15ml/1 tbsp chopped galangal
   2 lemon grass stalks, chopped
   3 kaffir lime leaves, chopped
   4 fresh coriander (cilantro) roots
   10 black peppercorns
   good pinch of ground cinnamon
   5ml/1 tsp ground turmeric
   2.5ml/¹/₂ tsp shrimp paste
   5ml/1 tsp salt
   30ml/2 tbsp vegetable oil

1 Make the curry paste. Dry-fry the coriander and cumin seeds for 1–2 minutes, then put in a mortar or food processor with the remaining ingredients, except the oil, and pound or process to a paste.

2 Add the oil, a little at a time, mixing or processing well after each addition. Transfer to a jar and keep in the refrigerator until ready to use.

3 Pour half of the coconut milk into a large, heavy pan. Bring the milk to the boil, stirring constantly until it has separated.

4 Stir in 30ml/2 tbsp of the red curry paste and cook the mixture for 2–3 minutes, stirring constantly. The remaining red curry paste can be kept in the refrigerator for up to 3 months.

5 Add the chicken pieces, Thai fish sauce and sugar to the pan. Stir well, then cook for 5–6 minutes, until the chicken changes colour and is cooked through, stirring constantly to prevent the mixture from sticking to the base of the pan.

6 Pour the remaining coconut milk into the pan, then add the sliced bamboo shoots and torn kaffir lime leaves. Bring the curry back to the boil over a medium heat, stirring constantly to prevent the mixture from sticking, then taste and season with salt and pepper if necessary.

7 To serve, spoon the curry into a warmed serving dish and garnish with chopped chillies and kaffir lime leaves. Boiled Thai jasmine rice would be a good accompaniment.

VARIATION
Instead of, or as well as, bamboo shoots, use straw mushrooms. These are available in cans from Asian stores and supermarkets. Drain well and then stir into the curry at the end of the recipe.

COOK'S TIP
It is essential to use chicken breast portions, rather than any other cut, for this curry, as it is cooked very quickly. Look for diced chicken or strips of chicken (which are often labelled "stir-fry chicken") in the supermarket.

Per portion: Energy 261Kcal/1105kJ; Protein 29.6g; Carbohydrate 19.6g, of which sugars 18.3g; Fat 7.8g, of which saturates 1.5g; Cholesterol 79mg; Calcium 95mg; Fibre 1.1g; Sodium 837mg.

SPANISH PORK *AND* SAUSAGE CASSEROLE

THIS DISH IS FROM THE CATALAN REGION OF SPAIN, AND COMBINES PORK CHOPS WITH SPICY BUTIFARRA SAUSAGES IN A RICH TOMATO SAUCE. YOU CAN FIND THESE SAUSAGES IN SOME SPANISH DELICATESSENS BUT, IF NOT, SWEET ITALIAN SAUSAGES WILL DO.

SERVES FOUR

INGREDIENTS

30ml/2 tbsp olive oil
4 boneless pork chops, about
  175g/6oz each
4 butifarra or sweet Italian sausages
1 onion, chopped
2 garlic cloves, chopped
120ml/4fl oz/½ cup dry white wine
6 plum tomatoes, chopped
1 bay leaf
30ml/2 tbsp chopped fresh parsley
salt and ground black pepper
baked potatoes and green salad,
  to serve

1 Heat the oil in a large, deep frying pan. Cook the pork chops over a high heat until browned on both sides, then transfer to a plate.

2 Add the sausages, onion and garlic to the pan and cook over a medium heat until the sausages are browned and the onion softened, turning the sausages two or three times during cooking. Return the chops to the pan.

3 Stir in the wine, tomatoes, bay leaf and parsley. Season. Cover the pan and cook for 30 minutes.

4 Remove the sausages and cut into thick slices. Return them to the pan and heat through. Serve with baked potatoes and a green salad.

Per portion: Energy 431Kcal/1803kJ; Protein 44.3g; Carbohydrate 12.5g, of which sugars 6.9g; Fat 20.8g, of which saturates 6.5g; Cholesterol 127mg; Calcium 78mg; Fibre 2.4g; Sodium 618mg.

POTATO AND SAUSAGE CASSEROLE

YOU WILL FIND NUMEROUS VARIATIONS OF THIS TRADITIONAL SUPPER DISH THROUGHOUT IRELAND, BUT THE BASIC INGREDIENTS ARE THE SAME WHEREVER YOU GO — POTATOES, SAUSAGES AND BACON.

SERVES FOUR

INGREDIENTS
  15ml/1 tbsp vegetable oil
  4 bacon rashers (strips), cut into
    2.5cm/1in pieces
  2 large onions, chopped
  2 garlic cloves, crushed
  8 large pork sausages
  4 large baking potatoes,
    thinly sliced
  1.5ml/¼ tsp fresh sage
  300ml/½ pint/1¼ cups
    vegetable stock
  salt and ground black pepper
  freshly baked soda bread,
    to serve (optional)

1 Preheat the oven to 180°C/350°F/
Gas 4. Grease a large ovenproof dish
and set aside.

2 Heat the oil in a frying pan. Add the
bacon and cook for 2 minutes, then add
the onions and cook for 5–6 minutes,
until golden. Add the garlic and cook for
1 minute, then remove the mixture
from the pan and set aside.

3 Add the sausages to the pan and
cook for 5–6 minutes, until golden.

4 Arrange the potatoes in the base of
the prepared dish. Spoon the bacon
and onion mixture on top. Season with
the salt and pepper and sprinkle
with the fresh sage.

5 Pour on the stock and top with the
sausages. Cover and bake for 1 hour.
Serve hot with soda bread if you like.

Per portion: Energy 553Kcal/2305kJ; Protein 17.4g; Carbohydrate 48.7g, of which sugars 10g; Fat 33.4g, of which saturates 11.8g; Cholesterol 51mg; Calcium 74mg; Fibre 4g; Sodium 1019mg.

LAMB'S LIVER AND BACON CASSEROLE

BOILED NEW POTATOES TOSSED IN LOTS OF BUTTER GO WELL WITH THIS SIMPLE CASSEROLE. THE TRICK WHEN COOKING LIVER IS TO SEAL IT QUICKLY, THEN SIMMER IT GENTLY AND BRIEFLY. PROLONGED AND/OR FIERCE COOKING MAKES LIVER HARD AND GRAINY.

SERVES FOUR

INGREDIENTS

30ml/2 tbsp sunflower oil
225g/8oz rindless unsmoked back (lean) bacon rashers (strips), cut into pieces
2 onions, halved and sliced
175g/6oz/2⅓ cups chestnut mushrooms, halved
450g/1lb lamb's liver, trimmed and sliced
25g/1oz/2 tbsp butter
15ml/1 tbsp soy sauce
30ml/2 tbsp plain (all-purpose) flour
150ml/¼ pint/⅔ cup chicken stock
salt and ground black pepper

1 Heat the oil in a frying pan and cook the bacon until crisp. Add the onions to the pan and cook for about 10 minutes, stirring frequently, or until softened. Add the mushrooms to the pan and cook for a further 1 minute.

2 Use a slotted spoon to remove the bacon and vegetables from the pan and set aside. Add the liver to the pan and cook over a high heat for 3–4 minutes, turning once to seal the slices on both sides. Remove the liver from the pan and keep warm.

3 Melt the butter in the pan, add the soy sauce and flour and blend together. Stir in the stock and bring to the boil, stirring until thickened. Return the liver and vegetables to the pan and heat through for 1 minute. Season with salt and pepper to taste, and serve with new potatoes and lightly cooked green beans.

Per portion: Energy 434Kcal/1809kJ; Protein 34.7g; Carbohydrate 13g, of which sugars 3.9g; Fat 27.4g, of which saturates 9.4g; Cholesterol 527mg; Calcium 43mg; Fibre 1.6g; Sodium 1258mg.

LAMB AND NEW POTATO CURRY

THIS DISH MAKES THE MOST OF AN ECONOMICAL CUT OF MEAT BY COOKING IT SLOWLY UNTIL THE MEAT IS FALLING FROM THE BONE. CHILLIES AND COCONUT CREAM GIVE IT LOTS OF FLAVOUR.

SERVES FOUR

INGREDIENTS

25g/1oz/2 tbsp butter
4 garlic cloves, crushed
2 onions, sliced into rings
2.5ml/½ tsp each ground cumin,
   ground coriander, turmeric and
   cayenne pepper
2–3 fresh red chillies, seeded and
   finely chopped
300ml/½ pint/1¼ cups hot
   chicken stock
200ml/7fl oz/scant 1 cup
   coconut cream
4 lamb shanks, trimmed of fat
450g/1lb new potatoes, halved
6 ripe tomatoes, quartered
salt and ground black pepper
fresh coriander (cilantro) leaves,
   to garnish
spicy rice, to serve

2 Stir in the hot stock and coconut cream. Place the lamb shanks in the liquid and cover the casserole with foil. Cook in the oven for 2 hours, turning the shanks twice, first after about an hour or so and again about half an hour later.

3 Par-boil the potatoes for 10 minutes, drain and add to the casserole with the tomatoes, then cook uncovered in the oven for a further 35 minutes. Season to taste, garnish with coriander leaves and serve with the spicy rice.

1 Preheat the oven to 160°C/325°F/Gas 3. Melt the butter in a large flameproof casserole, add the garlic and onions and cook over a low heat for 15 minutes, until golden. Stir in the cumin, ground coriander, turmeric, cayenne and chillies, then cook for a further 2 minutes.

COOK'S TIP
Make this dish a day in advance if possible. Cool and chill overnight, then it will be easy to skim off the excess fat that has risen to the surface and solidified. Reheat the curry thoroughly before you serve it.

Per portion: Energy 364Kcal/1528kJ; Protein 23.5g; Carbohydrate 30.5g, of which sugars 12.1g; Fat 17.4g, of which saturates 8.8g; Cholesterol 89mg; Calcium 58mg; Fibre 3.5g; Sodium 205mg.

LAMB STEW WITH SHALLOTS AND NEW POTATOES

THIS FRESH LEMON-SEASONED STEW IS FINISHED WITH AN ITALIAN MIXTURE OF CHOPPED GARLIC, PARSLEY AND LEMON RIND KNOWN AS GREMOLATA, THE TRADITIONAL TOPPING FOR OSSO BUCCO.

SERVES SIX

INGREDIENTS

1kg/2¼lb boneless shoulder of lamb, trimmed of fat and cut into 5cm/ 2in cubes
1 garlic clove, finely chopped
finely grated rind of ½ lemon and juice of 1 lemon
90ml/6 tbsp olive oil
45ml/3 tbsp plain (all-purpose) flour
1 large onion, sliced
5 anchovy fillets in olive oil, drained
2.5ml/½ tsp caster (superfine) sugar
300ml/½ pint/1¼ cups white wine
475ml/16fl oz/2 cups lamb stock or half stock and half water
1 fresh bay leaf
fresh thyme sprig
fresh parsley sprig
500g/1¼lb small new potatoes
250g/9oz shallots, peeled but left whole
45ml/3 tbsp double (heavy) cream (optional)
salt and ground black pepper
For the gremolata
1 garlic clove, finely chopped
finely shredded rind of ½ lemon
45ml/3 tbsp chopped fresh flat leaf parsley

1 Mix the lamb with the garlic and the rind and juice of ½ lemon. Season with pepper and mix in 15ml/1 tbsp olive oil, then leave to marinate for 12–24 hours.

2 Drain the lamb, reserving the marinade, and pat the lamb dry with kitchen paper. Preheat the oven to 180°C/350°F/Gas 4.

COOK'S TIP
A mezzaluna (double-handled, half-moon shaped, curved chopping blade) makes a very good job of chopping gremolata ingredients. If using a food processor or electric chopper, take care not to overprocess the mixture as it is easy to reduce the ingredients to a paste.

3 Heat 30ml/2 tbsp olive oil in a large, heavy frying pan. Season the flour with salt and pepper and toss the lamb in it to coat, shaking off any excess. Seal the lamb on all sides in the hot oil. Do this in batches, transferring each batch of lamb to an ovenproof pan or flameproof casserole as you brown it. You may need to add an extra 15ml/1 tbsp olive oil to the pan.

4 Reduce the heat, add another 15ml/ 1 tbsp oil to the pan and cook the onion gently over a very low heat, stirring frequently, for 10 minutes, until softened and golden but not browned. Add the anchovies and caster sugar and cook, mashing the anchovies into the soft onion with a wooden spoon.

5 Add the reserved marinade, increase the heat a little and cook for about 1–2 minutes, then pour in the wine and stock or stock and water and bring to the boil. Simmer gently for about 5 minutes, then pour over the lamb.

6 Tie the bay leaf, thyme and parsley together and add to the lamb. Season with salt and pepper, then cover tightly and cook in the oven for 1 hour. Stir the potatoes into the stew and cook for a further 20 minutes.

7 Meanwhile, to make the gremolata, chop all the ingredients together finely. Place in a dish, cover and set aside.

8 Heat the remaining oil in a frying pan and brown the shallots on all sides, then stir them into the lamb. Cover and cook for a further 30–40 minutes, until the lamb is tender. Transfer the lamb and vegetables to a dish and keep warm. Discard the herbs.

9 Boil the cooking juices to reduce and concentrate them, then add the cream, if using, and simmer for 2–3 minutes. Adjust the seasoning, adding a little lemon juice to taste. Pour this sauce over the lamb, sprinkle the gremolata on top and serve immediately.

Per portion: Energy 553Kcal/2311kJ; Protein 37g; Carbohydrate 26.2g, of which sugars 5.3g; Fat 30.6g, of which saturates 10.4g; Cholesterol 128mg; Calcium 79mg; Fibre 2.7g; Sodium 261mg.

SPICED LAMB WITH TOMATOES AND PEPPERS

SELECT LEAN TENDER LAMB FROM THE LEG FOR THIS LIGHTLY SPICED CURRY WITH SUCCULENT PEPPERS AND ONION WEDGES. SERVE WITH WARM NAAN BREAD TO MOP UP THE TOMATO-RICH JUICES.

SERVES SIX

INGREDIENTS

1.5kg/3¼lb boneless lamb, cubed
250ml/8fl oz/1 cup natural
  (plain) yogurt
30ml/2 tbsp sunflower oil
3 onions
2 red (bell) peppers, seeded and cut
  into chunks
3 garlic cloves, finely chopped
1 red chilli, seeded and chopped
2.5cm/1in piece fresh root ginger,
  peeled and chopped
30ml/2 tbsp mild curry paste
2 x 400g/14oz cans tomatoes
large pinch of saffron threads
800g/1¾lb plum tomatoes, halved,
  seeded and cut into chunks
salt and ground black pepper
chopped fresh coriander (cilantro),
  to garnish

1 Mix the lamb with the yogurt in a bowl. Cover and chill for about 1 hour. (Marinating in yogurt helps to tenderize the meat and reduce the cooking time.)

2 Heat the oil in a karahi, wok or large pan. Drain the lamb and reserve the yogurt, then cook the lamb, in batches, until it is golden on all sides – this takes about 15 minutes in total. Remove from the pan and set aside.

3 Cut two of the onions into wedges (six from each onion) and add to the oil remaining in the pan. Cook the onion wedges over a medium heat for about 10 minutes, or until they are beginning to colour. Add the peppers and cook for a further 5 minutes. Use a slotted spoon to remove the vegetables from the pan and set aside.

4 Meanwhile, chop the remaining onion. Add it to the oil remaining in the pan with the garlic, chilli and ginger, and cook, stirring frequently, until softened.

5 Stir in the curry paste and canned tomatoes with the reserved yogurt marinade. Replace the lamb, add seasoning to taste and stir well. Bring to the boil, reduce the heat and simmer for about 30 minutes.

6 Pound the saffron to a powder in a mortar, then stir in a little boiling water to dissolve it. Add this liquid to the curry. Replace the onion and pepper mixture. Stir in the fresh tomatoes and bring back to simmering point, then cook for 15 minutes. Garnish with chopped coriander to serve.

Per portion: Energy 587Kcal/2456kJ; Protein 54.7g; Carbohydrate 19.5g, of which sugars 17.7g; Fat 33g, of which saturates 13.8g; Cholesterol 191mg; Calcium 143mg; Fibre 4g; Sodium 318mg.

OSSO BUCCO WITH RISOTTO MILANESE

LITERALLY MEANING BONE WITH A HOLE, OSSO BUCCO IS A TRADITIONAL MILANESE STEW OF VEAL, ONIONS AND LEEKS IN WHITE WINE. MANY OF TODAY'S VERSIONS ALSO INCLUDE TOMATOES. RISOTTO MILANESE IS THE ARCHETYPAL ITALIAN RISOTTO AND THE CLASSIC ACCOMPANIMENT FOR OSSO BUCCO.

SERVES FOUR

INGREDIENTS
  50g/2oz/¼ cup butter
  15ml/1 tbsp olive oil
  1 large onion, chopped
  1 leek, finely chopped
  45ml/3 tbsp plain (all-purpose) flour
  4 large portions of veal shin (shank)
  600ml/1 pint/2½ cups dry white wine
  salt and ground black pepper
For the risotto
  25g/1oz/2 tbsp butter
  1 onion, finely chopped
  350g/12oz/1⅔ cups risotto rice
  1 litre/1¾ pints/4 cups boiling
    chicken stock
  2.5ml/½ tsp saffron threads
  60ml/4 tbsp white wine
  50g/2oz/⅔ cup Parmesan cheese,
    coarsely grated
For the gremolata
  grated rind of 1 lemon
  30ml/2 tbsp chopped fresh parsley
  1 garlic clove, finely chopped

1 Heat the butter and oil until sizzling in a large frying pan. Add the onion and leek, and cook gently for about 5 minutes without browning the onions. Season the flour and toss the veal in it, then add it to the pan and cook over a high heat until browned.

COOK'S TIP
When buying veal shin, ask for the pieces to be cut thickly so that they will retain the marrow during cooking (or check that they are prepared this way if purchasing prepacked meat).

2 Gradually stir in the wine and heat until simmering. Cover the pan and simmer for 1½ hours, stirring occasionally, or until the meat is very tender. Use a slotted spoon to transfer the veal to a warm serving dish, then boil the sauce rapidly until reduced and thickened to the required consistency.

3 Make the risotto about 30 minutes before the end of the cooking time for the stew. Melt the butter in a large pan and cook the onion until softened.

4 Stir in the rice to coat all the grains in butter. Add a ladleful of boiling chicken stock and mix well. Continue adding the boiling stock a ladleful at a time, letting each portion be absorbed before adding the next. The whole process takes about 20 minutes.

5 Pound the saffron threads in a mortar, then stir in the wine. Add the saffron-scented wine to the risotto and cook for a final 5 minutes. Remove the pan from the heat and stir in the Parmesan.

6 Mix the lemon rind, parsley and garlic for the gremolata. Spoon some risotto on to each plate, then add the veal. Sprinkle with gremolata and serve immediately.

Per portion: Energy 901Kcal/3764kJ; Protein 49.1g; Carbohydrate 92g, of which sugars 8g; Fat 25.9g, of which saturates 13.7g; Cholesterol 130mg; Calcium 248mg; Fibre 2.9g; Sodium 350mg.

BEEF CARBONADE

THIS RICH, DARK STEW OF BEEF, COOKED SLOWLY WITH LOTS OF ONIONS, GARLIC AND BEER,
IS A CLASSIC CASSEROLE FROM THE NORTH OF FRANCE AND NEIGHBOURING BELGIUM.

3 Reduce the heat and return the onions to the pan. Add the garlic, cook briefly, then add the beer or ale, water and sugar. Tie the thyme and bay leaf together and add to the pan with the celery. Bring to the boil, stirring, then season with salt and pepper.

4 Pour the sauce over the beef and mix well. Cover tightly, then place in the oven for 2½ hours. Check the beef once or twice to make sure that it is not too dry, adding a little water, if necessary. Test for tenderness, allowing an extra 30–40 minutes' cooking if necessary.

SERVES SIX

INGREDIENTS
    45ml/3 tbsp vegetable oil or
      beef dripping (drippings)
    3 onions, sliced
    45ml/3 tbsp plain (all-purpose) flour
    2.5ml/½ tsp mustard powder
    1kg/2¼lb boneless beef shin (shank)
      or chuck, cut into large cubes
    2–3 garlic cloves, finely chopped
    300ml/½ pint/1¼ cups dark beer or ale
    150ml/¼ pint/⅔ cup water
    5ml/1 tsp dark brown sugar
    1 fresh thyme sprig
    1 fresh bay leaf
    1 piece celery stick
    salt and ground black pepper
For the topping
    50g/2oz/¼ cup butter
    1 garlic clove, crushed
    15ml/1 tbsp Dijon mustard
    45ml/3 tbsp chopped fresh parsley
    6–12 slices baguette or ficelle loaf

1 Preheat the oven to 160°C/325°F/ Gas 3. Heat 30ml/2 tbsp of the oil or dripping in a frying pan and cook the onions over a low heat until softened. Remove from the pan and set aside.

2 Meanwhile, mix together the flour and mustard and season. Toss the beef in the flour. Add the remaining oil or dripping to the pan and heat over a high heat. Brown the beef all over, then transfer it to a casserole.

5 To make the topping, cream the butter with the garlic, mustard and 30ml/2 tbsp of the parsley. Spread the butter thickly over the bread. Increase the oven temperature to 190°C/375°F/ Gas 5. Taste and season the casserole, then arrange the bread slices, buttered side uppermost, on top. Bake for 20–25 minutes, until the bread is browned and crisp. Sprinkle the remaining parsley over the top and serve immediately.

Per portion: Energy 577Kcal/2410kJ; Protein 42.8g; Carbohydrate 32.8g, of which sugars 9.6g; Fat 28.8g, of which saturates 11.5g; Cholesterol 114mg; Calcium 87mg; Fibre 2.1g; Sodium 414mg.

CHILLI CON CARNE

ORIGINALLY MADE WITH FINELY CHOPPED BEEF, CHILLIES AND KIDNEY BEANS BY HUNGRY LABOURERS WORKING ON THE TEXAN RAILROAD, THIS FAMOUS TEX-MEX STEW HAS BECOME AN INTERNATIONAL FAVOURITE. SERVE WITH RICE OR BAKED POTATOES TO COMPLETE THIS HEARTY MEAL.

SERVES EIGHT

INGREDIENTS
1.2kg/2½lb lean braising steak
30ml/2 tbsp sunflower oil
1 large onion, chopped
2 garlic cloves, finely chopped
15ml/1 tbsp plain (all-purpose) flour
300ml/½ pint/1¼ cups red wine
300ml/½ pint/1¼ cups beef stock
30ml/2 tbsp tomato purée (paste)
fresh coriander (cilantro) leaves
salt and ground black pepper
For the beans
30ml/2 tbsp olive oil
1 onion, chopped
1 red chilli, seeded and chopped
2 x 400g/14oz cans red kidney
 beans, drained and rinsed
400g/14oz can chopped tomatoes
For the topping
6 tomatoes, peeled and chopped
1 green chilli, seeded and chopped
30ml/2 tbsp chopped fresh chives
30ml/2 tbsp fresh coriander (cilantro)
150ml/¼ pint/⅔ cup sour cream

2 Use a slotted spoon to remove the onion from the pan, then add the floured beef and cook over a high heat until browned on all sides. Remove from the pan and set aside, then flour and brown another batch of meat.

3 When the last batch of meat is browned, return the first batches with the onion to the pan. Stir in the wine, stock and tomato purée. Bring to the boil, reduce the heat and simmer for 45 minutes, or until the beef is tender.

4 Meanwhile, for the beans, heat the olive oil in a frying pan and cook the onion and chilli until softened. Add the kidney beans and tomatoes and simmer gently for 20–25 minutes, or until thickened and reduced.

5 Mix the tomatoes, chilli, chives and coriander for the topping. Ladle the meat mixture on to warmed plates. Add a layer of bean mixture and tomato topping. Finish with sour cream and garnish with coriander leaves.

1 Cut the meat into thick strips and then cut it crossways into small cubes. Heat the oil in a large, flameproof casserole. Add the chopped onion and garlic, and cook until softened but not coloured. Meanwhile, season the flour and place it on a plate, then toss a batch of meat in it.

VARIATION
This stew is equally good served with tortillas instead of rice. Wrap the tortillas in foil and warm through in the oven.

Per portion: Energy 470Kcal/1969kJ; Protein 42g; Carbohydrate 28.4g, of which sugars 11.2g; Fat 18.9g, of which saturates 6.9g; Cholesterol 106mg; Calcium 124mg; Fibre 8.2g; Sodium 517mg.

STOVE-TOP DISHES

It is remarkable how many main meals can be cooked entirely on top of the stove, from Classic Fish and Chips to steamed specialities like Sea Bass with Orange Chilli Salsa. This is very much hands-on cooking and often achieves better results than when food is cooked in the oven, largely because the cook is more likely to stir and check the dish regularly. The aroma of the cooking food stimulates the appetite, doubling the enjoyment of those lucky enough to tuck into such tasty dishes as Bang Bang Chicken or Pot-roasted Brisket.

MOULES PROVENÇALES

EATING THESE DELECTABLE MUSSELS IS A MESSY AFFAIR, WHICH IS PART OF THEIR CHARM. HAND ROUND PLENTY OF CRUSTY FRENCH BREAD FOR MOPPING UP THE JUICES AND DON'T FORGET FINGERBOWLS OF WARM WATER AND A PLATE FOR DISCARDED SHELLS.

SERVES FOUR

INGREDIENTS
30ml/2 tbsp olive oil
200g/7oz rindless unsmoked streaky (fatty) bacon, cubed
1 onion, finely chopped
3 garlic cloves, finely chopped
1 bay leaf
15ml/1 tbsp chopped fresh mixed Provençal herbs, such as thyme, marjoram, basil, oregano and savory
15–30ml/1–2 tbsp sun-dried tomatoes in oil, chopped
4 large, very ripe tomatoes, peeled, seeded and chopped
50g/2oz/½ cup pitted black olives, chopped
105ml/7 tbsp dry white wine
2.25kg/5–5¼lb fresh mussels, scrubbed and bearded
salt and ground black pepper
60ml/4 tbsp coarsely chopped fresh parsley, to garnish

1 Heat the oil in a large pan. Cook the bacon until golden and crisp. Remove with a slotted spoon; set aside. Add the onion and garlic to the pan and cook gently until softened. Add the herbs, with both types of tomatoes. Cook gently for 5 minutes, stirring frequently. Stir in the olives and season.

2 Put the wine and mussels in another pan. Cover and shake over a high heat for 5 minutes, until the mussels open. Discard any that remain closed.

3 Strain the mussel cooking liquid into the pan containing the tomato sauce through a sieve lined with muslin (cheesecloth) and boil until the mixture is reduced by about one-third. Add the mussels and stir to coat them thoroughly with the sauce. Remove and discard the bay leaf.

4 Divide the mussels and sauce among four heated dishes. Sprinkle over the fried bacon and chopped parsley and serve piping hot.

Per portion: Energy 439Kcal/1836kJ; Protein 34.9g; Carbohydrate 12.8g, of which sugars 6.9g; Fat 25.9g, of which saturates 6.2g; Cholesterol 123mg; Calcium 112mg; Fibre 2.4g; Sodium 1467mg.

FRENCH MUSSELS

THIS IS A TRADITIONAL DISH OF MUSSELS COOKED WITH SHALLOTS, GARLIC AND SAFFRON FROM THE WEST ATLANTIC COAST OF FRANCE. IT TASTES AS SUPERB AS IT LOOKS.

SERVES SIX

INGREDIENTS

  2kg/4½lb fresh mussels, scrubbed
    and bearded
  250g/9oz shallots, finely chopped
  300ml/½ pint/1¼ cups medium white
    wine, such as Vouvray
  generous pinch of saffron threads
    (about 12 strands)
  75g/3oz/6 tbsp butter
  2 celery sticks, finely chopped
  5ml/1 tsp fennel seeds,
    lightly crushed
  2 large garlic cloves, finely chopped
  250ml/8fl oz/1 cup fish or stock
  1 bay leaf
  pinch of cayenne pepper
  2 large (US extra large) egg yolks
  150ml/¼ pint/⅔ cup double
    (heavy) cream
  juice of ½–1 lemon
  30–45ml/2–3 tbsp chopped
    fresh parsley
  salt and ground black pepper

1 Discard any mussels that do not shut when tapped sharply.

2 Place 30ml/2 tbsp of the shallots with the wine in a wide pan and bring to the boil. Add half the mussels and cover, then boil rapidly for 1 minute, shaking the pan once. Remove all the mussels, discarding any that remain closed. Repeat with the remaining mussels. Remove the top half-shell from each mussel. Strain the cooking liquid through a fine sieve into a bowl and stir in the saffron, then set aside.

3 Melt 50g/2oz/4 tbsp of the butter in a heavy pan. Add the remaining shallots and celery and cook over a low heat, stirring occasionally, for 5–6 minutes, until softened but not browned. Add the fennel seeds and half of the garlic, then cook for another 2–3 minutes.

4 Pour in the reserved mussel liquid, bring to the boil and then simmer for 5 minutes before adding the stock, bay leaf and cayenne. Season with salt and pepper to taste, then simmer, uncovered, for 5–10 minutes.

5 Beat the egg yolks with the cream, then whisk in a ladleful of the hot liquid followed by the juice of ½ lemon. Whisk this mixture back into the sauce. Cook over a very low heat, without allowing it to boil, for 5–10 minutes until slightly thickened. Taste for seasoning and add more lemon juice if necessary.

6 Stir the remaining garlic, butter and most of the parsley into the sauce with the mussels and reheat for 30–60 seconds. Distribute the mussels among six soup plates and ladle the sauce over. Sprinkle with the remaining parsley and serve.

Per portion: Energy 568Kcal/2360kJ; Protein 26g; Carbohydrate 9.9g, of which sugars 5.4g; Fat 42.1g, of which saturates 23.6g; Cholesterol 272mg; Calcium 149mg; Fibre 1.4g; Sodium 632mg.

STEAMED FISH <u>WITH</u> FIVE WILLOW SAUCE

A FISH KETTLE WILL COME IN USEFUL FOR THIS RECIPE. CARP IS TRADITIONALLY USED, BUT ANY CHUNKY FISH THAT CAN BE COOKED WHOLE, SUCH AS SALMON OR SEA BREAM, CAN BE GIVEN THIS TREATMENT. MAKE SURE YOU HAVE A SUITABLE LARGE PLATTER FOR SERVING THIS SPECTACULAR DISH.

SERVES FOUR

INGREDIENTS

- 1–2 carp or similar whole fish, total weight about 1kg/2¼ lb, cleaned and scaled
- 2.5cm/1in piece fresh root ginger, peeled and thinly sliced
- 4 spring onions (scallions), cut into thin strips
- 2.5ml/½ tsp salt

For the five willow sauce

- 375g/13oz jar chow chow (Chinese sweet mixed pickles)
- 300ml/½ pint/1¼ cups water
- 30ml/2 tbsp rice vinegar
- 25ml/1½ tbsp sugar
- 25ml/1½ tbsp cornflour (cornstarch)
- 15ml/1 tbsp light soy sauce
- 15ml/1 tbsp rice wine or medium-dry sherry
- 1 small green (bell) pepper, seeded and diced
- 1 carrot, peeled and cut into batons
- 1 tomato, peeled, seeded and diced

2 Fold up one or two pieces of foil to make a long wide strip. You will need one for each fish. Place the fish on the foil and then lift the fish on to the trivet. Lower the trivet into the fish kettle and tuck the ends of the foil over the fish.

3 Pour boiling water into the fish kettle to a depth of 2.5cm/1in. Bring to a full rolling boil, then lower the heat and cook the fish until the flesh flakes, topping up the kettle with boiling water as necessary. (See Cook's Tip for cooking times.)

5 In a small bowl, mix the cornflour to a paste with the remaining water. Stir in the soy sauce and rice wine or sherry.

6 Add the mixture to the sauce and bring to the boil, stirring until it thickens and becomes glossy. Add all the vegetables, the chopped pickles and the pickle liquid and cook over a gentle heat for 2 minutes.

7 Using the foil strips as a support, carefully transfer the cooked fish to a platter, then ease the foil away. Spoon the warm sauce over the fish and serve.

1 Rinse the fish inside and out. Dry with kitchen paper. Create a support for each fish by placing a broad strip of oiled foil on the work surface. Place the fish on the foil. Mix the ginger, spring onions and salt, then tuck the mixture into the body cavity.

4 Meanwhile, prepare the sauce. Tip the chow chow into a sieve placed over a bowl and reserve the liquid. Cut each of the pickles in half. Pour 250ml/8fl oz/ 1 cup of the water into a pan and bring to the boil. Add the vinegar and sugar and stir until dissolved.

COOK'S TIP
If using one large fish that is too long to fit in a fish kettle, cut it in half and cook it on a rack placed over a large roasting pan. Pour in a similar quantity of boiling water as for the fish kettle, cover with foil and cook on top of the stove. Allow about 20–25 minutes for a 1kg/2¼ lb fish; 15–20 minutes for a 675g/1½lb fish. Reassemble the halved fish before coating it with the sauce.

Per portion: Energy 156Kcal/655kJ; Protein 19.1g; Carbohydrate 7.8g, of which sugars 6.3g; Fat 5.1g, of which saturates 1g; Cholesterol 67mg; Calcium 77mg; Fibre 2.4g; Sodium 739mg.

CHINESE-STYLE STEAMED FISH

THIS IS A CLASSIC CHINESE WAY OF COOKING WHOLE FISH, WITH GARLIC, SPRING ONIONS, GINGER AND BLACK BEANS. THE FISH MAKES A SPLENDID CENTREPIECE FOR A CHINESE MEAL OR IT CAN BE SERVED MORE SIMPLY, WITH BOILED RICE AND SOME STIR-FRIED CHINESE GREENS.

SERVES FOUR TO SIX

INGREDIENTS

2 sea bass, or trout, each weighing
    about 675–800g/1½–1¾lb
25ml/1½ tbsp salted black beans
2.5ml/½ tsp sugar
30ml/2 tbsp finely shredded fresh
    root ginger
4 garlic cloves, thinly sliced
30ml/2 tbsp Chinese rice wine or
    dry sherry
30ml/2 tbsp light soy sauce
4–6 spring onions (scallions), finely
    shredded or sliced diagonally
45ml/3 tbsp groundnut (peanut) oil
10ml/2 tsp sesame oil

1 Wash the fish inside and out under cold running water, then pat them dry on kitchen paper. Using a sharp knife, slash three or four deep cross shapes on each side of each fish.

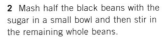

2 Mash half the black beans with the sugar in a small bowl and then stir in the remaining whole beans.

3 Place a little ginger and garlic inside the cavity of each fish and then lay them on a plate or dish that will fit inside a large steamer. Rub the bean mixture into the fish, especially into the slashes, then sprinkle the remaining ginger and garlic over the top. Cover and chill for 30 minutes.

4 Place the steamer over a pan of boiling water. Sprinkle the rice wine or sherry and half the soy sauce over the fish and steam them for 15–20 minutes, or until just cooked.

5 Sprinkle with the remaining soy sauce and sprinkle the spring onions over the fish.

6 In a small pan, heat the groundnut oil until smoking, then trickle it over the spring onions. Sprinkle with the sesame oil and serve immediately.

Per portion: Energy 415Kcal/1741kJ; Protein 54.7g; Carbohydrate 1.6g, of which sugars 1.5g; Fat 20.3g, of which saturates 4.3g; Cholesterol 224mg; Calcium 90mg; Fibre 0.2g; Sodium 739mg.

SEA BASS WITH ORANGE CHILLI SALSA

THE CHILLI CITRUS SALSA HAS A FRESHNESS WHICH PROVIDES THE PERFECT CONTRAST TO THE WONDERFUL FLAVOUR OF FRESH SEA BASS.

SERVES FOUR

INGREDIENTS
    4 sea bass fillets
    salt and ground black pepper
    fresh coriander (cilantro), to garnish
For the salsa
    2 fresh green chillies
    2 oranges or pink grapefruit
    1 small onion

1 Make the salsa. Roast the chillies in a dry griddle pan until the skins are blistered, being careful not to let the flesh burn. Put them in a strong plastic bag and tie the top to keep the steam in. Set aside for 20 minutes.

COOK'S TIP
If the fish has not been scaled, do this by running the back of a small filleting knife against the grain of the scales. They should come away cleanly. Rinse and pat dry with kitchen paper.

2 Slice the top and bottom off each orange or grapefruit and cut off all the peel and pith. Cut between the membranes and put each segment in a bowl.

3 Remove the chillies from the bag and peel off the skins. Cut off the stalks, then slit the chillies and scrape out the seeds. Chop the flesh finely. Cut the onion in half and slice it thinly. Add the onion and chillies to the orange pieces and mix lightly. Season and chill.

4 Season the sea bass fillets. Line a steamer with greaseproof (waxed) paper, allowing extra to hang over the sides to help lift out the fish after cooking. Place the empty steamer over a pan of water and bring to the boil.

5 Place the fish in a single layer in the steamer. Cover with a lid and steam for about 8 minutes, or until just cooked. Garnish with fresh coriander and serve with the salsa and a vegetable side dish of your choice.

Per portion: Energy 181Kcal/763kJ; Protein 30.2g; Carbohydrate 6.6g, of which sugars 6.3g; Fat 3.9g, of which saturates 0.6g; Cholesterol 120mg; Calcium 232mg; Fibre 1.3g; Sodium 108mg.

FILLETS OF TURBOT WITH OYSTERS

THIS LUXURIOUS DISH IS PERFECT FOR SPECIAL OCCASIONS. IT IS WORTH BUYING A WHOLE TURBOT AND ASKING THE FISHMONGER TO FILLET AND SKIN IT FOR YOU. KEEP THE HEAD, BONES AND TRIMMINGS FOR STOCK. SOLE, BRILL AND HALIBUT CAN ALL BE SUBSTITUTED FOR THE TURBOT.

SERVES FOUR

INGREDIENTS

12 Pacific (rock) oysters
115g/4oz/½ cup butter
2 carrots, cut into julienne strips
200g/7oz celeriac, cut into
  julienne strips
the white parts of 2 leeks, cut into
  julienne strips
375ml/13fl oz/generous 1½ cups
  Champagne or dry white sparkling
  wine (about ½ bottle)
105ml/7 tbsp whipping cream
1 turbot, about 1.75kg/4–4½lb,
  filleted and skinned
salt and ground white pepper

1 Using an oyster knife, open the oysters over a bowl to catch the juices, then carefully remove them from their shells, discarding the shells, and place them in a separate bowl. Set aside until required.

2 Melt 25g/1oz/2 tbsp of the butter in a shallow pan, add the vegetable julienne and cook over a low heat until tender but not coloured. Pour in half the Champagne or sparkling wine and cook very gently until all the liquid has evaporated. Keep the heat low so that the vegetables do not colour.

3 Strain the oyster juices into a small pan and add the cream and the remaining Champagne or sparkling wine. Place over a medium heat until the mixture has reduced to the consistency of thin cream. Dice half the remaining butter and whisk it into the sauce, one piece at a time, until smooth. Season to taste, then pour the sauce into a blender and process until velvety smooth.

4 Return the sauce to the pan, bring it to just below boiling point, then drop in the oysters. Poach for about 1 minute, to warm but barely cook. Keep warm, but do not let the sauce boil.

5 Season the turbot fillets with salt and pepper. Heat the remaining butter in a large frying pan until foaming, then cook the fillets over a medium heat for about 2–3 minutes on each side, until cooked through and golden.

6 Cut each turbot fillet into three pieces and arrange on individual warmed plates. Pile the vegetable julienne on top, place three oysters around the turbot fillets on each plate and pour the sauce around the edge.

Per portion: Energy 752Kcal/3125kJ; Protein 66.7g; Carbohydrate 9.2g, of which sugars 8g; Fat 44.1g, of which saturates 23.9g; Cholesterol 106mg; Calcium 252mg; Fibre 1.4g; Sodium 370mg.

COD CARAMBA

THIS COLOURFUL MEXICAN DISH, WITH ITS CONTRASTING CRUNCHY TOPPING AND TENDER FISH FILLING, CAN BE MADE WITH ANY ECONOMICAL WHITE FISH, SUCH AS COLEY OR HADDOCK.

SERVES FOUR TO SIX

INGREDIENTS
450g/1lb cod fillets
225g/8oz smoked cod fillets
300ml/½ pint/1¼ cups fish stock
50g/2oz/¼ cup butter
1 onion, sliced
2 garlic cloves, crushed
1 green and 1 red (bell) pepper,
   seeded and diced
2 courgettes (zucchini), diced
115g/4oz/⅔ cup drained canned or
   thawed frozen corn kernels
2 tomatoes, peeled and chopped
juice of 1 lime
Tabasco sauce
salt, ground black pepper and
   cayenne pepper
For the topping
75g/3oz tortilla chips
50g/2oz/½ cup grated
   Cheddar cheese
coriander (cilantro) sprigs, to garnish
lime wedges, to serve

1 Lay the fish in a shallow pan and pour over the fish stock. Bring to the boil, lower the heat, cover and poach for about 8 minutes, until the flesh flakes easily when tested with the tip of a sharp knife. Leave to cool slightly, then remove the skin and separate the flesh into large flakes. Keep hot.

2 Melt the butter in a pan, add the onion and garlic and cook over a low heat until soft. Add the peppers, stir and cook for 2 minutes. Stir in the courgettes and cook for 3 minutes more, until all the vegetables are tender.

3 Mix the corn and tomatoes, then add lime juice and Tabasco to taste. Add to the pan, season with salt, black pepper and cayenne. Cook for 2 minutes to heat the corn and tomatoes, then stir in the fish and transfer to a dish that can safely be used under the grill (broiler).

4 Preheat the grill. Make the topping by crushing the tortilla chips, then mixing in the grated cheese. Add cayenne pepper to taste and sprinkle over the fish. Place the dish under the grill until the topping is crisp and brown. Garnish with coriander sprigs and lime wedges.

Per portion: Energy 439Kcal/1834kJ; Protein 39.8g; Carbohydrate 23.7g, of which sugars 11.3g; Fat 20.8g, of which saturates 10.4g; Cholesterol 116mg; Calcium 185mg; Fibre 4.8g; Sodium 1391mg.

CLASSIC FISH AND CHIPS

NOTHING BEATS A PIECE OF COD COOKED TO A CRISP WITH FRESHLY MADE CHIPS ON THE SIDE.
THE BATTER SHOULD BE LIGHT AND CRISP, BUT NOT TOO GREASY AND THE FISH SHOULD MELT
IN THE MOUTH. SERVE WITH LEMON WEDGES, OR LIME WEDGES IF YOU REALLY WANT TO SHOW OFF.
THE SECRET OF COOKING FISH AND CHIPS SUCCESSFULLY IS TO MAKE SURE THE OIL IS FRESH AND
CLEAN. HEAT THE OIL TO THE CORRECT TEMPERATURE BEFORE COOKING THE CHIPS AND AGAIN
BEFORE YOU ADD THE FISH. SERVE THE DISH IMMEDIATELY, WHILE STILL CRISP AND PIPING HOT.

SERVES FOUR

INGREDIENTS
   450g/1lb potatoes
   groundnut (peanut) oil for deep-frying
   4 x 175g/6oz cod fillets, skinned
For the batter
   75g/3oz/⅔ cup plain (all-
     purpose) flour
   1 egg yolk
   10ml/2 tsp oil
   175ml/6fl oz/¾ cup water
   salt

1 Cut the potatoes into 5mm/¼in thick slices. Cut each slice again to make 5mm/¼in chips (French fries).

2 Heat the oil in a deep-fryer to 180°C/350°F. Add the chips to the fryer and cook for 3 minutes, then remove from the pan and shake off all fat and set to one side.

3 To make the batter, sift the flour into a bowl and add the remaining ingredients with a pinch of salt. Beat well until smooth. Set aside until ready to use.

4 Cook the chips again in the fat for a further 5 minutes or so, until they are really nice and crisp. Drain on kitchen paper and season with salt. Keep hot in a low oven while you cook the pieces of fish.

VARIATION
Although cod is the traditional choice for fish and chips, you can also use haddock. Rock salmon, sometimes sold as huss or dogfish, also has a good flavour. It has a central length of cartilage which cannot be removed before cooking – otherwise the pieces of fish will fall apart – but can be easily prised out once the fish is served.

5 Dip the fish into the batter, making sure they are evenly coated, and shake off any excess.

6 Carefully lower the fish into the fat and cook for 5 minutes. Drain on kitchen paper. Serve with lemon wedges and the chips.

COOK'S TIPS
• Use fresh rather than frozen fish for the very best texture and flavour. If you have to use frozen fish, thaw it thoroughly and make sure it is dry before coating with batter.
• Ideally, you should use fresh oil for deep-frying each time, but it can usually be safely re-used once more. Do not use the same oil repeatedly, as it gradually breaks down and will smoke or even ignite quite easily. Long storage may cause it to turn rancid. After the first use, cool, then strain the oil to remove any debris. Remember, too, that the oil will be flavoured, to some extent, by the food first cooked in it.
• People keeping an eye on their fat intake may not realize that deep-fried foods absorb less fat during cooking than shallow-fried foods. This is because the initial submersion in the oil, providing it has been heated to the correct temperature, quickly seals the outside, preventing any more fat from being absorbed by the food.

Per portion: Energy 740Kcal/3093kJ; Protein 32.8g; Carbohydrate 61g, of which sugars 0.8g; Fat 42.2g, of which saturates 4.2g; Cholesterol 0mg; Calcium 134mg; Fibre 3.6g; Sodium 313mg.

TANDOORI CHICKEN

THE WORD TANDOORI REFERS TO A METHOD OF COOKING IN A CHARCOAL-FIRED CLAY OVEN CALLED A TANDOOR. IN NORTHERN INDIA AND PAKISTAN, A WIDE VARIETY OF FOODS IS COOKED IN THIS TYPE OF OVEN, BUT IN WESTERN COUNTRIES THE METHOD IS MOST POPULAR FOR CHICKEN. WARM NAAN BREAD AND MANGO CHUTNEY MAY BE OFFERED WITH THE CHICKEN AND RICE.

SERVES FOUR

INGREDIENTS
  30ml/2 tbsp vegetable oil
  2 small onions, cut into wedges
  2 garlic cloves, sliced
  4 skinless, boneless chicken breast
    portions, cut into cubes
  100ml/3½fl oz/⅓ cup water
  300g/11oz jar tandoori sauce
  salt and ground black pepper
  coriander (cilantro) sprigs, to garnish
To serve
  5ml/1 tsp ground turmeric
  350g/12oz/1⅔ cups basmati rice

1 Heat the oil in a flameproof casserole. Add the onions and garlic, and cook for about 3 minutes, or until the onion is beginning to soften, stirring frequently.

2 Add the cubes of chicken to the casserole and cook for 6 minutes. Stir the water into the tandoori sauce and pour it over the chicken. Bring to the boil, then reduce the heat and simmer for 10 minutes, or until the chicken pieces are cooked through and the sauce is slightly reduced and thickened.

3 Meanwhile, bring a large pan of lightly salted water to the boil, add the turmeric and rice and bring back to the boil. Stir once, reduce the heat to prevent the water from boiling over and simmer the rice for 12 minutes, or according to the time suggested on the packet, until tender.

4 Drain the rice well and serve with the tandoori chicken on warmed individual serving plates, garnished with sprigs of fresh coriander.

COOK'S TIP
You will find jars of ready-made tandoori sauce in large supermarkets.

Per portion: Energy 592Kcal/2479kJ; Protein 44g; Carbohydrate 77.5g, of which sugars 4.5g; Fat 11.4g, of which saturates 1.1g; Cholesterol 105mg; Calcium 54mg; Fibre 0.4g; Sodium 826mg.

CHICKEN AND VEGETABLE TAGINE

MOROCCAN TAGINES ARE USUALLY SERVED WITH COUSCOUS, BUT RICE MAKES AN EQUALLY DELICIOUS ACCOMPANIMENT. HERE, COUSCOUS IS STIRRED INTO THE RICE TO CREATE AN UNUSUAL AND TASTY DISH, ALTHOUGH YOU COULD USE RICE BY ITSELF.

SERVES FOUR

INGREDIENTS
    30ml/2 tbsp groundnut (peanut) oil
    4 skinless, boneless chicken breast
      portions, cut into large pieces
    1 large onion, chopped
    2 garlic cloves, crushed
    1 parsnip, cut into 2.5cm/1in pieces
    1 turnip, cut into 2cm/¾in pieces
    3 carrots, cut into 4cm/1½in pieces
    4 tomatoes, chopped
    1 cinnamon stick
    4 cloves
    5ml/1 tsp ground ginger
    1 bay leaf
    1.5–2.5ml/¼–½ tsp cayenne pepper
    350ml/12fl oz/1½ cups chicken stock
    400g/14oz can chickpeas, drained
      and skinned
    1 red (bell) pepper, seeded
      and sliced
    150g/5oz green beans, halved
    1 piece of preserved lemon peel,
      thinly sliced
    20–30 pitted brown or green olives
    salt
For the rice and couscous
    750ml/1¼ pints/3 cups chicken stock
    225g/8oz/generous 1 cup
      long grain rice
    115g/4oz/⅔ cup couscous
    45ml/3 tbsp chopped fresh
      coriander (cilantro)

1 Heat half of the oil in a large, flameproof casserole and cook the chicken pieces for a few minutes until evenly browned. Transfer to a plate.

2 Heat the remaining oil and cook the onion, garlic, parsnip, turnip and carrots together over a medium heat for 4–5 minutes until the vegetables are lightly flecked with brown, stirring frequently. Lower the heat, cover and sweat the vegetables for 5 minutes more, stirring occasionally.

3 Add the tomatoes, cook for a few minutes, then add the cinnamon stick, cloves, ginger, bay leaf and cayenne. Cook for 1–2 minutes.

4 Pour in the chicken stock, add the chickpeas and browned chicken pieces, and season with salt. Cover and simmer for 25 minutes.

5 Meanwhile, cook the rice and couscous mixture. Bring the chicken stock to the boil. Add the rice and simmer for about 5 minutes until almost tender. Remove the pan from the heat, stir in the couscous, cover tightly and leave for about 5 minutes.

6 When the vegetables in the tagine are almost tender, stir in the pepper slices and green beans and simmer for 10 minutes. Add the preserved lemon and olives, stir well and cook for 5 minutes more, or until the vegetables are perfectly tender.

7 Stir the chopped coriander into the rice and couscous mixture and pile it on to a plate. Serve the chicken tagine in the traditional dish, if you have one, or in a casserole.

BANG BANG CHICKEN

*WHAT A DESCRIPTIVE NAME THIS SPECIAL DISH FROM SICHUAN HAS! USE TOASTED SESAME PASTE
TO GIVE THE SAUCE AN AUTHENTIC FLAVOUR, ALTHOUGH CRUNCHY PEANUT BUTTER CAN BE USED
INSTEAD. BANG BANG CHICKEN IS PERFECT FOR PARTIES AND IDEAL FOR A BUFFET.*

SERVES FOUR

INGREDIENTS
 3 skinless, boneless chicken
   breast portions, total weight
   about 450g/1lb
 1 garlic clove, crushed
 2.5ml/½ tsp black peppercorns
 1 small onion, halved
 1 large cucumber, peeled, seeded
   and cut into thin strips
 salt and ground black pepper
For the sauce
 45ml/3 tbsp toasted sesame paste
 15ml/1 tbsp light soy sauce
 15ml/1 tbsp wine vinegar
 2 spring onions (scallions),
   finely chopped
 2 garlic cloves, crushed
 5 × 1cm/2 × ½in piece fresh
   root ginger, peeled and cut
   into thin batons
 15ml/1 tbsp Sichuan peppercorns,
   dry-fried and crushed
 5ml/1 tsp light brown sugar
For the chilli oil
 60ml/4 tbsp groundnut (peanut) oil
 5ml/1 tsp chilli powder

1 Place the chicken in a large, heavy
pan. Pour in sufficient water just to
cover, add the garlic, peppercorns and
onion and bring to the boil over a
medium heat. Skim off any foam that
rises to the surface, stir in salt and
pepper to taste, then cover the pan.
Lower the heat and cook for about
25 minutes, or until the chicken is just
tender. Drain, reserving the stock.

2 Make the sauce by mixing the
toasted sesame paste with 45ml/3 tbsp
of the chicken stock, saving the rest for
soup. Add the soy sauce, vinegar,
spring onions, garlic, ginger and
crushed peppercorns to the sesame
mixture. Stir in sugar to taste.

3 Make the chilli oil by gently heating
the oil and chilli powder together until
foaming. Simmer for 2 minutes, cool,
then strain off the red-coloured oil and
discard the sediment.

4 Spread out the cucumber batons
on a platter. Cut the chicken breast
portions into pieces of about the same
size as the cucumber strips and arrange
them on top. Pour over the sauce,
drizzle on the chilli oil and serve.

VARIATION
Crunchy peanut butter can be used
instead of sesame paste, if you like. Mix
it with 30ml/2 tbsp sesame oil and
proceed as in Step 2.

Per portion: Energy 297Kcal/1239kJ; Protein 29.7g; Carbohydrate 2.3g, of which sugars 1.8g; Fat 18.9g, of which saturates 2.6g; Cholesterol 79mg; Calcium 94mg; Fibre 1.4g; Sodium 339mg.

POT-COOKED DUCK AND GREEN VEGETABLES

PREPARE THE INGREDIENTS FOR THIS JAPANESE DISH BEFOREHAND, SO THAT THE COOKING CAN BE DONE AT THE TABLE. USE A HEAVY PAN OR FLAMEPROOF CASSEROLE WITH A PORTABLE STOVE.

SERVES FOUR

INGREDIENTS
    4 duck breast fillets, about 800g/
    1¾lb total weight
    8 large shiitake mushrooms, stalks
    removed, a cross cut into each cap
    2 leeks, trimmed and cut diagonally
    into 6cm/2½in lengths
    ½ hakusai, stalk part removed and
    cut into 5cm/2in squares
    500g/1¼lb shungiku or mizuna, root
    part removed, cut in half crossways
For the stock
    raw bones from 1 chicken, washed
    1 egg shell
    200g/7oz/scant 1 cup short grain
    rice, washed and drained
    120ml/4fl oz/½ cup sake
    about 10ml/2 tsp coarse sea salt
For the sauce
    75ml/5 tbsp shoyu
    30ml/2 tbsp sake
    juice of 1 lime
    8 white peppercorns, crushed
For the soup
    130g/4½oz Chinese egg noodles,
    cooked and loosened
    1 egg, beaten
    1 bunch of chives
    ground white pepper

1 To make the stock, put the chicken bones into a pan three-quarters full of water. Bring to the boil and drain when it reaches boiling point. Wash the pan and the bones again, then return to the pan with the same amount of water. Add the egg shell and then bring to the boil. Simmer, uncovered, for 1 hour, skimming frequently. Remove the bones and egg shell. Add the rice, sake and salt, then simmer for 30 minutes. Remove from the heat and set aside.

2 Heat a heavy frying pan until just smoking. Remove from the heat for 1 minute, then add the duck breasts, skin side down. Return to a medium heat and sear for 3–4 minutes, or until crisp. Turn over and sear the other side for 1 minute. Remove from the heat.

3 When cool, wipe the duck fat with kitchen paper and cut the breast and skin into 5mm/¼in thick slices. Arrange on a large serving plate with all the prepared vegetables.

4 Heat through all the ingredients for the sauce in a small pan and transfer to a small jug (pitcher) or bowl.

5 Prepare four dipping bowls, four serving bowls and chopsticks. At the table, bring the pan of soup stock to the boil, then reduce to medium-low. Add half of the shiitake and leeks. Wait for 5 minutes and put in half of the stalk part of the hakusai. Add half of the duck and cook for 1–2 minutes for rare or 5–8 minutes for well-done meat.

6 Each person prepares some duck and vegetables in a serving bowl and drizzles over a little sauce. Add the soft hakusai leaves, shungiku and mizuna to the stock as you eat, adjusting the heat as you go. When the stock is less than a quarter of the pot's volume, top up with 3 parts water to 1 part sake.

7 When the duck has been eaten, bring the reduced stock to the boil. Skim the oil from the surface, and reduce the heat to medium. Add the noodles, cook for 1–2 minutes and check the seasoning. Add more salt if required. Pour in the beaten egg and swirl in the stock. Cover, turn off the heat, then leave to stand for 1 minute. Decorate with the chopped chives and serve with ground pepper.

Per portion: Energy 676Kcal/2846kJ; Protein 53.4g; Carbohydrate 81.6g, of which sugars 9.8g; Fat 19.4g, of which saturates 4.1g; Cholesterol 277mg; Calcium 126mg; Fibre 9.3g; Sodium 1296mg.

LAMB POT-ROASTED WITH TOMATOES, BEANS AND ONIONS

THIS SLOW-BRAISED DISH OF LAMB AND TOMATOES, SPICED WITH CINNAMON AND STEWED WITH GREEN BEANS, SHOWS A GREEK INFLUENCE. IT IS ALSO GOOD MADE WITH COURGETTES INSTEAD OF BEANS.

SERVES EIGHT

INGREDIENTS
  1kg/2¼lb lamb on the bone
  8 garlic cloves, chopped
  2.5–5ml/½–1 tsp ground cumin
  45ml/3 tbsp olive oil
  juice of 1 lemon
  2 onions, thinly sliced
  about 500ml/17fl oz/2¼ cups
    lamb, beef or vegetable stock
  75–90ml/5–6 tbsp tomato
    purée (paste)
  1 cinnamon stick
  2–3 large pinches of ground
    allspice or ground cloves
  15–30ml/1–2 tbsp sugar
  400g/14oz/scant 3 cups
    green beans
  salt and ground black pepper
  15–30ml/1–2 tbsp chopped
    fresh parsley, to garnish

1 Preheat the oven to 160°C/325°F/Gas 3. Coat the lamb with the garlic, cumin, olive oil, lemon juice, salt and pepper.

2 Heat a flameproof casserole. Sear the lamb on all sides. Add the onions and pour the stock over the meat to cover. Stir in the tomato purée, spices and sugar. Cover and cook in the oven for 2–3 hours.

3 Remove the casserole from the oven and pour the stock into a pan. Move the onions to the side of the dish and return to the oven, uncovered, for 20 minutes.

4 Meanwhile, add the beans to the hot stock and cook until the beans are tender and the sauce has thickened. Slice the meat and serve with the pan juices and beans. Garnish with parsley.

Per portion: Energy 333Kcal/1394kJ; Protein 39.1g; Carbohydrate 8.2g, of which sugars 6.9g; Fat 16.2g, of which saturates 5.4g; Cholesterol 125mg; Calcium 41mg; Fibre 2g; Sodium 109mg.

POT-ROASTED BRISKET

THIS JEWISH, POT-ROASTED MEAT DISH INCLUDES THE TRADITIONAL KISHKE, A HEAVY, SAUSAGE-SHAPED DUMPLING, WHICH IS ADDED TO THE POT AND COOKED WITH THE MEAT. SERVE WITH KASHA — MEAT GRAVY WITH KASHA IS ONE OF LIFE'S PERFECT COMBINATIONS.

SERVES SIX TO EIGHT

INGREDIENTS
  5 onions, sliced
  3 bay leaves
  1–1.6kg/2¼–3½lb beef brisket
  1 garlic bulb, broken into cloves
  4 carrots, thickly sliced
  5–10ml/1–2 tsp paprika
  about 500ml/17fl oz/2¼ cups
    beef stock
  3–4 baking potatoes, peeled
    and quartered
  salt and ground black pepper
For the kishke
  about 90cm/36in sausage casing
    (see Cook's Tip)
  250g/9oz/2¼ cups plain
    (all-purpose) flour
  120ml/4fl oz/½ cup semolina
    or couscous
  10–15ml/2–3 tsp paprika
  1 carrot, grated and 2 carrots,
    diced (optional)
  250ml/8fl oz/1 cup rendered
    chicken fat
  30ml/2 tbsp crisp, fried onions
  ½ onion, grated and 3 onions,
    thinly sliced
  3 garlic cloves, chopped
  salt and ground black pepper

2 Pour in enough stock to fill the dish to about 5–7.5cm/2–3in and cover with foil. Cook in the oven for 2 hours.

3 Meanwhile, make the kishke. In a bowl, combine all the ingredients and stuff the mixture into the casing, leaving enough space for the mixture to expand. Tie into sausage-shaped lengths.

4 When the meat has cooked for about 2 hours, add the kishke and potatoes to the pan, re-cover and cook for a further 1 hour, or until the meat and potatoes are tender.

5 Remove the foil from the dish and increase the oven temperature to 190–200°C/375–400°F/Gas 5–6. Move the onions away from the top of the meat to the side of the dish and return to the oven for a further 30 minutes, or until the meat, onions and potatoes are beginning to brown and become crisp. Serve hot or cold.

COOK'S TIP
Traditionally, sausage casings are used for kishke but, if unavailable, use cooking-strength clear film (plastic wrap) or a piece of muslin (cheesecloth).

1 Preheat the oven to 180°C/350°F/Gas 4. Put one-third of the onions and a bay leaf in an ovenproof dish, then top with the brisket. Sprinkle over the garlic, carrots and the remaining bay leaves, sprinkle with salt, pepper and paprika, then top with the remaining onions.

Per portion: Energy 781Kcal/3271kJ; Protein 44.2g; Carbohydrate 74g, of which sugars 12.7g; Fat 36.4g, of which saturates 14.4g; Cholesterol 113mg; Calcium 124mg; Fibre 5g; Sodium 124mg.

TACOS WITH SHREDDED BEEF

IN MEXICO, TACOS ARE MOST OFTEN MADE WITH SOFT CORN TORTILLAS, WHICH ARE FILLED AND FOLDED IN HALF. IT IS UNUSUAL TO SEE THE CRISP SHELLS OF CORN WHICH ARE SO WIDELY USED IN TEX-MEX COOKING. TACOS ARE ALWAYS EATEN IN THE HAND.

3 Put the meat on a board, let it cool slightly, then shred it, using two forks. Put the meat in a bowl. Divide the tortilla dough into six equal balls.

4 Open a tortilla press and line both sides with plastic (this can be cut from a new plastic sandwich bag). Put each ball on the press and flatten it into a 15–20cm/6–8in round.

5 Heat a griddle or frying pan until hot. Cook each tortilla for 15–20 seconds on each side, and then for a further 15 seconds on the first side. Keep the tortillas warm and soft by folding them inside a slightly damp dishtowel.

6 Add the oregano and cumin to the shredded meat and mix well. Heat the oil in a frying pan and cook the onion and garlic for 3–4 minutes, until softened. Add the meat mixture and toss over the heat until heated through.

7 Place some shredded lettuce on a tortilla, top with shredded beef and salsa, fold in half and serve with lime wedges. Garnish with fresh coriander.

SERVES SIX

INGREDIENTS
    450g/1lb rump (round) steak, diced
    150g/5oz/1 cup masa harina
    2.5ml/½ tsp salt
    120ml/4fl oz/½ cup warm water
    10ml/2 tsp dried oregano
    5ml/1 tsp ground cumin
    30ml/2 tbsp oil
    1 onion, thinly sliced
    2 garlic cloves, crushed
    fresh coriander (cilantro), to garnish
    shredded lettuce, lime wedges and
        tomato salsa, to serve

1 Put the steak in a deep frying pan and pour over water to cover. Bring to the boil, then lower the heat and simmer for 1–1½ hours.

2 Meanwhile, make the tortilla dough. Mix the masa harina and salt in a large mixing bowl. Add the warm water, a little at a time, to make a dough that can be worked into a ball. Knead the dough on a lightly floured surface for 3–4 minutes until smooth, then wrap the dough in clear film (plastic wrap) and leave to rest for 1 hour.

Per portion: Energy 232Kcal/975kJ; Protein 18.6g; Carbohydrate 21.4g, of which sugars 1.8g; Fat 8.6g, of which saturates 2.6g; Cholesterol 46mg; Calcium 44mg; Fibre 1.1g; Sodium 198mg.

BEEF ENCHILADAS WITH RED SAUCE

ENCHILADAS ARE USUALLY MADE WITH CORN TORTILLAS, ALTHOUGH IN PARTS OF NORTHERN MEXICO WHEAT FLOUR TORTILLAS ARE SOMETIMES USED.

SERVES THREE TO FOUR

INGREDIENTS

500g/1¼lb rump (round) steak, cut
   into 5cm/2in cubes
2 ancho chillies, seeded
2 pasilla chillies, seeded
2 garlic cloves, crushed
10ml/2 tsp dried oregano
2.5ml/½ tsp ground cumin
30ml/2 tbsp vegetable oil
7 fresh corn tortillas
shredded onion and flat leaf parsley
   to garnish
mango salsa, to serve

1 Put the steak in a deep frying pan and cover with water. Bring to the boil, then lower the heat and simmer for 1–1½ hours, or until very tender.

2 Meanwhile, put the dried chillies in a bowl and pour over the hot water. Leave to soak for 30 minutes, then tip the contents of the bowl into a blender and process to a smooth paste.

3 Drain the steak and let it cool, reserving 250ml/8fl oz/1 cup of the cooking liquid. Meanwhile, cook the garlic, oregano and cumin in the oil for 2 minutes.

4 Stir in the chilli paste and the reserved cooking liquid from the steak. Tear one of the tortillas into small pieces and add it to the mixture. Bring to the boil, then lower the heat. Simmer for 10 minutes, stirring occasionally, until thickened. Shred the steak, using two forks, stir it into the sauce and heat through for a few minutes.

5 Spoon some of the meat mixture on to each tortilla and roll it up to make an enchilada. Keep the enchiladas in a warmed dish until you have rolled them all. Garnish with shreds of onion and fresh flat leaf parsley and then serve immediately with the mango salsa.

VARIATION
For a richer version place the rolled enchiladas side by side in a gratin dish. Pour over 300ml/½ pint/1¼ cups sour cream and 75g/3oz/¾ cup grated Cheddar cheese. Place under a preheated grill (broiler) for 5 minutes, or until the cheese melts and the sauce begins to bubble. Serve with the salsa.

Per portion: Energy 477Kcal/2004kJ; Protein 40.6g; Carbohydrate 39.9g, of which sugars 0.9g; Fat 18.3g, of which saturates 5.5g; Cholesterol 102mg; Calcium 85mg; Fibre 1.6g; Sodium 261mg.

GRILLS AND
GRIDDLED DISHES

Whether you grill (broil) inside the oven, on a ridged griddle

pan or over an open fire, this is an excellent cooking method.

Grilled food looks good, with an all-over tan or the attractive

stripes that mark the means of its cooking. There's often a

contrast in textures, the outside gaining a crisp crust beneath

which the food is beautifully tender. Finally — and perhaps

most importantly — grilled food is healthy, as only a minimum

amount of oil is used in the process. This chapter includes

kebabs, patties and superb grilled vegetable dishes.

GRILLED AUBERGINE PARCELS

THESE ARE DELICIOUS LITTLE ITALIAN BUNDLES OF PLUM TOMATOES, MOZZARELLA CHEESE AND FRESH BASIL LEAVES, WRAPPED IN SLICES OF AUBERGINE.

SERVES FOUR

INGREDIENTS

    2 large, long aubergines (eggplant)
    225g/8oz mozzarella cheese
    2 plum tomatoes
    16 large fresh basil leaves
    30ml/2 tbsp olive oil
    salt and ground black pepper
For the dressing
    60ml/4 tbsp olive oil
    5ml/1 tsp balsamic vinegar
    15ml/1 tbsp sun-dried tomato paste
    15ml/1 tbsp lemon juice
For the garnish
    30ml/2 tbsp roasted pine nuts
    torn basil leaves

1 Remove and discard the stalks from the aubergines and cut them lengthways into thin slices – the aim is to get 16 slices in total (disregarding the first and last slices), each about 5mm/¼in thick.

2 Bring a large pan of salted water to the boil and cook the aubergine slices for about 2 minutes, until just softened. Drain, then dry on kitchen paper.

3 Cut the mozzarella cheese into eight slices. Cut each tomato into eight slices, not counting the first and last slices.

4 Place two aubergine slices on a baking sheet in a cross. Place a tomato slice in the centre, season, then add a basil leaf, followed by a slice of mozzarella, a basil leaf, a tomato slice and more seasoning.

5 Fold the ends of the aubergine slices around the filling to make a neat parcel. Repeat with the rest of the ingredients to make eight parcels. Chill for about 20 minutes. Preheat the grill (broiler).

6 To make the tomato dressing, whisk all the ingredients together and season to taste.

7 Brush the parcels with the oil and cook for about 5 minutes on each side, until golden. Serve, with the dressing, sprinkled with pine nuts and basil.

Per portion: Energy 370Kcal/1532kJ; Protein 12.9g; Carbohydrate 4.4g, of which sugars 4.2g; Fat 33.6g, of which saturates 10.6g; Cholesterol 33mg; Calcium 219mg; Fibre 2.7g; Sodium 237mg.

GRILLED POLENTA WITH CARAMELIZED ONIONS, RADICCHIO AND TALEGGIO CHEESE

SLICES OF GRILLED POLENTA, ONE OF THE STAPLES OF NORTH ITALIAN COOKING, ARE TASTY TOPPED WITH SLOWLY CARAMELIZED ONIONS AND BUBBLING TALEGGIO, ALSO FROM NORTH ITALY.

SERVES FOUR

INGREDIENTS
900ml/1½ pints/3¾ cups water
5ml/1 tsp salt
150g/5oz/generous 1 cup polenta
  or cornmeal
50g/2oz/⅓ cup freshly grated
  Parmesan cheese
5ml/1 tsp chopped fresh thyme
90ml/6 tbsp olive oil
675g/1½lb onions, halved and sliced
2 garlic cloves, chopped
a few fresh thyme sprigs
5ml/1 tsp brown sugar
15–30ml/1–2 tbsp balsamic vinegar
2 heads radicchio, cut into thick
  slices or wedges
225g/8oz Taleggio cheese, sliced
salt and ground black pepper

1 In a large pan, bring the water to the boil and add the salt. Adjust the heat so that it simmers. Stirring constantly, add the polenta in a steady stream, then bring to the boil. Cook over a very low heat, stirring frequently, for about 30–40 minutes, until thick and smooth.

2 Beat in the Parmesan and chopped thyme, then turn on to a work surface or tray. Spread evenly, then leave to cool.

3 Heat 30ml/2 tbsp of the oil in a frying pan over a moderate heat. Add the onions and stir to coat in the oil, then cover and cook over a very low heat for 15 minutes, stirring occasionally.

4 Add the garlic and most of the thyme sprigs and cook, uncovered, for another 10 minutes, or until light brown.

5 Add the sugar, 15ml/1 tbsp of the vinegar and salt and pepper. Cook for another 5–10 minutes, until soft and well-browned. Taste and add more vinegar and seasoning as necessary.

6 Preheat the grill (broiler). Cut the polenta into thick slices and brush with a little of the remaining oil, then grill (broil) until crusty and lightly browned.

7 Turn over the polenta and add the radicchio to the grill rack or pan. Season the radicchio and brush with a little oil. Grill for about 5 minutes, until the polenta and radicchio are browned. Drizzle a little vinegar over the radicchio.

8 Heap the onions on to the polenta. Sprinkle the cheese and a few sprigs of thyme over both polenta and radicchio. Grill until the cheese is bubbling. Season with pepper and serve immediately.

Per portion: Energy 608Kcal/2522kJ; Protein 22.3g; Carbohydrate 42.7g, of which sugars 11.4g; Fat 37.5g, of which saturates 15.2g; Cholesterol 65mg; Calcium 352mg; Fibre 3.7g; Sodium 456mg.

YUCATAN-STYLE SHARK STEAK

A FIRM-FLESHED FISH, SHARK IS WIDELY AVAILABLE, EITHER FRESH OR FROZEN. IT NEEDS CAREFUL WATCHING, AS OVERCOOKING WILL MAKE IT DRY AND TOUGH, BUT THE FLAVOUR IS EXCELLENT.

SERVES FOUR

INGREDIENTS

    grated rind and juice of 1 orange
    juice of 1 small lime
    45ml/3 tbsp white wine
    30ml/2 tbsp olive oil
    2 garlic cloves, crushed
    10ml/2 tsp ground achiote seed
    (annatto powder)
    2.5ml/½ tsp cayenne pepper
    2.5ml/½ tsp dried marjoram
    5ml/1 tsp salt
    4 shark steaks
    fresh oregano leaves, to garnish
    4 wheat-flour tortillas and any
    suitable salsa, to serve

COOK'S TIP
Shark freezes successfully, with little or no loss of flavour on thawing, so use frozen steaks if you can't find fresh.

1 Put the orange rind and juice in a shallow non-metallic dish which is large enough to hold all the shark steaks in a single layer. Add the lime juice, white wine, olive oil, garlic, ground achiote (annatto powder), cayenne, marjoram and salt. Mix well.

2 Add the shark steaks to the dish and spoon the marinade over them. Cover and set aside for 1 hour, turning once.

3 Heat a griddle pan until very hot and cook the marinated shark steaks for 2–3 minutes on each side. Alternatively, they are very good cooked on the barbecue, as long as they are cooked after the coals have lost their fierce initial heat. Do not overcook.

4 Garnish the shark steaks with oregano and serve with the tortillas and salsa. A green vegetable would also go well.

Per portion: Energy 239Kcal/1006kJ; Protein 40.6g; Carbohydrate 0.7g, of which sugars 0.1g; Fat 7.5g, of which saturates 1.2g; Cholesterol 77mg; Calcium 33mg; Fibre 0.2g; Sodium 246mg.

SEARED TUNA STEAKS
WITH RED ONION SALSA

RED ONIONS ARE IDEAL FOR THIS SALSA, NOT ONLY FOR THEIR MILD AND SWEET FLAVOUR, BUT ALSO BECAUSE THEY LOOK SO APPETIZING. SALAD, RICE OR BREAD AND A BOWL OF THICK YOGURT FLAVOURED WITH CHOPPED FRESH HERBS ARE GOOD ACCOMPANIMENTS.

SERVES FOUR

INGREDIENTS

4 tuna steaks, each weighing about
    175–200g/6–7oz
5ml/1 tsp cumin seeds, toasted
    and crushed
pinch of dried red chilli flakes
grated rind and juice of 1 lime
30–60ml/2–4 tbsp extra virgin
    olive oil
salt and ground black pepper
lime wedges and fresh coriander
    (cilantro) sprigs, to garnish
For the salsa
1 small red onion, finely chopped
200g/7oz red or yellow cherry
    tomatoes, coarsely chopped
1 avocado, peeled, stoned
    (pitted) and chopped
2 kiwi fruit, peeled and chopped
1 fresh red chilli, seeded and
    finely chopped
15g/½oz fresh coriander
    (cilantro), chopped
6 fresh mint sprigs, leaves
    only, chopped
5–10ml/1–2 tsp Thai fish sauce
about 5ml/1 tsp muscovado
    (molasses) sugar

1 Wash the tuna steaks and pat dry. Sprinkle with half the cumin, the dried chilli, salt, pepper and half the lime rind. Rub in 30ml/2 tbsp of the oil and set aside in a glass or china dish for about 30 minutes.

2 Meanwhile, make the salsa. Mix the onion, tomatoes, avocado, kiwi fruit, fresh chilli, chopped coriander and mint. Add the remaining cumin, the rest of the lime rind and half the lime juice. Season with Thai fish sauce and sugar to taste. Set aside for 15–20 minutes, then add more Thai fish sauce, lime juice and olive oil if required.

3 Heat a ridged, cast–iron griddle pan. Cook the tuna, allowing about 2 minutes on each side for rare tuna or a little longer for a medium result.

4 Serve the tuna steaks garnished with lime wedges and coriander sprigs. Serve the salsa separately or spoon on to the plates with the tuna.

Per portion: Energy 389Kcal/1628kJ; Protein 43.2g; Carbohydrate 7.9g, of which sugars 6.8g; Fat 20.7g, of which saturates 4.4g; Cholesterol 49mg; Calcium 55mg; Fibre 2.5g; Sodium 180mg.

GRILLED SKEWERED CHICKEN

THESE JAPANESE-STYLE KEBABS, SERVED WITH DELICIOUS YAKITORI SAUCE FOR DIPPING, ARE PERFECT FOR EASY ENTERTAINING AND ABSOLUTELY IDEAL FOR A BARBECUE PARTY. FOR AUTHENTICITY, SERVE WITH JAPANESE CONDIMENTS AND SMALL DRINKING BOWLS OF WARM RICE WINE.

SERVES FOUR

INGREDIENTS
  8 chicken thighs with skin, boned
  8 large, thick spring onions
    (scallions), trimmed
For the yakitori sauce
  60ml/4 tbsp sake
  75ml/5 tbsp shoyu
  15ml/1 tbsp mirin
  15ml/1 tbsp caster (superfine) sugar
To serve
  shichimi togarashi, sansho or
    lemon wedges

1 First, make the yakitori sauce. Mix all the ingredients together in a small pan. Bring to the boil, then reduce the heat and simmer for 10 minutes, or until the sauce has thickened.

2 Cut the chicken into 2.5cm/1in cubes with a sharp knife. Cut the spring onions into 2.5cm/1in long sticks.

3 To grill (broil), preheat the grill (broiler) to high. Oil the wire rack and spread out the chicken cubes on it. Grill both sides of the chicken until the juices run, then dip the pieces in the sauce and put back on the rack. Grill for 30 seconds on each side, repeating the dipping process twice more.

4 Set aside and keep warm. Gently grill the spring onions until soft and slightly brown outside. Do not dip. Thread about four pieces of chicken and three spring onion pieces on to each of eight bamboo skewers.

5 Alternatively, to cook on a barbecue, soak eight bamboo skewers overnight in water. This prevents the skewers from burning. Prepare the barbecue. Thread the chicken and spring onion pieces on to skewers, as above. Place the sauce in a small bowl.

6 Cook the skewered chicken on the barbecue. Keep the skewer handles away from the fire, turning them frequently until the juices start to run. Brush the chicken with sauce. Return to the coals and repeat this process twice more until the chicken is well cooked.

7 Arrange the skewers on a platter or individual plates and serve sprinkled with shichimi togarashi or sansho, or accompanied by lemon wedges.

Per portion: Energy 132Kcal/558kJ; Protein 21.6g; Carbohydrate 5.2g, of which sugars 5.1g; Fat 2.9g, of which saturates 0.8g; Cholesterol 105mg; Calcium 18mg; Fibre 0.3g; Sodium 715mg.

GRILLED CHICKEN BALLS COOKED ON BAMBOO SKEWERS

THESE TASTY CHICKEN BALLS, KNOWN AS TSUKUNE, *ARE A YAKITORI BAR REGULAR IN JAPAN, AS WELL AS A FAVOURITE FAMILY DISH, AS THEY ARE EASY FOR CHILDREN TO EAT DIRECTLY FROM THE SKEWER. YOU CAN MAKE THE BALLS IN ADVANCE UP TO THE END OF STEP 2, AND THEY FREEZE VERY WELL.*

SERVES FOUR

INGREDIENTS

    300g/11oz skinless chicken,
      minced (ground)
    2 eggs
    2.5ml/½ tsp salt
    10ml/2 tsp plain (all-purpose) flour
    10ml/2 tsp cornflour (cornstarch)
    90ml/6 tbsp dried breadcrumbs
    2.5cm/1in piece fresh root
      ginger, grated
For the "tare" yakitori sauce
    60ml/4 tbsp sake
    75ml/5 tbsp shoyu
    15ml/1 tbsp mirin
    15ml/1 tbsp caster (superfine) sugar
    2.5ml/½ tsp cornflour (cornstarch)
      blended with 5ml/1 tsp water
To serve
    shichimi togarashi or
      sansho (optional)

1 Soak eight bamboo skewers overnight in water. Put all the ingredients for the chicken balls, except the ginger, in a food processor and blend well.

2 Wet your hands and scoop about a tablespoonful of the mixture into your palm. Shape it into a small ball about half the size of a golf ball. Make a further 30–32 balls in the same way.

3 Squeeze the juice from the grated ginger into a small mixing bowl. Discard the pulp.

4 Add the ginger juice to a small pan of boiling water. Add the chicken balls, and boil for about 7 minutes, or until the colour of the meat changes and the balls float to the surface. Scoop out using a slotted spoon and drain on a plate covered with kitchen paper.

5 In a small pan, mix all the ingredients for the yakitori sauce, except for the cornflour liquid. Bring to the boil, then reduce the heat and simmer for about 10 minutes, or until the sauce has slightly reduced. Add the cornflour liquid and stir until the sauce is thick. Transfer to a small bowl.

6 Thread three or four balls on to each skewer. Cook under a medium grill (broiler) or on a barbecue, keeping the skewer handles away from the fire. Turn them frequently for a few minutes, or until the balls start to brown. Brush with sauce and return to the heat. Repeat the process twice. Serve, sprinkled with shichimi togarashi or sansho, if you like.

Per portion: Energy 223Kcal/942kJ; Protein 24.2g; Carbohydrate 23.9g, of which sugars 5.1g; Fat 4.1g, of which saturates 1g; Cholesterol 148mg; Calcium 54mg; Fibre 0.6g; Sodium 1031mg.

TURKEY PATTIES

MINCED TURKEY MAKES DELICIOUSLY LIGHT PATTIES, WHICH ARE IDEAL FOR SUMMER MEALS. THE RECIPE IS A FLAVOURFUL VARIATION ON A CLASSIC BURGER. THE PATTIES CAN ALSO BE MADE USING MINCED LAMB, PORK OR BEEF. SERVE THEM IN SPLIT AND TOASTED BUNS OR PIECES OF CRUSTY BREAD, WITH CHUTNEY, SALAD LEAVES AND CHUNKY FRIES.

SERVES SIX

INGREDIENTS
  675g/1½lb minced (ground) turkey
  1 small red onion, finely chopped
  grated rind and juice of 1 lime
  small handful of fresh thyme leaves
  15–30ml/1–2 tbsp olive oil
  salt and ground black pepper

VARIATIONS
• You could try chopped fresh oregano, parsley or basil in place of the thyme, and lemon rind instead of lime.
• Substitute minced (ground) chicken for the turkey.

1 Mix together the turkey, onion, lime rind and juice, thyme and seasoning. Cover and chill for up to 4 hours to allow the flavours to infuse, then divide the mixture into six equal portions and shape into round patties.

2 Preheat a griddle pan. Brush the patties with oil, then place them on the pan and cook for 10–12 minutes. Turn the patties over, brush with more oil and cook for 10–12 minutes on the second side, or until cooked through.

Per portion: Energy 141Kcal/596kJ; Protein 24.8g; Carbohydrate 0.8g, of which sugars 0.6g; Fat 4.4g, of which saturates 1.1g; Cholesterol 69mg; Calcium 15mg; Fibre 0.2g; Sodium 62mg.

TURKEY BREASTS WITH TOMATO-CORN SALSA

ALTHOUGH AN ECONOMICAL AND USEFUL MEAT, TURKEY CAN BE DISAPPOINTINGLY BLAND, SO
MARINATING IT BEFORE COOKING AND SERVING WITH A SPICY SALSA IS THE IDEAL APPROACH.

SERVES FOUR

INGREDIENTS

    4 skinless boneless turkey breast
      halves, about 175g/6oz each
    30ml/2 tbsp fresh lemon juice
    30ml/2 tbsp olive oil
    2.5ml/½ tsp ground cumin
    2.5ml/½ tsp dried oregano
    5ml/1 tsp coarse black pepper
    salt
For the salsa
    1 fresh hot green chilli
    450g/1lb tomatoes, seeded
      and chopped
    250g/9oz/1½ cups corn kernels,
      freshly cooked or thawed frozen
    3 spring onions (scallions), chopped
    15ml/1 tbsp chopped fresh parsley
    30ml/2 tbsp chopped fresh
      coriander (cilantro)
    30ml/2 tbsp fresh lemon juice
    45ml/3 tbsp olive oil
    5ml/1 tsp salt

1 With a meat mallet, pound the turkey breasts between two sheets of greaseproof (waxed) paper until thin.

2 In a shallow dish, combine the lemon juice, oil, cumin, oregano and pepper. Add the turkey and turn to coat. Cover and marinate for at least 2 hours, or overnight in the refrigerator.

COOK'S TIP
Use the flat side of a meat mallet to pound the turkey. If you don't have a meat mallet, use the side of a wooden rolling pin.

3 For the salsa, roast the chilli over a gas flame, holding it with tongs, until charred on all sides. Alternatively, char the skin under the hot grill (broiler). Leave to cool for 5 minutes. Wearing rubber gloves, carefully rub off the charred skin. For a less hot flavour, discard the seeds. Chop the chilli finely and place in a bowl.

4 Add the remaining salsa ingredients and toss well to blend. Set aside.

5 Remove the turkey from the marinade. Season lightly on both sides with salt to taste.

6 Heat a ridged griddle pan. When hot, add the turkey breasts and cook for about 3 minutes, until browned on the undersides. Turn and cook the meat on the other side for a further 3–4 minutes, until it is cooked through. Serve the turkey immediately, accompanied by tomato-corn salsa.

VARIATION
Use the cooked turkey, thinly sliced and combined with the salsa, as a filling for warmed flour tortillas.

Per portion: Energy 407Kcal/1711kJ; Protein 45.7g; Carbohydrate 20.6g, of which sugars 9.9g; Fat 16.4g, of which saturates 2.7g; Cholesterol 100mg; Calcium 36mg; Fibre 2.5g; Sodium 761mg.

PORK CHOPS WITH SOUR GREEN CHILLI SALSA

THIN CHOPS OR LOIN STEAKS ARE DELICIOUSLY TENDER AND COOK VERY QUICKLY, SO THIS TASTY DISH IS IDEAL FOR A MIDWEEK FAMILY SUPPER.

SERVES FOUR

INGREDIENTS
30ml/2 tbsp vegetable oil
15ml/1 tbsp fresh lemon juice
10ml/2 tsp ground cumin
5ml/1 tsp dried oregano
8 pork loin chops, about
   5mm/¼in thick
salt and ground black pepper
For the salsa
2 fresh hot green chillies
2 green (bell) peppers, seeded
   and chopped
1 tomato, peeled and seeded
½ onion, coarsely chopped
4 spring onions (scallions)
1 pickled jalapeño chilli
30ml/2 tbsp olive oil
30ml/2 tbsp fresh lime juice
45ml/3 tbsp cider vinegar
5ml/1 tsp salt

1 In a small bowl, combine the vegetable oil, lemon juice, cumin and oregano. Add pepper to taste and stir to mix well.

2 Arrange the pork chops in one layer in a shallow dish. Brush each of them with the oil mixture on both sides. Cover them with clear film (plastic wrap) and set aside to marinate for 2–3 hours or in the refrigerator overnight.

3 For the salsa, roast the chillies over a gas flame, holding them with tongs, until charred on all sides. Alternatively, char the skins under the grill (broiler). Leave to cool for 5 minutes. Wearing rubber gloves, remove the skin. For a less hot flavour, discard the seeds.

4 Place the chillies in a food processor or blender. Add the remaining salsa ingredients. Process until finely chopped but do not purée.

5 Transfer the salsa to a small, heavy pan and simmer 15 minutes, stirring occasionally. Set aside.

6 Season the pork chops to taste with salt and pepper. Heat a ridged griddle pan. Alternatively, preheat the grill (broiler). When hot, add the pork chops and cook for about 5 minutes, until browned on the undersides. Turn and continue cooking for a further 5–7 minutes, until done. Work in batches, if necessary.

7 Serve immediately, with the sour green chilli salsa.

Per portion: Energy 341Kcal/1427kJ; Protein 38.9g; Carbohydrate 5.2g, of which sugars 4.7g; Fat 18.5g, of which saturates 4g; Cholesterol 110mg; Calcium 30mg; Fibre 2.2g; Sodium 623mg.

PORK AND LEEK SAUSAGES WITH MUSTARD MASHED POTATO AND ONION GRAVY

LONG, SLOW COOKING IS THE TRICK TO REMEMBER FOR GOOD ONION GRAVY AS THIS REDUCES AND CARAMELIZES THE ONIONS TO CREATE A WONDERFULLY SWEET FLAVOUR. DO NOT BE ALARMED AT THE NUMBER OF ONIONS — THEY REDUCE DRAMATICALLY IN VOLUME DURING COOKING.

SERVES FOUR

INGREDIENTS
  12 pork and leek sausages
  salt and ground black pepper
For the onion gravy
  30ml/2 tbsp olive oil
  25g/1oz/2 tbsp butter
  8 onions, sliced
  5ml/1 tsp caster sugar
  15ml/1 tbsp plain (all-purpose) flour
  300ml/½ pint/1¼ cups beef stock
For the mash
  1.5kg/3¼lb potatoes
  50g/2oz/¼ cup butter
  150ml/¼ pint/⅔ cup whipping cream
  15ml/1 tbsp wholegrain mustard

1 Heat the oil and butter in a large pan until foaming. Add the onions and mix well to coat them in the fat. Cover and cook gently for about 30 minutes, stirring frequently. Add the sugar and cook for a further 5 minutes, or until the onions are softened, reduced and caramelized.

2 Remove the pan from the heat and stir in the flour, then gradually stir in the stock. Return the pan to the heat. Bring to the boil, stirring, then simmer for 3 minutes, or until thickened. Season.

VARIATION
Pesto and garlic mash is also good with sausages. Instead of the mustard, add 15ml/1 tbsp pesto, 2 crushed garlic cloves and a little olive oil.

3 Meanwhile, cook the potatoes and the pork and leek sausages. First, cook the potatoes in a pan of salted boiling water for 20 minutes, or until tender.

4 Drain the potatoes well and mash them with the butter, whipping cream and wholegrain mustard. Season with salt and pepper to taste.

5 Meanwhile, preheat the grill (broiler) to medium. Arrange the sausages on the grill rack and cook for 15–20 minutes, or until cooked, turning frequently so that they turn an even golden brown all over.

6 Serve the sausages with the creamy mash and plenty of onion gravy.

Per portion: Energy 939Kcal/3913kJ; Protein 19.9g; Carbohydrate 85g, of which sugars 16.7g; Fat 60g, of which saturates 28.6g; Cholesterol 133mg; Calcium 179mg; Fibre 6.6g; Sodium 942mg.

PORK CHOPS <u>WITH</u> CHILLI-NECTARINE RELISH

A FRUITY SALSA MAKES AN INTERESTING AND TASTY CHANGE FROM THE MORE USUAL APPLE SAUCE.

SERVES FOUR

INGREDIENTS
    250ml/8fl oz/1 cup fresh
      orange juice
    45ml/3 tbsp olive oil
    2 garlic cloves, ground
    5ml/1 tsp ground cumin
    15ml/1 tbsp coarsely ground
      black pepper
    8 pork loin chops, about 2cm/¾in
      thick, well trimmed
    salt
For the relish
    1 small fresh green chilli
    2 nectarines
    30ml/2 tbsp clear honey
    juice of ½ lemon
    250ml/8fl oz/1 cup chicken stock
    1 garlic clove, finely chopped
    ½ onion, finely chopped
    5ml/1 tsp grated fresh root ginger
    1.5ml/¼ tsp salt
    15ml/1 tbsp chopped fresh
      coriander (cilantro)

1 For the relish, roast the chilli over a gas flame, holding it with tongs, until charred on all sides. Alternatively, char the skin under the grill (broiler). Leave to cool for 5 minutes.

2 Wearing rubber gloves, carefully remove the charred skin of the chilli. Discard the seeds if you like a less hot flavour. Finely chop the chilli and place in a heavy pan. Halve the nectarines and remove and discard the stones (pits). Chop the flesh and add to the pan with the chilli.

3 Add the honey, lemon juice, chicken stock, garlic, onion, ginger and salt. Bring to the boil, then simmer, stirring occasionally, for about 30 minutes. Stir in the coriander and set aside.

4 In a small bowl, combine the orange juice, oil, garlic, cumin and pepper. Stir to mix well.

5 Arrange the pork chops, in a single layer, in a shallow, non-metallic dish. Pour over the orange juice mixture and turn to coat. Cover with clear film (plastic wrap) and leave in a cool place to marinate for at least 1 hour or in the refrigerator overnight.

6 Remove the pork chops from the marinade and pat dry with kitchen paper. Season lightly with salt.

7 Heat a ridged griddle pan. When hot, add the pork chops and cook for about 5 minutes, until the undersides are browned. Turn and cook on the other side for a further 10 minutes, until browned. Work in batches if necessary. Serve the chops immediately, with the chilli-nectarine relish.

Per portion: Energy 315Kcal/1321kJ; Protein 43.4g; Carbohydrate 11.4g, of which sugars 11g; Fat 10.9g, of which saturates 3.2g; Cholesterol 126mg; Calcium 28mg; Fibre 0.6g; Sodium 144mg.

ROMANIAN KEBABS

KEBABS ARE POPULAR WORLDWIDE, LARGELY BECAUSE THEY ARE SO EASILY ADAPTED TO SUIT EVERYONE'S TASTE. IN THIS RECIPE, LEAN LAMB IS MARINATED, THEN COOKED WITH CHUNKS OF VEGETABLES TO PRODUCE A DELICIOUS, COLOURFUL AND HEALTHY MEAL.

SERVES SIX

INGREDIENTS

675g/1½lb lean lamb, cut into
   4cm/1½in cubes
12 button (pearl) onions
2 green (bell) peppers, seeded and
   cut into 12 pieces
12 cherry tomatoes
12 button (white) mushrooms
lemon slices and fresh rosemary
   sprigs, to garnish
freshly cooked rice and crusty bread,
   to serve
For the marinade
   juice of 1 lemon
   120ml/4fl oz/½ cup red wine
   1 onion, finely chopped
   60ml/4 tbsp olive oil
   2.5ml/½ tsp dried sage
   2.5ml/½ tsp chopped fresh rosemary
   salt and ground black pepper

VARIATIONS
• Use rump (round) steak instead of lamb. Cut it into strips, marinate it as suggested, then interleave the strips on the skewers, with the onions, cherry tomatoes and mushrooms. Omit the green (bell) peppers.
• These kebabs are just as delicious cooked on a barbecue.

1 For the marinade, combine the lemon juice, red wine, onion, olive oil, herbs and seasoning in a bowl. Stir the cubes of lamb into the marinade. Cover and chill in the refrigerator for 2–12 hours, stirring occasionally.

2 Remove the lamb pieces from the marinade and thread on six skewers with the onions, peppers, tomatoes and mushrooms. Preheat the grill (broiler).

3 Brush the kebabs with marinade and grill (broil) for 10–15 minutes, turning once. Arrange on cooked rice, with lemon and rosemary. Serve with crusty bread.

Per portion: Energy 259Kcal/1083kJ; Protein 23.6g; Carbohydrate 4g, of which sugars 3.4g; Fat 16.7g, of which saturates 6.5g; Cholesterol 86mg; Calcium 22mg; Fibre 1.9g; Sodium 104mg.

JERUSALEM BARBECUE LAMB KEBABS

IN THE EARLY DAYS OF THE MODERN STATE OF ISRAEL, THE DAYS OF AUSTERITY, "LAMB" KEBABS WOULD HAVE BEEN MADE WITH TURKEY AND A LITTLE LAMB FAT, AND "VEAL" KEBABS WITH CHICKEN AND A SMALL AMOUNT OF VEAL. TURKEY, CHICKEN, BEEF AND VEAL CAN ALL BE COOKED IN THIS WAY.

SERVES FOUR TO SIX

INGREDIENTS

800g/1¾lb tender lamb, cubed
1.5ml/¼ tsp ground allspice
1.5ml/¼ tsp ground cinnamon
1.5ml/¼ tsp ground black pepper
1.5ml/¼ tsp ground cardamom
45–60ml/3–4 tbsp chopped
  fresh parsley
2 onions, chopped
5–8 garlic cloves, chopped
juice of ½ lemon or 45ml/3 tbsp dry
  white wine
45ml/3 tbsp extra virgin olive oil
sumac, for sprinkling (optional)
30ml/2 tbsp pine nuts
salt
For serving
  flat breads, such as pitta bread,
    tortillas or naan bread
  tahini
  crunchy vegetable salad

1 Put the lamb, allspice, cinnamon, black pepper, cardamom, half the parsley, half the onions, the garlic, lemon juice or wine and olive oil in a bowl and mix together. Season with salt now, if you like, or sprinkle on after cooking. Set aside and leave to marinate.

2 Meanwhile, light the barbecue and leave for about 40 minutes. When the coals are white and grey, the barbecue is ready for cooking. If using wooden skewers, soak them in water for about 30 minutes to prevent them from burning.

3 Thread the cubes of meat on to wooden or metal skewers, then cook on the barbecue for 2–3 minutes on each side, turning occasionally, until cooked evenly and browned.

4 Transfer the kebabs to a serving dish and sprinkle with the reserved onions, parsley, sumac, if using, pine nuts and salt, if you like. Serve the kebabs with warmed flat breads to wrap the kebabs in, a bowl of tahini for drizzling over and a vegetable salad.

COOK'S TIPS
• If sumac is available, its tangy flavour is fresh and invigorating, and its red colour is appealing.
• These kebabs can also be cooked under a hot grill (broiler).

Per portion: Energy 513Kcal/2137kJ; Protein 41.4g; Carbohydrate 6.4g, of which sugars 4.7g; Fat 36g, of which saturates 11.9g; Cholesterol 152mg; Calcium 51mg; Fibre 1.6g; Sodium 177mg.

STEAK BÉARNAISE

BÉARNAISE, AFTER BÉARN IN SOUTH-WEST FRANCE, IS A CREAMY EGG AND BUTTER SAUCE FLAVOURED WITH FRESH TARRAGON. IT IS A CLASSIC COMPLEMENT TO GRIDDLED, GRILLED OR PAN-FRIED STEAK AND ALSO EXCELLENT WITH ROAST BEEF. ROASTED VEGETABLES MAKE A GOOD ACCOMPANIMENT.

SERVES FOUR

INGREDIENTS
4 sirloin steaks, each weighing about
   225g/8oz, trimmed
15ml/1 tbsp sunflower oil (optional)
salt and ground black pepper
For the Béarnaise sauce
90ml/6 tbsp white wine vinegar
12 black peppercorns
2 bay leaves
2 shallots, finely chopped
4 fresh tarragon sprigs
4 egg yolks
225g/8oz/1 cup unsalted (sweet)
   butter at room temperature, diced
30ml/2 tbsp chopped fresh tarragon
ground white pepper

1 Start by making the sauce. Put the vinegar, peppercorns, bay leaves, shallots and tarragon sprigs in a small pan and simmer until reduced to 30ml/2 tbsp. Strain the vinegar through a fine sieve.

2 Beat the egg yolks with salt and freshly ground white pepper in a small, heatproof bowl. Stand the bowl over a pan of very gently simmering water, then gradually beat the strained vinegar into the yolks.

3 Gradually beat in the butter, one piece at a time, allowing each addition to melt before adding the next. Do not allow the water to heat beyond a gentle simmer or the sauce will overheat and curdle.

4 While cooking the sauce, heat a griddle or grill until very hot.

COOK'S TIP
If you are confident about preparing egg and butter sauces, the best method is to reduce the flavoured vinegar before cooking the steak, then finish the sauce while the steak is cooking. This way, the sauce does not have to be kept hot and there is less risk of overheating it or allowing it to become too thick.

5 Beat the chopped fresh tarragon into the sauce and remove the pan from the heat. The sauce should be smooth, thick and glossy.

6 Cover the surface of the sauce with clear film (plastic wrap) or dampened greaseproof (waxed) paper to prevent a skin forming and leave over the pan of hot water, still off the heat, to keep hot while you cook the steak.

7 Season the steaks with salt and plenty freshly ground black pepper.

8 A pan is not usually oiled before cooking steak, but if it is essential to grease the pan, add only the minimum oil. Cook the steaks for 2–4 minutes on each side. The cooking time depends on the thickness of the steaks and the extent to which you want to cook them. As a guide, 2–4 minutes will give a medium-rare result.

9 Serve the steaks on warmed plates. Peel the clear film or dampened greaseproof paper off the sauce and stir it lightly, then spoon it over the steaks.

Per portion: Energy 796Kcal/3297kJ; Protein 51.1g; Carbohydrate 0.5g, of which sugars 0.4g; Fat 65.5g, of which saturates 37.2g; Cholesterol 459mg; Calcium 50mg; Fibre 0.2g; Sodium 450mg.

STUFFED BUTTERFLY OF BEEF WITH CHEESE AND CHILLI SAUCE

THIS RECIPE HAD ITS ORIGINS IN NORTHERN MEXICO OR IN NEW MEXICO, WHICH IS BEEF COUNTRY. IT IS A GOOD WAY TO COOK STEAKS, EITHER UNDER THE GRILL OR ON THE BARBECUE.

SERVES FOUR

INGREDIENTS

    4 fresh serrano chillies
    115g/4oz/½ cup full-fat soft cheese
    30ml/2 tbsp reposada tequila
    30ml/2 tbsp oil
    1 onion
    2 garlic cloves
    5ml/1 tsp dried oregano
    2.5ml/½ tsp salt
    2.5ml/½ tsp ground black pepper
    175g/6oz/1½ cups grated medium
      Cheddar cheese
    4 fillet steaks, at least 2.5cm/
      1in thick

3 Put the full-fat soft cheese in a small heavy pan and stir over a very low heat until it has melted. Add the chilli strips and the tequila and stir to make a smooth sauce. Keep warm over a very low heat.

6 Cut each steak almost but not quite in half across its width, so that it can be opened out, butterfly-fashion. Preheat the grill (broiler) to its highest setting.

1 Dry-roast the chillies in a griddle pan over a moderate heat, turning them frequently until the skins are blistered but not burnt. Put them in a strong plastic bag and tie the top to keep the steam in. Set aside for 20 minutes.

4 Heat the oil in a frying pan and cook the onion, garlic and oregano for about 5 minutes over a moderate heat, stirring frequently until the onion has browned. Season with the salt and pepper.

7 Spoon a quarter of the cheese and onion filling on to one side of each steak and close the other side over it. Place the steaks in a grill pan and grill (broil) for 3–5 minutes on each side, depending on how you like your steak. Serve on heated plates with the vegetables of your choice, and with the cheese and chilli sauce poured over.

2 Remove the chillies from the bag, slit them and scrape out the seeds with a sharp knife. Cut the flesh into long narrow strips, then cut each strip into several shorter strips.

5 Remove the pan from the heat and add the grated Cheddar cheese, in two or three batches. Stir well so that it melts into the onion and garlic mixture without becoming rubbery.

COOK'S TIP
One of the easiest ways of testing whether a steak is cooked is by touch. A steak that is very rare or "blue" will feel soft to the touch; the meat will be relaxed. A rare steak will feel like a sponge, and will spring back when lightly pressed. A medium-rare steak offers more resistance, while a well-cooked steak will feel very firm.

Per portion: Energy 580Kcal/2412kJ; Protein 51.1g; Carbohydrate 3g, of which sugars 2.2g; Fat 39.5g, of which saturates 20.6g; Cholesterol 175mg; Calcium 372mg; Fibre 0.5g; Sodium 735mg.

LONE STAR STEAK WITH POTATO DINNER

*THIS TRADITIONAL AMERICAN MEAL IS USUALLY SERVED WITH CORN ON THE COB, BUT A CRISP,
GREEN SALAD WOULD MAKE A LIGHTER ALTERNATIVE ACCOMPANIMENT.*

SERVES FOUR

INGREDIENTS
    45ml/3 tbsp olive oil
    5 large garlic cloves, crushed
    5ml/1 tsp coarse black pepper
    2.5ml/½ tsp ground allspice
    5ml/1 tsp ground cumin
    2.5ml/½ tsp chilli powder
    10ml/2 tsp dried oregano
    15ml/1 tbsp cider vinegar
    4 boneless sirloin steaks, about
        2cm/¾in thick
    salt
To serve
    tomato salsa
    freshly cooked corn on the
        cob (optional)
For the potatoes
    50ml/2fl oz/¼ cup vegetable oil
    1 onion, chopped
    5ml/1 tsp salt
    900g/2lb potatoes, boiled and diced
    30–75ml/2–5 tbsp chopped canned
        or bottled green chillies, according
        to taste

3 Add the pepper, allspice, cumin, chilli powder, oregano and vinegar to the garlic and stir to blend thoroughly. If necessary, add just enough water to obtain a fairly thick paste.

6 Season the steaks on both sides with salt to taste. Heat a ridged griddle pan. When hot, add the steaks and cook, turning once, until done to your taste. Allow about 1–2 minutes on each side for rare, 2–3 minutes for medium-rare, and 3–4 minutes for well done.

4 Add the steaks to the dish and turn to coat evenly on both sides with the spice mixture. Cover and leave to marinate for 2 hours or place in the refrigerator overnight. Bring the steaks to room temperature 30 minutes before cooking.

7 If necessary, briefly reheat the potatoes. Serve immediately, with the tomato salsa and corn, if using.

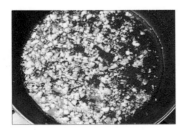

1 Heat the olive oil in a heavy frying pan. When hot, add the garlic and cook, stirring frequently, for about 3 minutes, until tender and just brown. Do not let the garlic burn, as it will become bitter.

2 Transfer the garlic and oil to a shallow dish large enough to hold the steaks in a single layer.

5 To make the potatoes, heat the oil in a large non-stick frying pan. Add the onion and salt. Cook over a medium heat for 5 minutes, until softened. Add the potatoes and chillies. Cook, stirring occasionally, for 15–20 minutes.

VARIATION
The steaks can also be cooked on a barbecue. Prepare the fire, and when the coals are glowing red and covered with grey ash, spread them in a single layer. Cook the steaks in the centre of an oiled grill rack set about 13cm/5in above the coals for 1 minute per side to sear them. Move them away from the centre and cook for 10–12 minutes, or longer for medium-rare, turning once.

Per portion: Energy 560Kcal/2346kJ; Protein 45.4g; Carbohydrate 39.2g, of which sugars 5g; Fat 25.6g, of which saturates 5.9g; Cholesterol 89mg; Calcium 32mg; Fibre 2.8g; Sodium 640mg.

ROASTS

Although far fewer families sit down to a regular roast dinner every weekend, the fact remains that this is one of the easiest ways of cooking a well-balanced meal — and one of the most delicious. The important thing to remember is that taste really does tell, so it is worth buying the best meat, game, poultry and fish you can afford. Cultivate a good butcher and fish supplier or buy from a recommended source specializing in free-range, additive-free or organic meat or fish. Regard dishes such as Marmalade-glazed Goose or Roast Rib of Beef as special treats and you'll enjoy them all the more.

ROASTED VEGETABLES WITH SALSA VERDE

THERE ARE ENDLESS VARIATIONS OF THE ITALIAN SALSA VERDE, WHICH MEANS "GREEN SAUCE". USUALLY A BLEND OF FRESH CHOPPED HERBS, GARLIC, OLIVE OIL, ANCHOVIES AND CAPERS, THIS IS A SIMPLIFIED VERSION. HERE, IT IS SERVED WITH VEGETABLES AND A RICE DISH FROM CYPRUS.

SERVES FOUR

INGREDIENTS
    3 courgettes (zucchini),
        sliced lengthways
    1 large fennel bulb, cut
        into wedges
    450g/1lb butternut squash, cut into
        2cm/¾in chunks
    12 shallots
    2 red (bell) peppers, seeded
        and cut lengthways into
        thick slices
    4 plum tomatoes, halved and seeded
    45ml/3 tbsp olive oil
    2 garlic cloves, crushed
    5ml/1 tsp balsamic vinegar
    salt and ground black pepper
For the salsa verde
    45ml/3 tbsp chopped fresh mint
    90ml/6 tbsp chopped fresh flat
        leaf parsley
    15ml/1 tbsp Dijon mustard
    juice of ½ lemon
    30ml/2 tbsp olive oil
For the rice
    15ml/1 tbsp vegetable or olive oil
    75g/3oz/¾ cup vermicelli, broken
        into short lengths
    225g/8oz/generous 1 cup long
        grain rice
    900ml/1½ pints/3¾ cups
        vegetable stock

1 To make the salsa verde, place all the ingredients, with the exception of the olive oil, in a food processor or blender. Blend to a coarse paste, then add the oil, a little at a time, until the mixture forms a smooth purée.

2 Transfer the salsa to a bowl, season to taste with salt and pepper, cover and set aside.

3 Preheat the oven to 220°C/425°F/ Gas 7. To roast the vegetables, toss the courgettes, fennel, squash, shallots, peppers and tomatoes in the olive oil, garlic and balsamic vinegar. Set aside for 10 minutes to allow all the flavours to combine.

4 Place all the vegetables – apart from the squash and tomatoes – on a large baking sheet, brush with half the oil and vinegar mixture and season.

5 Roast the vegetables for 25 minutes, then remove the baking sheet from the oven. Using a fork, turn all the vegetables over and brush with the rest of the oil and vinegar mixture. Add the butternut squash and plum tomatoes, return to the oven and cook for a further 20–25 minutes, until all the vegetables are tender and lightly charred around the edges.

VARIATIONS
• Substitute 45ml/3 tbsp watercress for half the parsley in the salsa.
• Use sherry vinegar instead of balsamic vinegar to flavour the vegetables.
• If you like, add a medium aubergine (eggplant), cut into chunks, to the mixture of roasted vegetables.

6 Meanwhile, prepare the rice. Heat the oil in a heavy pan. Add the vermicelli and cook for about 3 minutes, or until golden and crisp. Season to taste.

7 Rinse the rice under cold running water, then drain well and add it to the vermicelli. Cook for 1 minute, stirring to coat it in the oil.

8 Add the vegetable stock, then cover the pan and allow to cook for about 12 minutes, until all the liquid is absorbed. Stir the rice, then cover and leave to stand for 10 minutes. Serve the warm rice with the roasted vegetables and salsa verde.

COOK'S TIP
The salsa verde will keep for up to 1 week if stored in an airtight container in the refrigerator.

Per portion: Energy 519Kcal/2160kJ; Protein 12.1g; Carbohydrate 75.3g, of which sugars 14.7g; Fat 18.7g, of which saturates 2.8g; Cholesterol 0mg; Calcium 151mg; Fibre 6.9g; Sodium 27mg.

ROASTED COD WITH FRESH TOMATO SAUCE

REALLY FRESH COD HAS A SWEET, DELICATE FLAVOUR AND A PURE WHITE FLAKY FLESH. SERVED WITH AN AROMATIC TOMATO SAUCE, IT MAKES A DELICIOUS MEAL.

SERVES FOUR

INGREDIENTS

350g/12oz ripe plum tomatoes
75ml/5 tbsp olive oil
2.5ml/½ tsp sugar
2 strips of pared orange rind
1 fresh thyme sprig
6 fresh basil leaves
900g/2lb fresh cod fillet, skin on
salt and ground black pepper
steamed green beans, to serve

COOK'S TIP
Cod is becoming increasingly rare and expensive. You can substitute any firm white fish fillets in this dish. Try haddock, pollock, or that excellent and underrated fish, coley. When raw, coley flesh looks grey, but it turns white on cooking.

1 Preheat the oven to 230°C/450°F/ Gas 8. Coarsely chop the tomatoes.

2 Heat 15ml/1 tbsp of the olive oil in a heavy pan, add the tomatoes, sugar, orange rind, thyme and basil, and simmer for about 5 minutes, until the tomatoes are soft.

3 Press the tomato mixture through a fine sieve, discarding the solids that remain in the sieve. Pour into a small pan and heat gently.

4 Scale the cod fillet and cut on the diagonal into four pieces. Season well.

5 Heat the remaining oil in a heavy frying pan and cook the cod, skin side down, until the skin is crisp. Place the fish on a greased baking sheet, skin side up, and roast in the oven for 8–10 minutes, until the fish is cooked through. Serve the fish on the steamed green beans with the tomato sauce.

Per portion: Energy 319Kcal/1330kJ; Protein 41.8g; Carbohydrate 2.7g, of which sugars 2.7g; Fat 15.6g, of which saturates 2.3g; Cholesterol 104mg; Calcium 27mg; Fibre 0.9g; Sodium 143mg.

ROAST MONKFISH WITH GARLIC

MONKFISH TIED UP AND COOKED IN THIS WAY IS KNOWN IN FRENCH AS A "GIGOT", BECAUSE IT RESEMBLES A LEG OF LAMB. THE COMBINATION OF MONKFISH AND GARLIC IS SUPERB. FOR A CONTRAST IN COLOUR, SERVE IT WITH VIBRANT GREEN BEANS.

SERVES FOUR TO SIX

INGREDIENTS
   1kg/2¼lb monkfish tail, skinned
   14 fat garlic cloves
   5ml/1 tsp fresh thyme leaves
   30ml/2 tbsp olive oil
   juice of 1 lemon
   2 bay leaves
   salt and ground black pepper

1 Preheat the oven to 220°C/425°F/ Gas 7. Remove any membrane from the monkfish tail and cut out the central bone. Peel two garlic cloves and cut them into thin slivers. Sprinkle a quarter of these and half the thyme leaves over the cut side of the fish, then close it up and use fine kitchen string to tie it into a neat shape, like a boned piece of meat. Pat dry with kitchen paper.

2 Make incisions on either side of the fish and push in the remaining garlic slivers. Heat half the olive oil in a frying pan which can safely be used in the oven. When the oil is hot, put in the monkfish and brown it all over for about 5 minutes, until evenly coloured. Season with salt and pepper, sprinkle with lemon juice and then sprinkle over the remaining thyme.

3 Tuck the bay leaves under the monkfish, arrange the remaining (unpeeled) garlic cloves around it and drizzle the remaining olive oil over the fish and the garlic. Transfer the frying pan to the oven and roast the monkfish for 20–25 minutes, until the flesh is cooked through.

4 Place on a warmed serving dish with the garlic and some green beans. To serve, remove the string and cut the monkfish into 2cm/¾in thick slices.

COOK'S TIPS
• The garlic heads can be used whole.
• When serving the monkfish, invite each guest to pop out the soft garlic pulp with a fork and spread it over the monkfish.
• Use two smaller monkfish tails.

Per portion: Energy 253Kcal/1065kJ; Protein 45.2g; Carbohydrate 3.1g, of which sugars 0.3g; Fat 6.6g, of which saturates 1.1g; Cholesterol 40mg; Calcium 26mg; Fibre 0.8g; Sodium 51mg.

ROASTED CHICKEN WITH GRAPES AND FRESH ROOT GINGER

THIS DISH, WITH ITS BLEND OF SPICES AND SWEET FRUIT, IS INSPIRED BY MOROCCAN FLAVOURS. SERVE WITH COUSCOUS, MIXED WITH A HANDFUL OF COOKED CHICKPEAS.

SERVES FOUR

INGREDIENTS
1–1.6kg/2¼–3½lb chicken
115–130g/4–4½oz fresh root
  ginger, grated
6–8 garlic cloves, coarsely chopped
juice of 1 lemon
about 30ml/2 tbsp olive oil
2–3 large pinches of ground cinnamon
500g/1¼lb seeded red and
  green grapes
500g/1¼lb seedless green grapes
5–7 shallots, chopped
about 250ml/8fl oz/1 cup chicken stock
salt and ground black pepper

1 Rub the chicken with half of the ginger, the garlic, half of the lemon juice, the olive oil, cinnamon, salt and lots of pepper. Leave to marinate.

2 Meanwhile, cut the red and green seeded grapes in half, remove the seeds and set aside. Add the whole green seedless grapes to the halved ones.

3 Preheat the oven to 180°C/350°F/Gas 4. Heat a heavy frying pan or flameproof casserole until hot.

4 Remove the chicken from the marinade, add to the pan and cook until browned on all sides. (There should be enough oil on the chicken to brown it but, if not, add a little extra.)

5 Put some of the shallots into the chicken cavity with the garlic and ginger from the marinade and as many of the red and green grapes that will fit inside. Roast in the oven for 40–60 minutes, or until the chicken is tender.

VARIATIONS
• This dish is good made with duck in place of the chicken. Marinate and roast as above, adding 15–30ml/1–2 tbsp honey to the pan sauce as it cooks.
• Use boneless chicken breast portions, with the skin still attached, instead of a whole chicken. Pan-fry the chicken portions, rather than roasting them.

6 Remove the chicken from the pan and keep warm. Pour off any oil from the pan, reserving any sediment in the base of the pan. Add the remaining shallots to the pan and cook for about 5 minutes until softened.

7 Add half the remaining red and green grapes, the remaining ginger, the stock and any juices from the roast chicken and cook over a medium-high heat until the grapes have cooked down to a thick sauce. Season with salt, ground black pepper and the remaining lemon juice to taste.

8 Serve the chicken on a warmed serving dish, surrounded by the sauce and the reserved grapes.

COOK'S TIP
Seeded Italia or muscat grapes have a delicious, sweet fragrance and are perfect for using in this recipe.

Per portion: Energy 454Kcal/1891kJ; Protein 31.6g; Carbohydrate 19.5g, of which sugars 19.5g; Fat 28.1g, of which saturates 7g; Cholesterol 165mg; Calcium 28mg; Fibre 1g; Sodium 116mg.

GALVESTON CHICKEN

A LIGHTLY SPICED MARINADE TURNS ORDINARY ROAST CHICKEN INTO A SPECIAL MEAL WITH SCARCELY ANY EXTRA EFFORT DEMANDED OF THE COOK. WHAT COULD BE BETTER?

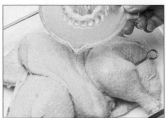

2 Insert a skewer through the chicken, at the thighs, to keep it flat during cooking. Place the chicken in a shallow, non-metallic dish and pour over the lemon juice.

3 In a small bowl, combine the garlic, cayenne, paprika, oregano, pepper, and oil. Mix well. Rub the mixture evenly over the surface of the chicken.

4 Cover and set aside to marinate for 2–3 hours at room temperature or in the refrigerator overnight. Bring the chicken back to room temperature 30 minutes before roasting.

5 Season the chicken well with salt on both sides. Transfer it to a shallow roasting pan.

SERVES FOUR

INGREDIENTS

1.5kg/3½ lb chicken
juice of 1 lemon
4 garlic cloves, crushed
15ml/1 tbsp cayenne
15ml/1 tbsp paprika
15ml/1 tbsp dried oregano
2.5ml/½ tsp coarse black pepper
10ml/2 tsp olive oil
5ml/1 tsp salt

COOK'S TIP
Roasting chicken in an oven that has not been preheated produces a particularly crispy skin.

1 With a sharp knife or poultry shears, remove the backbone from the chicken. Turn it breast side up. With the heel of your hand, press down to break the breastbone, and open the chicken flat like a book.

6 Put the roasting pan in a cold oven and set the temperature to 200°C/400°F/Gas 6. Roast until the chicken is done, about 1–1½ hours, turning occasionally and basting with the roasting juices. To test if it is cooked through, insert a skewer into the thickest part. If the juices that run out are clear, it is ready.

Per portion: Energy 407Kcal/1688kJ; Protein 37.2g; Carbohydrate 0g, of which sugars 0g; Fat 28.5g, of which saturates 7.7g; Cholesterol 198mg; Calcium 12mg; Fibre 0g; Sodium 626mg.

ROASTED DUCKLING
ON A BED OF HONEYED POTATOES

THE RICH FLAVOUR OF DUCK COMBINED WITH THESE SWEETENED POTATOES GLAZED WITH HONEY MAKES AN EXCELLENT TREAT FOR A DINNER PARTY OR SPECIAL OCCASION.

SERVES FOUR

INGREDIENTS

1 duckling, giblets removed
60ml/4 tbsp light soy sauce
150ml/¼ pint/⅔ cup fresh
  orange juice
3 large floury potatoes, cut
  into chunks
30ml/2 tbsp clear honey
15ml/1 tbsp sesame seeds
salt and ground black pepper

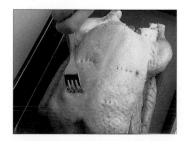

1 Preheat the oven to 200°C/400°F/ Gas 6. Place the duckling in a roasting pan. Prick the skin well.

2 Mix the soy sauce and orange juice together and pour over the duck. Cook for 20 minutes.

3 Place the potato chunks in a bowl, stir in the honey and toss to mix well. Remove the duckling from the oven and spoon the potatoes all around and under the duckling.

4 Roast for 35 minutes and remove from the oven. Toss the potatoes in the juices so the underside will be cooked and turn the duck over. Put back in the oven and cook for a further 30 minutes.

5 Remove the duckling from the oven and carefully scoop off the excess fat, leaving the juices behind.

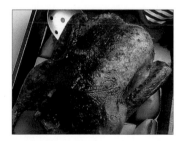

6 Sprinkle the sesame seeds over the potatoes, season and turn the duckling back over, breast side up, and cook for a further 10 minutes. Remove the duckling and potatoes from the oven and keep warm, allowing the duck to stand for a few minutes.

7 Pour off the excess fat and simmer the juices on the hob (stovetop) for a few minutes. Serve the juices with the carved duckling and potatoes.

Per portion: Energy 806Kcal/3341kJ; Protein 20.8g; Carbohydrate 32.3g, of which sugars 6.4g; Fat 66.8g, of which saturates 17.9g; Cholesterol 0mg; Calcium 53mg; Fibre 2.1g; Sodium 403mg.

MARMALADE-GLAZED GOOSE

SUCCULENT ROAST GOOSE IS THE CLASSIC CENTREPIECE FOR A TRADITIONAL CHRISTMAS LUNCH.
RED CABBAGE COOKED WITH LEEKS, AND BRAISED FENNEL ARE TASTY ACCOMPANIMENTS.

SERVES EIGHT

INGREDIENTS

4.5kg/10lb oven-ready goose
1 cooking apple, peeled, cored and
   cut into eighths
1 large onion, cut into eighths
bunch of fresh sage, plus extra sprigs
   to garnish
30ml/2 tbsp ginger
   marmalade, melted
salt and ground black pepper
For the stuffing
25g/1oz/2 tbsp butter
1 onion, finely chopped
15ml/1 tbsp ginger marmalade
450g/1lb/2 cups ready-to-eat
   prunes, chopped
45ml/3 tbsp Madeira
225g/8oz/4 cups fresh
   white breadcrumbs
30ml/2 tbsp chopped fresh sage
For the gravy
1 onion, chopped
15ml/1 tbsp plain (all-purpose) flour
150ml/¼ pint/⅔ cup Madeira
600ml/1 pint/2½ cups chicken stock

1 Preheat the oven to 200°C/400°F/
Gas 6. Prick the skin of the goose all
over with a fork and season the bird
generously, both inside and out.

COOK'S TIP

Red cabbage goes well with goose. Cook
1 small leek, sliced, in 75g/3oz/6 tbsp
butter, add 1kg/2¼lb/9 cups shredded
red cabbage, with the grated rind of
1 orange, and cook for 2 minutes. Add
30ml/2 tbsp Madeira and 15ml/1 tbsp
brown sugar and cook for 15 minutes.

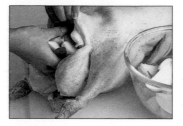

2 Mix the apple, onion and sage leaves
and spoon the mixture into the rump
end of the goose.

3 To make the stuffing, melt the butter
in a large pan and cook the onion for
about 5 minutes, or until softened but
not coloured. Remove the pan from
the heat and stir in the marmalade,
chopped prunes, Madeira, breadcrumbs
and chopped sage.

4 Stuff the neck end of the goose with
some of the stuffing, and set the
remaining stuffing aside in the
refrigerator. Sew up the bird or secure it
with skewers to prevent the stuffing
from escaping during cooking.

5 Place the goose in a large roasting
pan. Butter a piece of foil and use to
cover the goose loosely, then place in
the oven for 2 hours.

6 Baste the goose frequently during
cooking and remove excess fat from the
pan as necessary, using a small ladle or
serving spoon. (Strain, cool and chill the
fat in a covered container: it is excellent
for roasting potatoes.)

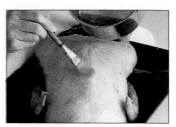

7 Remove the foil from the goose and
brush the melted ginger marmalade
over the goose, then roast for
30–40 minutes more, or until cooked
through. To check if the goose is cooked,
pierce the thick part of the thigh with a
metal skewer; the juices will run clear
when the bird is cooked. Remove from
the oven and cover with foil, then leave
to stand for 15 minutes before carving.

8 While the goose is cooking, shape the
remaining stuffing into walnut-size balls
and place them in an ovenproof dish.
Spoon 30ml/2 tbsp of the goose fat over
the stuffing balls and bake for about
15 minutes before the goose is cooked.

9 To make the gravy, pour off all but
15ml/1 tbsp of fat from the roasting
pan, leaving the meat juices behind.
Add the onion and cook for about
3–5 minutes, or until softened but not
coloured. Sprinkle in the flour and then
gradually stir in the Madeira and stock.
Bring to the boil, stirring constantly,
then simmer for 3 minutes, or until
thickened and glossy. Strain the gravy
and serve it with the carved goose and
stuffing. Garnish with sage leaves.

Per portion: Energy 823Kcal/3443kJ; Protein 57.6g; Carbohydrate 47.1g, of which sugars 23.8g; Fat 43.3g, of which saturates 14g; Cholesterol 177mg; Calcium 106mg; Fibre 4.5g; Sodium 395mg.

SOMERSET CIDER-GLAZED HAM

WILLIAM THE CONQUEROR INTRODUCED CIDER MAKING TO ENGLAND FROM NORMANDY IN 1066. THIS WONDERFUL OLD WEST-COUNTRY HAM GLAZED WITH CIDER IS TRADITIONALLY SERVED WITH CRANBERRY SAUCE AND IS IDEAL FOR CHRISTMAS FEASTING.

SERVES EIGHT TO TEN

INGREDIENTS
  2kg/4½lb middle gammon
    (cured ham) in a single piece
  1.3 litres/2¼ pints/5⅔ cups medium-
    dry (hard) cider
  1 large or 2 small onions
  about 30 whole cloves
  3 bay leaves
  10 black peppercorns
  45ml/3 tbsp soft light brown sugar
  bunch of flat leaf parsley, to garnish
For the cranberry sauce
  2 clementines
  350g/12oz/3 cups cranberries
  175g/6oz/¾ cup soft light brown sugar
  30ml/2 tbsp port

1 Weigh the ham and calculate the cooking time at 20 minutes per 450g/1lb, then place it in a large casserole or pan. Stud the onion or onions with 5–10 of the cloves and add to the casserole or pan with the bay leaves and peppercorns.

2 Add 1.2 litres/2 pints/5 cups of the cider and enough water just to cover the ham. Heat until simmering and then carefully skim off the scum that rises to the surface using a large spoon or ladle. Start timing the cooking from the moment the stock begins to simmer.

VARIATION
Use honey in place of the soft brown sugar for the glaze and serve the ham with redcurrant sauce or jelly.

3 Cover with a lid or foil and simmer gently for the calculated time. Towards the end of the cooking time, preheat the oven to 220°C/425°F/Gas 7.

4 Heat the sugar and remaining cider in a pan; stir until the sugar has dissolved.

5 Simmer for 5 minutes to make a dark, sticky glaze. Remove the pan from the heat and leave to cool for 5 minutes.

6 Lift the ham out of the casserole or pan using a slotted spoon and a large fork. Carefully and evenly, cut the rind from the ham, then score the fat into a neat diamond pattern. Place the ham in a roasting pan or ovenproof dish.

7 Press a clove into the centre of each diamond, then carefully spoon over the glaze. Roast for 20–25 minutes, or until the fat is brown, glistening and crisp.

8 Grate the rind and squeeze the juice from the clementines. Simmer all the cranberry sauce ingredients in a heavy pan for 15–20 minutes, stirring frequently. Transfer the sauce to a jug (pitcher). Serve the ham hot or cold, garnished with parsley and with the cranberry sauce.

COOK'S TIPS
• A large stock pot or preserving pan can be used in place of the casserole or pan for cooking the ham.
• Leave the ham until it is just cool enough to handle before removing the rind. Snip off the string using a sharp knife or scissors, then carefully slice off the rind, leaving a thin, even layer of fat. Use a narrow-bladed, sharp knife for the best results – a filleting knife, or a long, slim ham knife would be ideal.

ROAST PORK WITH SAGE AND ONION STUFFING

SAGE AND ONION MAKE A CLASSIC STUFFING FOR ROAST PORK, DUCK AND TURKEY, WITH THE SAGE COUNTERACTING THE FATTINESS OF THE RICH MEATS. SERVE WITH APPLE SAUCE AND ROAST POTATOES.

SERVES SIX TO EIGHT

INGREDIENTS
1.3–1.6kg/3–3½lb boneless loin of pork
60ml/4 tbsp fine, dry breadcrumbs
10ml/2 tsp chopped fresh sage
25ml/1½ tbsp plain (all-purpose) flour
300ml/½ pint/1¼ cups (hard) cider
150ml/¼ pint/⅔ cup water
5–10ml/1–2 tsp crab apple or redcurrant jelly
salt and ground black pepper
fresh thyme sprigs, to garnish
For the stuffing
25g/1oz/2 tbsp butter
50g/2oz bacon, finely chopped
2 large onions, finely chopped
75g/3oz/1½ cups fresh white breadcrumbs
30ml/2 tbsp chopped fresh sage
5ml/1 tsp chopped fresh thyme
10ml/2 tsp finely grated lemon rind
1 small (US medium) egg, beaten

1 Preheat the oven to 220°C/425°F/Gas 7. To make the stuffing, melt the butter in a pan and cook the bacon until it begins to brown, then add the onions and cook gently until softened. Mix with the breadcrumbs, sage, thyme, lemon rind and egg, then season well.

2 Cut the rind off the piece of pork in one piece and score it well. Cooking the rind separately makes crisper crackling than leaving it on the pork.

3 Place the pork fat side down, and season. Add a layer of stuffing, then roll up and tie neatly.

4 Lay the rind over the pork and rub in 5ml/1 tsp salt. Roast for 2–2½ hours, basting with the pork fat once or twice. Reduce the temperature to 190°C/375°F/Gas 5 after 20 minutes. Shape the remaining stuffing into balls and add to the roasting pan for the last 30 minutes.

5 Remove the rind from the pork. Increase the oven temperature to 220°C/425°F/Gas 7 and roast the rind for a further 20–25 minutes, until crisp.

6 Mix the dry breadcrumbs and sage and press them into the fat. Cook the pork for 10 minutes, then cover and set aside in a warm place for 15–20 minutes.

7 Remove all but 30–45ml/2–3 tbsp of the fat from the roasting pan and place it on the hob (stovetop). Stir in the flour, followed by the cider and water. Bring to the boil and then cook gently for 10 minutes. Strain the gravy into a clean pan, add the crab apple or redcurrant jelly, and cook for another 5 minutes. Adjust the seasoning.

8 Serve the pork cut into thick slices and the crisp crackling cut into strips with the cider gravy, garnished with thyme.

Per portion: Energy 426Kcal/1789kJ; Protein 52.4g; Carbohydrate 23.7g, of which sugars 5.3g; Fat 14.1g, of which saturates 5.7g; Cholesterol 180mg; Calcium 67mg; Fibre 1.4g; Sodium 475mg.

ROASTED AND MARINATED PORK

*YUAN, A SAUCE MADE FROM SAKE, SHOYU, MIRIN AND CITRUS FRUIT, IS OFTEN USED IN JAPAN TO
MARINATE INGREDIENTS EITHER BEFORE OR AFTER COOKING. IN THIS RECIPE, THE SAUCE GIVES A
DELICATE FLAVOUR TO PORK. IF POSSIBLE, LEAVE THE MEAT TO MARINATE OVERNIGHT.*

SERVES FOUR

INGREDIENTS
600g/1lb 5oz pork fillet (tenderloin)
1 garlic clove, crushed
generous pinch of salt
4 spring onions (scallions), trimmed,
  white part only
10g/¼oz dried wakame, soaked in
  water for 20 minutes and drained
10cm/4in celery stick, trimmed and
  cut in half crossways
1 carton salad cress
For the yuan sauce
  105ml/7 tbsp shoyu
  45ml/3 tbsp sake
  60ml/4 tbsp mirin
  1 lime, sliced into thin rings

1 Preheat the oven to 200°C/400°F/
Gas 6. Rub the pork with crushed garlic
and salt, and leave for 15 minutes.

2 Roast the pork for 20 minutes, then
turn the meat over and reduce the oven
temperature to 180°C/350°F/Gas 4.
Cook for a further 20 minutes, or until
the pork is cooked. Test by inserting a
skewer or the point of a sharp knife into
the meat. If the juices run clear, the
meat is cooked. If there are any traces
of pink in the juices, roast the pork for
a little longer.

3 Meanwhile, mix the yuan sauce
ingredients in a container that is big
enough to hold the pork. When the
meat is cooked, immediately put it in
the sauce, and leave it to marinate for
at least 2 hours, or overnight.

4 Cut the white part of the spring
onions in half crossways, then in half
lengthways. Remove the round cores,
then lay the spring onion quarters flat
on a chopping board. Slice them very
thinly lengthways to make fine shreds.

5 Soak the shreds in a bowl of ice-cold
water. Repeat with the remaining parts
of the spring onions. When the shreds
curl up, drain and gather them into a
louse ball.

6 Cut the drained wakame into 2.5cm/
1in squares or narrow strips. Slice the
celery very thinly lengthways. Soak in
cold water, then drain and gather
together as before.

7 Remove the pork from the marinade
and wipe with kitchen paper. Slice it
very thinly. Strain the marinade and
keep it in a gravy boat or jug (pitcher).
Arrange the sliced pork on a large
serving plate with the vegetables around
it. Serve cold with the yuan sauce.

Per portion: Energy 188Kcal/787kJ; Protein 32.5g; Carbohydrate 0.7g, of which sugars 0.6g; Fat 6.1g, of which saturates 2.1g; Cholesterol 95mg; Calcium 18mg; Fibre 0.2g; Sodium 377mg.

ROAST LEG OF LAMB

WHEN YOUNG LAMB WAS SEASONAL TO SPRINGTIME, A ROAST LEG WAS AN EASTER SPECIALITY, SERVED WITH A SAUCE USING THE FIRST SPRIGS OF MINT OF THE YEAR AND EARLY NEW POTATOES. ROAST LAMB IS NOW WELL ESTABLISHED AS A YEAR-ROUND FAMILY FAVOURITE FOR SUNDAY LUNCH, OFTEN SERVED WITH CRISP ROAST POTATOES.

SERVES SIX

INGREDIENTS
   1.5kg/3¼lb leg of lamb
   4 garlic cloves, sliced
   2 fresh rosemary sprigs
   30ml/2 tbsp light olive oil
   300ml/½ pint/1¼ cups red wine
   5ml/1 tsp clear honey
   45ml/3 tbsp redcurrant jelly
   salt and ground black pepper
For the roast potatoes
   45ml/3 tbsp white vegetable fat
      or lard
   1.3kg/3lb potatoes, such as Desirée,
      cut into chunks
For the mint sauce
   about 15g/½oz fresh mint
   10ml/2 tsp caster (superfine) sugar
   15ml/1 tbsp boiling water
   30ml/2 tbsp white wine vinegar

1 Preheat the oven to 220°C/425°F/ Gas 7. Make small slits into the lamb all over the leg. Press a slice of garlic and a few rosemary leaves into each slit, then place the lamb in a roasting pan and season well. Drizzle the oil over the lamb and roast for about 1 hour.

COOK'S TIP
To make a quick and tasty gravy from the pan juices, add about 300ml/½ pint/ 1¼ cups red wine, stock or water and boil, stirring occasionally, until reduced and well-flavoured. Season to taste, then strain into a sauce boat to serve.

2 Meanwhile, mix the wine, honey and redcurrant jelly in a small pan and heat, stirring, until the jelly melts. Bring to the boil, then reduce the heat and simmer until reduced by half. Spoon this glaze over the lamb and return it to the oven for 30–45 minutes.

3 To make the potatoes, put the fat in a roasting pan on the oven shelf above the meat. Boil the potatoes for about 5–10 minutes, then drain them and fluff up the surface of each with a fork.

4 Add the prepared potatoes to the hot fat and baste well, then roast them for 40–50 minutes, or until they are crisp.

5 Meanwhile, make the mint sauce. Place the mint on a chopping board and sprinkle the sugar over the top. Chop the mint finely, then transfer the mint and sugar to a bowl.

6 Add the boiling water and stir until the sugar has dissolved. Add 15ml/ 1 tbsp vinegar and taste the sauce before adding the remaining vinegar. (You may want to add slightly less or more than the suggested quantity.) Leave the mint sauce to stand until you are ready to serve the meal.

7 Cover the lamb with foil and set it aside in a warm place to rest for 10–15 minutes before carving. Serve with the crisp roast potatoes, mint sauce and a selection of seasonal vegetables.

Per portion: Energy 732Kcal/3080kJ; Protein 78g; Carbohydrate 36.4g, of which sugars 4.2g; Fat 31.6g, of which saturates 12.7g; Cholesterol 257mg; Calcium 36mg; Fibre 2.2g; Sodium 182mg.

ROAST VEAL WITH PARSLEY STUFFING

COOKING THIS LOIN OF VEAL, WITH ITS FRAGRANT PARSLEY AND LEEK STUFFING, IN A ROASTING BAG MAKES SURE THAT IT IS SUCCULENT AND FULL FLAVOURED WHEN SERVED.

SERVES SIX

INGREDIENTS

25g/1oz/2 tbsp butter
15ml/1 tbsp sunflower oil
1 leek, finely chopped
1 celery stick, finely chopped
50g/2oz/1 cup fresh
    white breadcrumbs
50g/2oz/½ cup chopped fresh flat
    leaf parsley
900g/2lb boned loin of veal
salt and ground black pepper

VARIATION
Other mild herbs can be used in the stuffing instead of parsley. Try tarragon, chervil and chives, but avoid strong-flavoured herbs, such as marjoram, oregano and thyme, which tend to overpower the delicate flavour of veal.

1 Preheat the oven to 180°C/350°F/ Gas 4. Heat the butter and oil in a frying pan until foaming. Cook the leek and celery until they are just starting to colour, then remove the pan from the heat and stir in the breadcrumbs, parsley and seasoning.

2 Lay the loin of veal out flat. Spread the stuffing over the meat, then roll it up carefully and tie the roll at regular intervals to secure it in a neat shape.

3 Place the veal in a roasting bag and close the bag with an ovenproof tie, then place it in a roasting pan. Roast the veal for 1¼ hours.

4 Pierce the meat with a metal skewer to check whether it is cooked: when cooked the meat juices will run clear. Leave the veal to stand for about 10–15 minutes, then carve it into thick slices and serve with gravy, sautéed potatoes, asparagus and sugar snaps.

ESCALOPES OF VEAL WITH CREAM SAUCE

THIS QUICK, EASY DINNER-PARTY DISH IS DELICIOUS SERVED WITH BUTTERED TAGLIATELLE AND LIGHTLY STEAMED GREEN VEGETABLES.

SERVES FOUR

INGREDIENTS

15ml/1 tbsp plain (all-purpose) flour
4 veal escalopes (US scallops), each
    weighing about 75–115g/3–4oz
30ml/2 tbsp sunflower oil
1 shallot, chopped
150g/5oz/2 cups oyster
    mushrooms, sliced
30ml/2 tbsp Marsala or
    medium-dry sherry
200ml/7fl oz/scant 1 cup
    crème fraîche
30ml/2 tbsp chopped fresh tarragon
salt and ground black pepper

COOK'S TIP
If the sauce seems to be too thick, add 30ml/2 tbsp water.

1 Season the flour and use to dust the veal escalopes, then set aside.

2 Heat the oil in a large frying pan and cook the shallot and mushrooms for 5 minutes. Add the escalopes and cook over a high heat for about 1½ minutes on each side. Pour in the Marsala or sherry and cook until reduced by half.

3 Use a spatula to remove the veal escalopes from the pan. Stir the crème fraîche, tarragon and seasoning into the juices remaining in the pan and simmer gently for 3–5 minutes, or until the sauce is thick and creamy.

4 Return the escalopes to the pan and heat through for 1 minute before serving.

Top per portion: Energy 233Kcal/981kJ; Protein 33.4g; Carbohydrate 7.6g, of which sugars 1.1g; Fat 7.9g, of which saturates 3.6g; Cholesterol 135mg; Calcium 49mg; Fibre 1.3g; Sodium 260mg.
Below per portion: Energy 376Kcal/1564kJ; Protein 25g; Carbohydrate 5.5g, of which sugars 1.5g; Fat 27.5g, of which saturates 14.9g; Cholesterol 108mg; Calcium 44mg; Fibre 0.6g; Sodium 73mg.

ROAST RIB OF BEEF

THIS ROAST LOOKS SPECTACULAR, AND SERVED IN TRADITIONAL STYLE, WITH YORKSHIRE PUDDINGS
AND HORSERADISH SAUCE, IT MAKES A PERFECT CELEBRATION MEAL.

SERVES EIGHT TO TEN

INGREDIENTS
  45ml/3 tbsp mixed peppercorns
  15ml/1 tbsp juniper berries
  2.75kg/6lb rolled rib of beef
  30ml/2 tbsp Dijon mustard
  15ml/1 tbsp olive oil
For the Yorkshire puddings
  150ml/¼ pint/⅔ cup water
  150ml/¼ pint/⅔ cup milk
  115g/4oz/1 cup plain (all-
    purpose) flour
  pinch of salt
  2 eggs, beaten
  60ml/4 tbsp lard, melted, or
    sunflower oil (optional)
For the caramelized shallots
  20 shallots
  5 garlic cloves, peeled
  60ml/4 tbsp light olive oil
  15ml/1 tbsp caster (superfine) sugar
For the gravy
  150ml/¼ pint/⅔ cup red wine
  600ml/1 pint/2½ cups beef stock
  salt and ground black pepper

1 Preheat the oven to 230°C/450°F/
Gas 8. Coarsely crush the peppercorns
and juniper berries. Sprinkle half the
spices over the meat, then transfer to a
roasting pan and roast for 30 minutes.

COOK'S TIP
If you prefer to cook beef on the bone,
buy a 3.6kg/8lb forerib. Trim off the
excess fat, sprinkle over the spices, then
follow the instructions in steps 1 and 2.
Roast at the lower temperature for
2 hours for rare beef, 2½ hours for
medium rare, and 3 hours for well done.

2 Reduce the oven temperature to
180°C/350°F/Gas 4. Mix the mustard
and oil into the remaining crushed spices
and spread the resulting paste over the
meat. Roast the meat for a further
1¼ hours if you like your meat rare,
1 hour 50 minutes for a medium-rare
result or 2 hours 25 minutes for a roast
that is medium to well done. Baste the
beef frequently during cooking.

3 Make the Yorkshire puddings as soon
as the beef is in the oven. Stir the water
into the milk. Sift the flour and salt into
a bowl. Make a well in the middle and
gradually whisk in the eggs followed by
the milk and water to make a smooth
batter. Cover and leave to stand for
about 1 hour. (The batter can be made
well in advance and chilled overnight in
the refrigerator if convenient.)

4 An hour before the beef is due to be
ready, mix the shallots and garlic cloves
with the light olive oil and spoon into
the roasting pan around the beef. After
30 minutes, sprinkle the caster sugar
over the shallots and garlic. Stir the
shallots and garlic two or three times
during cooking.

5 Transfer the meat to a large serving
platter, cover tightly with foil and
set aside in a warm place for
20–30 minutes. (This resting time
makes carving easier.) Increase the
oven temperature to 230°C/450°F/
Gas 8. Divide 60ml/4 tbsp dripping
from the meat or the lard or oil, if using,
among 10 individual Yorkshire pudding
tins (muffin pans) and heat in the oven
for 5 minutes.

6 Spoon the Yorkshire pudding batter
into the hot fat in the tins and bake
for 20–30 minutes, or until risen, firm
and a golden brown colour. The time
depends on the size of the tins: larger
Yorkshire puddings will take longer than
those in smaller tins.

7 Make the gravy while the Yorkshire
puddings are cooking. Simmer the red
wine and beef stock together in a pan
for about 5 minutes to intensify the
flavour of the gravy.

8 Skim the fat from the meat juices in
the roasting pan, then pour in the wine
mixture and simmer until the gravy is
reduced and thickened slightly to a
syrupy consistency. Stir frequently with
a wooden spoon to remove all of the
roasting residue from the roasting pan.
Season to taste.

9 Serve the beef with the individual
Yorkshire puddings, caramelized
shallots and gravy. Offer roast potatoes
or game chips as accompaniments,
along with a selection of lightly cooked,
seasonal vegetables.

Per portion: Energy 828Kcal/3444kJ; Protein 64.8g; Carbohydrate 14.2g, of which sugars 3.3g; Fat 55.7g, of which saturates 22.9g; Cholesterol 229mg; Calcium 74mg; Fibre 0.7g; Sodium 137mg.

BAKED DISHES

*Baking is a very versatile cooking method, as this eclectic
selection of recipes proves. Crunchy, golden toppings will prove
a hit with everyone, and slow baking brings out the full
flavour. For a family supper that is sure to please, choose
Roasted Ratatouille Moussaka or a hearty Country Meat Loaf.
Smoked Haddock and New Potato Pie is another excellent
choice, and you can ring the changes by choosing whatever fish
is readily available and therefore relatively inexpensive. Do try
Fillets of Brill in Red Wine Sauce, which proves once and for
all that red wine and fish can go beautifully together.*

ROASTED RATATOUILLE MOUSSAKA

BASED ON THE CLASSIC GREEK DISH, THIS MOUSSAKA REALLY HAS A TASTE OF THE MEDITERRANEAN. ROASTING BRINGS OUT THE DEEP RICH FLAVOURS OF THE VEGETABLES, WHICH GIVE A COLOURFUL CONTRAST TO THE LIGHT AND MOUTHWATERING EGG-AND-CHEESE TOPPING. THIS DISH IS PERFECT AS A VEGETARIAN MAIN COURSE, ALTHOUGH IT MAY BE SERVED AS A HEARTY WINTER SIDE DISH, TOO.

SERVES FOUR TO SIX

INGREDIENTS
  2 red (bell) peppers, seeded and cut
    into large chunks
  2 yellow (bell) peppers, seeded and
    cut into large chunks
  2 aubergines (eggplant), cut into
    large chunks
  3 courgettes (zucchini), thickly sliced
  45ml/3 tbsp olive oil
  3 garlic cloves, crushed
  400g/14oz can chopped tomatoes
  30ml/2 tbsp sun-dried tomato paste
  45ml/3 tbsp chopped fresh basil or
    15ml/1 tbsp dried basil
  15ml/1 tbsp balsamic vinegar
  1.5ml/¼ tsp soft light brown sugar
  salt and ground black pepper
  basil leaves, to garnish
For the topping
  25g/1oz/2 tbsp butter
  25g/1oz/¼ cup plain (all-
    purpose) flour
  300ml/½ pint/1¼ cups milk
  1.5ml/¼ tsp freshly grated nutmeg
  250g/9oz ricotta cheese
  3 eggs, beaten
  25g/1oz/⅓ cup freshly grated
    Parmesan cheese

1 Preheat the oven to 230°C/450°F/ Gas 8. Arrange the chunks of red and yellow peppers, aubergines and courgettes in an even layer in a large roasting pan. Season well with salt and ground black pepper.

2 Mix together the oil and crushed garlic cloves and pour them over the vegetables. Shake the roasting pan to thoroughly coat the vegetables in the garlic mixture.

3 Roast in the oven for 15–20 minutes, until slightly charred, lightly tossing the vegetables once during the cooking time. Remove the pan from the oven and set aside. Reduce the oven temperature to 200°C/400°F/Gas 6.

4 Put the chopped tomatoes, sun-dried tomato paste, basil, balsamic vinegar and brown sugar in a large, heavy pan and gently heat to boiling point. Reduce the heat and simmer, uncovered, for about 10–15 minutes, until reduced and thickened, stirring occasionally. Season with salt and freshly ground black pepper to taste.

5 Carefully tip the roasted vegetables out of their pan and into the pan of tomato sauce. Mix well, coating the vegetables thoroughly in the tomato sauce. Spoon into an ovenproof dish.

6 To make the topping, melt the butter in a large, heavy pan over a gentle heat. Stir in the flour and cook for 1 minute. Pour in the milk, stirring constantly, then whisk until blended. Add the nutmeg and continue whisking over a gentle heat until thickened. Cook for a further 2 minutes, then remove from the heat and leave to cool slightly.

7 Mix in the ricotta cheese and beaten eggs thoroughly. Season with salt and plenty of freshly ground black pepper to taste.

8 Level the surface of the roasted vegetable mixture with the back of a spoon. Spoon the moussaka topping over the vegetables and sprinkle with the Parmesan cheese. Bake for 30–35 minutes, until the topping is golden brown. Serve immediately, garnished with basil leaves.

VARIATION
Rather than baking this recipe in one large dish, divide the roasted vegetables and topping among individual gratin dishes. Reduce the baking time to 25 minutes. Individual portions can also be frozen and, when needed, simply removed from the freezer, left to thaw and baked for 30–35 minutes – ideal for those with a solitary vegetarian in the family, or for unexpected guests.

Per portion: Energy 570Kcal/2367kJ; Protein 22.1g; Carbohydrate 27.5g, of which sugars 21.7g; Fat 42.1g, of which saturates 20.3g; Cholesterol 223mg; Calcium 339mg; Fibre 7.1g; Sodium 447mg.

COD, BASIL, TOMATO AND POTATO PIE

FRESH AND SMOKED FISH MAKE A GREAT COMBINATION, ESPECIALLY WITH THE HINT OF TOMATO AND BASIL. SERVED WITH A GREEN SALAD, THIS MAKES AN IDEAL DISH FOR LUNCH OR A FAMILY SUPPER.

2 Melt 75g/3oz/6 tbsp of the butter in a large pan, add the onion and cook for about 5 minutes, until softened and tender but not browned. Sprinkle over the flour and half the chopped basil. Gradually add the reserved fish cooking liquid, adding a little more milk if necessary to make a fairly thin sauce, stirring constantly to make a smooth consistency. Bring to the boil, season with salt and pepper, and add the remaining basil.

3 Remove the pan from the heat, then add the fish and tomatoes and stir gently to combine. Pour into an ovenproof dish.

SERVES EIGHT

INGREDIENTS
   1kg/2¼lb smoked cod fillets
   1kg/2¼lb fresh cod fillets
   900ml/1½ pint/3¾ cups milk
   1.2litres/2 pints/5 cups water
   2 fresh basil sprigs
   1 fresh lemon thyme sprig
   150g/5oz/⅔ cup butter
   1 onion, chopped
   75g/3oz/⅔ cup plain
    (all-purpose) flour
   30ml/2 tbsp chopped fresh basil
   4 firm plum tomatoes, peeled
    and chopped
   12 medium floury potatoes
   salt and ground black pepper
   crushed black pepper corns,
    to garnish
   lettuce leaves, to serve

1 Place both kinds of fish in a roasting pan with 600ml/1 pint/2½ cups of the milk, the water and the herb sprigs. Bring to a simmer and cook gently for about 3–4 minutes. Remove from the heat and leave the fish to cool in the liquid for about 20 minutes. Drain the fish, reserving the cooking liquid for use in the sauce. Flake the fish, removing the skin and any remaining bones.

4 Preheat the oven to 180°C/350°F/ Gas 4. Cook the potatoes in boiling water until tender. Drain then add the remaining butter and milk and mash. Season to taste and spoon over the fish mixture, using a fork to create a pattern. You can freeze the pie at this stage. Bake for 30 minutes until the top is golden. Sprinkle with the crushed pepper corns and serve hot with lettuce.

Per portion: Energy 474Kcal/1989kJ; Protein 49.6g; Carbohydrate 30.7g, of which sugars 4.6g; Fat 17.8g, of which saturates 10.2g; Cholesterol 155mg; Calcium 62mg; Fibre 2.5g; Sodium 1672mg.

FISH PIE

*THIS DISH CAN BE VARIED TO SUIT YOUR TASTE AND POCKET. THIS IS A SIMPLE PIE, BUT YOU COULD
ADD PRAWNS OR HARD-BOILED EGGS, OR MIX THE POTATO TOPPING WITH SPRING ONIONS.*

SERVES FOUR

INGREDIENTS
    450g/1lb cod or haddock fillets
    225g/8oz smoked cod fillets
    300ml/½ pint/1¼ cups milk
    ½ lemon, sliced
    1 bay leaf
    1 fresh thyme sprig
    4–5 black peppercorns
    50g/2oz/¼ cup butter
    25g/1oz/¼ cup plain (all-
        purpose) flour
    30ml/2 tbsp chopped fresh parsley
    5ml/1 tsp anchovy essence (extract)
    150g/5oz/2 cups sliced mushrooms
    salt, ground black pepper and
        cayenne pepper
For the topping
    450g/1lb potatoes, cooked and
        mashed with milk
    50g/2oz/¼ cup butter
    2 tomatoes, sliced
    25g/1oz/¼ cup grated Cheddar
        cheese (optional)

1 Put the fish, skin side down, in a
shallow pan. Add the milk, lemon slices,
bay leaf, thyme and peppercorns. Bring
to the boil, then lower the heat and
poach gently for about 5 minutes, until
just cooked. Strain off and reserve the
milk. Remove the fish skin and flake the
flesh, discarding any bones.

2 Melt half the butter in a small pan,
stir in the flour and cook gently, stirring,
for 1 minute. Add the milk and boil,
whisking, until smooth and creamy. Stir
in the parsley and anchovy essence and
season to taste.

3 Heat the remaining butter in a frying
pan, add the sliced mushrooms and
sauté until tender. Season and add to
the flaked fish. Mix the sauce into the
fish and stir gently to combine. Transfer
the mixture to an ovenproof dish.

4 Preheat the oven to 200°C/400°F/
Gas 6. Beat the mashed potato with the
butter until very creamy. Season, then
spread the topping evenly over the fish.
Fork up the surface and arrange the
sliced tomatoes around the edge.
Sprinkle the exposed topping with the
grated cheese, if using.

5 Bake for 20–25 minutes, until the
topping is lightly browned. If you prefer,
finish browning under a grill (broiler).

VARIATION
Instead of using plain mashed potatoes,
try a mixture of mashed potato and
mashed swede (rutabaga) or celeriac.

Per portion: Energy 382Kcal/1600kJ; Protein 34.8g; Carbohydrate 24.3g, of which sugars 3.1g; Fat 16.8g, of which saturates 9.9g; Cholesterol 118mg; Calcium 62mg; Fibre 2.7g; Sodium 859mg.

SMOKED HADDOCK AND NEW POTATO PIE

SMOKED HADDOCK HAS A SALTY FLAVOUR AND CAN BE BOUGHT EITHER DYED OR UNDYED. THE DYED FISH HAS A STRONG YELLOW COLOUR, WHILE THE OTHER IS ALMOST CREAMY IN COLOUR.

SERVES FOUR

INGREDIENTS
  450g/1lb smoked haddock fillet
  475ml/16fl oz/2 cups semi-skimmed
    (low-fat) milk
  2 bay leaves
  1 onion, quartered
  4 cloves
  450g/1lb new potatoes
  butter, for greasing
  30ml/2 tbsp cornflour (cornstarch)
  60ml/4 tbsp double (heavy) cream
  30ml/2 tbsp chopped fresh chervil
  salt and ground black pepper
  mixed vegetables, to serve

VARIATIONS
Instead of using all smoked haddock for this pie, use half smoked and half fresh. Cook the two types together, as described in Step 1. A handful of peeled prawns (shrimp) is a good addition to this pie if you want to make it even more filling.

COOK'S TIP
The fish gives out liquid as it cooks, so it is best to start with a slightly thicker sauce than you might think is necessary.

1 Preheat the oven to 200°C/400°F/ Gas 6. Place the haddock in a deep-sided frying pan. Pour the milk over and add the bay leaves.

2 Stud the onion with the cloves and place it in the pan with the fish and milk. Cover the top and simmer for about 10 minutes or until the fish starts to flake.

3 Remove the fish with a slotted spoon and set aside to cool. Strain the liquid from the pan into a separate pan and set aside.

4 To prepare the potatoes, cut them into thin slices, leaving the skins on.

5 Blanch the potatoes in a large pan of lightly salted, boiling water for about 5 minutes. Drain.

6 Grease the base and sides of a 1.2 litre/2 pint/5 cup ovenproof dish. Then using a knife and fork, carefully flake the fish.

7 Reheat the milk in the pan. Mix the cornflour with a little water to form a paste and stir in the cream and the chervil. Add to the milk in the pan and cook until thickened.

8 Arrange one-third of the potatoes over the base of the dish and season with pepper. Lay half of the fish over. Repeat layering, finishing with a layer of potatoes on top.

9 Pour the sauce over the top, making sure that it sinks down through the mixture. Cover with foil and cook for 30 minutes. Remove the foil and cook for a further 10 minutes to brown the surface. Serve immediately with a selection of mixed vegetables.

Per portion: Energy 300Kcal/1266kJ; Protein 23.9g; Carbohydrate 32.4g, of which sugars 1.9g; Fat 9.3g, of which saturates 5.3g; Cholesterol 61mg; Calcium 56mg; Fibre 1.5g; Sodium 881mg.

BAKED SEA BREAM WITH TOMATOES

JOHN DORY, TURBOT OR SEA BASS CAN ALL BE COOKED THIS WAY. IF YOU PREFER TO USE FILLETED FISH, CHOOSE A CHUNKY FILLET, LIKE COD, AND BAKE IT SKIN SIDE UP. ROASTING THE TOMATOES BRINGS OUT THEIR SWEETNESS, WHICH CONTRASTS BEAUTIFULLY WITH THE FLAVOUR OF THE FISH.

2 Meanwhile, cut the potatoes into 1cm/½in slices. Par-boil for 5 minutes. Drain and set aside.

3 Grease an ovenproof dish with oil. Arrange the potatoes in a single layer with the lemon slices over; sprinkle on the bay leaf, thyme and basil. Season and drizzle with half the remaining olive oil. Lay the fish on top, season; pour over the wine and the rest of the oil. Arrange the tomatoes around the fish.

SERVES FOUR TO SIX

INGREDIENTS

   8 ripe tomatoes
   10ml/2 tsp caster (superfine) sugar
   200ml/7fl oz/scant 1 cup olive oil
   450g/1lb new potatoes
   1 lemon, sliced
   1 bay leaf
   1 fresh thyme sprig
   8 fresh basil leaves
   1 sea bream, about 900g–1kg/
     2–2¼lb, cleaned and scaled
   150ml/¼ pint/⅔ cup dry white wine
   30ml/2 tbsp fresh white breadcrumbs
   2 garlic cloves, crushed
   15ml/1 tbsp finely chopped
     fresh parsley
   salt and ground black pepper
   fresh flat parsley or basil leaves,
     chopped, to garnish

1 Preheat the oven to 240°C/475°F/ Gas 9. Using a sharp knife, cut the tomatoes in half lengthways and arrange them in a single layer in a large, ovenproof dish, cut side up. Sprinkle with the caster sugar, season to taste with salt and pepper and drizzle over a little of the olive oil. Roast for 30–40 minutes, until the tomatoes are soft and lightly browned on top.

4 Mix together the breadcrumbs, garlic and parsley and sprinkle over the fish. Bake for 30 minutes, until the flesh comes away easily from the bone. Garnish with chopped parsley or basil.

Per portion: Energy 571Kcal/2383kJ; Protein 25.9g; Carbohydrate 29.4g, of which sugars 7.2g; Fat 37.1g, of which saturates 4.9g; Cholesterol 48mg; Calcium 82mg; Fibre 3g; Sodium 224mg.

FILLETS OF BRILL IN RED WINE SAUCE

FORGET THE OLD MAXIM THAT RED WINE AND FISH DO NOT GO WELL TOGETHER. THE ROBUST SAUCE ADDS COLOUR AND RICHNESS TO THIS EXCELLENT DISH. TURBOT, HALIBUT AND JOHN DORY ARE ALSO GOOD COOKED THIS WAY.

SERVES FOUR

INGREDIENTS

4 brill fillets, about 175–200g/6–7oz each, skinned
150g/5oz/⅔ cup chilled butter, diced, plus extra for greasing
115g/4oz shallots, thinly sliced
200ml/7fl oz/scant 1 cup robust red wine
200ml/7fl oz/scant 1 cup fish stock
salt and ground white pepper
fresh chervil or flat leaf parsley leaves, to garnish

3 Using a fish slice or spatula, carefully lift the fish and shallots on to a serving dish, cover with foil and keep hot.

4 Transfer the dish to the hob (stovetop) and bring the cooking liquid to the boil over a high heat. Cook it until it has reduced by half. Lower the heat and whisk in the chilled butter, one piece at a time, to make a smooth, shiny sauce. Season with salt and ground white pepper, set aside and keep hot.

5 Divide the shallots among four warmed plates and lay the brill fillets on top. Pour the sauce over and around the fish and garnish with the chervil or flat leaf parsley.

1 Preheat the oven to 180°C/350°F/ Gas 4. Season the fish on both sides with salt and pepper. Generously butter a flameproof dish, which is large enough to take all the brill fillets in a single layer without overlapping. Spread the shallots over the base and lay the fish fillets on top. Season.

2 Pour in the red wine and fish stock, cover the dish and bring the liquid to just below boiling point. Transfer the dish to the oven and bake for 6–8 minutes, until just cooked.

Per portion: Energy 511Kcal/2123kJ; Protein 35.7g; Carbohydrate 1.3g, of which sugars 1.3g; Fat 36.7g, of which saturates 19.5g; Cholesterol 156mg; Calcium 97mg; Fibre 0.4g; Sodium 454mg.

SINIYA

The name of this classic Jewish Sephardi dish simply means fish and tahini sauce. In this version, the fish is first wrapped in vine leaves, then spread with tahini and baked. A final sprinkling of pomegranate seeds adds a fresh, invigorating flavour.

SERVES FOUR

INGREDIENTS

4 small fish, such as trout, sea
   bream, red mullet or snapper, each
   weighing about 300g/11oz, cleaned
at least 5 garlic cloves, chopped
juice of 2 lemons
75ml/5 tbsp olive oil
about 20 brined vine (grape) leaves
tahini, for drizzling
1–2 pomegranates
fresh mint and coriander (cilantro)
   sprigs, to garnish

VARIATION
Instead of whole fish, use fish fillets or
steaks such as fresh tuna. Make a bed
of vine (grape) leaves and top with the
fish and marinade. Bake for about
5–10 minutes, until the fish is half
cooked, then top with the tahini as above
and grill (broil) until golden brown and
lightly crusted on top.

1 Preheat the oven to 180°C/350°F/
Gas 4. Put the fish in a shallow, ovenproof
dish, large enough to fit all the fish
without touching each other. In a bowl,
combine the garlic, lemon juice and oil;
spoon over the fish. Turn the fish to coat.

2 Rinse the vine leaves well under cold
water, then wrap the fish in the leaves.
Arrange the fish in the same dish and
spoon any marinade in the dish over
the top of each. Bake for 30 minutes.

3 Drizzle the tahini over the top of each
wrapped fish, making a ribbon so that
the tops and tails of the fish and some
of the vine leaf wrapping still show.
Return to the oven and bake for a
further 5–10 minutes, until the top is
golden and slightly crusted.

4 Meanwhile, cut the pomegranates in
half and scoop out the seeds. Sprinkle
the seeds over the fish, garnish with
mint and coriander, and serve.

Per portion: Energy 402Kcal/1681kJ; Protein 46.8g; Carbohydrate 2.6g, of which sugars 2.6g; Fat 22.8g, of which saturates 4.1g; Cholesterol 192mg; Calcium 86mg; Fibre 0.5g; Sodium 176mg.

BACON-WRAPPED TROUT WITH OATMEAL AND ONION STUFFING

THIS STUFFING IS BASED ON A SCOTTISH SPECIALITY, A MIXTURE OF OATMEAL AND ONION CALLED SKIRLIE. HERRING CAN BE COOKED IN THE SAME WAY. THIS IS VERY GOOD WITH SLICES OF COOKED POTATOES, BRUSHED WITH OLIVE OIL AND GRILLED UNTIL GOLDEN ON EACH SIDE.

SERVES FOUR

INGREDIENTS
10 dry-cured streaky (fatty) bacon
  rashers (strips)
40g/1½oz/3 tbsp butter
1 onion, finely chopped
115g/4oz/1 cup oatmeal
30ml/2 tbsp chopped fresh parsley
30ml/2 tbsp chopped fresh chives
4 trout, about 350g/12oz each,
  gutted and boned
juice of ½ lemon
salt and ground black pepper
watercress, cherry tomatoes and
  lemon wedges, to serve
For the herb mayonnaise
6 watercress sprigs
15ml/1 tbsp chopped fresh chives
30ml/2 tbsp coarsely
  chopped parsley
90ml/6 tbsp lemon mayonnaise
30ml/2 tbsp crème fraîche
2.5–5ml/½–1 tsp tarragon mustard

1 Preheat oven to 190°C/375°F/Gas 5. Chop two of the bacon rashers. Melt 25g/1oz/2 tbsp of the butter in a large frying pan and cook the bacon briefly. Add the finely chopped onion and cook gently, stirring occasionally, for 5–8 minutes, until softened.

2 Add the oatmeal and cook until the oatmeal darkens and absorbs the fat, but do not allow it to overbrown. Stir in the parsley, chives and seasoning. Cool.

3 Wash and dry the trout, then stuff with the oatmeal mixture. Wrap each fish in two bacon rashers and place in an ovenproof dish. Dot with the remaining butter and sprinkle with the lemon juice. Bake for 20–25 minutes, until the bacon browns and crisps.

4 Meanwhile, make the mayonnaise. Place the watercress, chives and parsley in a sieve and pour boiling water over them. Drain, rinse under cold water, and drain well on kitchen paper.

5 Purée the herbs in a mortar with a pestle. (This is easier than using a food processor for this small quantity.) Stir the puréed herbs into the lemon mayonnaise together with the crème fraîche. Add tarragon mustard to taste and stir to combine.

6 When cooked, transfer the trout to warmed serving plates and serve immediately with watercress, tomatoes and lemon wedges, accompanied by the herb mayonnaise.

Per portion: Energy 870Kcal/3625kJ; Protein 65.9g; Carbohydrate 24.5g, of which sugars 2.6g; Fat 57.1g, of which saturates 17.8g; Cholesterol 300mg; Calcium 115mg; Fibre 2.5g; Sodium 1245mg.

BAKED SALMON WITH WATERCRESS SAUCE

WHOLE BAKED SALMON IS A CLASSIC DISH SERVED AT WEDDING PARTIES AND JUST ABOUT ANY OTHER BIG OCCASION. BAKING THE SALMON IN FOIL PRODUCES A FLESH RATHER LIKE THAT OF A POACHED FISH BUT WITH THE EASE OF BAKING. DECORATING THE FISH WITH THIN SLICES OF CUCUMBER LOOKS PRETTY AND WILL CONCEAL ANY FLESH THAT MAY LOOK RAGGED AFTER SKINNING.

SERVES SIX TO EIGHT

INGREDIENTS

2–3kg/4½–6¾lb salmon, cleaned, with head and tail left on
3–5 spring onions (scallions), thinly sliced
1 lemon, thinly sliced
1 cucumber, thinly sliced
fresh dill sprigs, to garnish
lemon wedges, to serve
For the watercress sauce
3 garlic cloves, chopped
200g/7oz watercress leaves, finely chopped
40g/1½oz fresh tarragon, finely chopped
300g/11oz mayonnaise
15–30ml/1–2 tbsp freshly squeezed lemon juice
200g/7oz/scant 1 cup unsalted (sweet) butter
salt and ground black pepper

1 Preheat the oven to 180°C/350°F/Gas 4. Rinse the salmon and lay it on a large piece of foil. Stuff the fish cavity with the sliced spring onions and layer the lemon slices inside and around the fish, then sprinkle with plenty of salt and ground black pepper.

2 Loosely fold the foil around the fish and fold the edges over to seal. Bake for about 1 hour.

3 Remove the fish from the oven and leave to stand, still wrapped in the foil, for about 15 minutes, then unwrap the parcel and leave the fish to cool.

4 When the fish is cool, carefully lift it on to a large plate, still covered with lemon slices. Cover the fish tightly with clear film (plastic wrap) and chill for several hours.

5 Before serving, discard the lemon slices around the fish. Using a blunt knife to lift up the edge of the skin, carefully peel the skin away from the flesh, avoiding tearing the flesh, and pull out any fins at the same time.

6 Arrange the cucumber slices in overlapping rows along the length of the fish, to resemble large fish scales.

COOK'S TIP
Do not prepare the sauce more than a few hours ahead of serving as the watercress will discolour it.

7 To make the sauce, put the garlic, watercress, tarragon, mayonnaise and lemon juice in a food processor or blender or a bowl, and process or mix to combine.

8 Melt the butter, then add to the watercress mixture, a little at a time, processing or stirring, until the butter has been incorporated and the sauce is thick and smooth. Cover and chill before serving. Serve the fish, garnished with dill, with the sauce and lemon wedges.

VARIATION
Instead of cooking a whole fish, prepare 6–8 salmon steaks. Place each fish steak on an individual square of foil, then top with a slice of onion and a slice of lemon and season generously with salt and ground black pepper. Loosely wrap the foil up around the fish, fold the edges to seal and place the parcels on a baking sheet. Bake as above for 10–15 minutes, or until the flesh is opaque. Serve cold with watercress sauce, garnished with slices of cucumber.

Per portion: Energy 1044Kcal/4323kJ; Protein 51.6g; Carbohydrate 1.4g, of which sugars 1.2g; Fat 92.4g, of which saturates 28.5g; Cholesterol 231mg; Calcium 135mg; Fibre 0.7g; Sodium 558mg.

BRAISED PORK CHOPS WITH ONION AND MUSTARD SAUCE

THE PIQUANT SAUCE ADDS PUNCH AND EXTRA FLAVOUR TO THIS SIMPLE SUPPER DISH. SERVE IT WITH CELERIAC AND POTATO MASH AND A GREEN VEGETABLE, SUCH AS BROCCOLI OR CABBAGE.

SERVES FOUR

INGREDIENTS

4 pork loin chops, at least
    2cm/¾in thick
30ml/2 tbsp plain (all-purpose) flour
45ml/3 tbsp olive oil
2 Spanish (Bermuda) onions, sliced
2 garlic cloves, finely chopped
250ml/8fl oz/1 cup dry (hard) cider
150ml/¼ pint/⅔ cup chicken stock
generous pinch of brown sugar
2 fresh bay leaves
6 fresh thyme sprigs
2 strips lemon rind
120ml/4fl oz/½ cup double
    (heavy) cream
30–45ml/2–3 tbsp wholegrain
    mustard
30ml/2 tbsp chopped fresh parsley
salt and ground black pepper

1 Preheat the oven to 200°C/400°F/Gas 6. Trim the chops of excess fat. Season the flour with salt and pepper and use to coat the chops. Heat 30ml/2 tbsp of the oil in a frying pan and brown the chops on both sides, then transfer them to an ovenproof dish.

2 Add the remaining oil to the pan and cook the onions over a fairly gentle heat until they soften and begin to brown at the edges. Add the garlic and cook for 2 minutes more.

3 Stir in any leftover flour, then gradually stir in the cider and stock. Season well with salt and pepper and add the brown sugar, bay leaves, thyme sprigs and lemon rind. Bring the sauce to the boil, stirring constantly, then pour over the chops.

4 Cover and cook in the oven for 20 minutes. Reduce the heat to 180°C/350°F/Gas 4 and continue cooking for another 30–40 minutes. Remove the foil for the last 10 minutes of the cooking time. Remove the chops from the dish and keep warm, covered with foil.

5 Tip the remaining contents of the dish into a pan or, if the dish is flameproof, place it over a direct heat. Discard the herbs and lemon rind, then bring to the boil.

6 Add the cream and continue to boil, stirring constantly. Taste for seasoning, adding a pinch more sugar if necessary. Finally, stir in the mustard to taste and pour the sauce over the braised chops. Sprinkle with the chopped parsley and serve immediately.

VARIATIONS
• For a less rich sauce, omit the cream and purée the sauce in a blender. Reheat, thinning with a little extra stock if necessary, then adjust the seasoning and add mustard to taste. This will produce a sharper tasting sauce that will need less mustard.
• If you prefer, you can use vegetable or pork stock instead of chicken.
• This recipe also works extremely well with veal chops.

Per portion: Energy 694Kcal/2881kJ; Protein 32g; Carbohydrate 19.8g, of which sugars 9.3g; Fat 53g, of which saturates 21.6g; Cholesterol 131mg; Calcium 80mg; Fibre 2.1g; Sodium 207mg.

PORK ESCALOPES BAKED WITH APPLE AND POTATO RÖSTI

THE JUICES FROM THE PORK COOK INTO THE APPLES AND POTATOES GIVING THEM A WONDERFUL FLAVOUR AS WELL AS MAKING A DELICIOUS SAUCE.

SERVES FOUR

INGREDIENTS
2 large potatoes, finely grated
1 medium cooking apple, grated
2 garlic cloves, crushed
1 egg, beaten
butter, for greasing
15ml/1 tbsp olive oil
4 large prosciutto slices
4 pork escalopes (US scallops), about
   175g/6oz each
4 sage leaves
1 medium cooking apple,
   cut into thin wedges
25g/1oz/2 tbsp butter, diced
salt and ground black pepper
caramelized apple wedges, to serve

COOK'S TIPS
• Do not be tempted to overcook the pork as it will start to dry out.
• If you can't find cooking apples, use an all-purpose eating variety, such as Granny Smith.

1 Preheat the oven to 200°C/400°F/ Gas 6. Squeeze out all the excess liquid from the grated potatoes and apple. Mix the grated ingredients together with the garlic, egg and seasoning.

2 Divide the potatoes into four portions and spoon each quarter on to a baking sheet that has been lined with foil and greased. Form a round with the potatoes and flatten out slightly with the back of a spoon. Drizzle with a little olive oil. Cook for 10 minutes.

3 Meanwhile, lay the prosciutto on a clean surface and place a pork escalope on top. Lay a sage leaf and apple wedges over each escalope and top each piece with the butter. Wrap the prosciutto around each piece of meat, making sure it is covered completely.

4 Remove the potatoes from the oven, place each pork parcel on top and return to the oven for 20 minutes. Carefully lift the pork and potatoes off the foil and serve with caramelized wedges of apple and any cooking juices on the side.

Per portion: Energy 396Kcal/1659kJ; Protein 42.7g; Carbohydrate 19.2g, of which sugars 4.4g; Fat 16.9g, of which saturates 6.7g; Cholesterol 177mg; Calcium 29mg; Fibre 1.5g; Sodium 310mg.

MOUSSAKA

THIS IS A TRADITIONAL EASTERN MEDITERRANEAN DISH, POPULAR IN BOTH GREECE AND TURKEY.
LAYERS OF MINCED LAMB, AUBERGINES, TOMATOES AND ONIONS ARE TOPPED WITH A CREAMY YOGURT
AND CHEESE SAUCE IN THIS DELICIOUS, AUTHENTIC RECIPE.

SERVES FOUR

INGREDIENTS
    450g/1lb aubergines (eggplant)
    150ml/¼ pint/²/₃ cup olive oil
    1 large onion, chopped
    2–3 garlic cloves, finely chopped
    675g/1½lb lean minced (ground) lamb
    15ml/1 tbsp plain (all-purpose) flour
    400g/14oz can chopped tomatoes
    30ml/2 tbsp chopped fresh herbs
    450g/1lb fresh tomatoes, sliced
    salt and ground black pepper
For the topping
    300ml/½ pint/1¼ cups yogurt
    2 eggs
    25g/1oz feta cheese, crumbled
    25g/1oz/⅓ cup freshly grated
      Parmesan cheese

1 Cut the aubergines into thin slices and layer them in a colander, sprinkling each layer with salt.

2 Cover the aubergines with a plate and a weight, then leave for about 30 minutes. Pat dry with kitchen paper.

3 Heat 45ml/3 tbsp of the oil in a large, heavy pan. Cook the onion and garlic until softened, but not coloured. Add the lamb and cook over a high heat, stirring frequently, until browned.

4 Stir in the flour until mixed, then stir in the canned tomatoes, herbs and seasoning. Bring to the boil, reduce the heat and simmer gently for 20 minutes.

5 Meanwhile, heat a little of the remaining oil in a large frying pan. Add as many aubergine slices as can be laid in the pan in a single layer, then cook until golden on both sides. Set the cooked aubergines aside. Heat more oil and continue cooking the aubergines, in batches, adding oil as necessary.

COOK'S TIP
Salting and drying the aubergines before cooking reduces the amount of fat that they absorb and helps them to brown more quickly.

6 Preheat the oven to 180°C/350°F/ Gas 4. Arrange half the aubergine slices in a large, shallow ovenproof dish, then add a layer of half the fresh tomatoes.

7 Top the slices with about half of the meat and tomato sauce mixture, then add a layer of the remaining aubergine slices, followed by the remaining tomato slices. Spread the remaining meat mixture over the aubergines and tomatoes.

8 Beat together the yogurt and eggs, then mix in the feta and Parmesan cheeses. Pour the mixture over the meat and spread it evenly.

9 Transfer the moussaka to the oven and bake for 35–40 minutes, or until golden and bubbling.

VARIATION
Use large courgettes (zucchini) instead of aubergines (eggplant), if you like. Cut them diagonally into fairly thick slices.

Per portion: Energy 753Kcal/3132kJ; Protein 46.2g; Carbohydrate 19.4g, of which sugars 17.6g; Fat 55.3g, of which saturates 17.6g; Cholesterol 237mg; Calcium 329mg; Fibre 4.9g; Sodium 425mg.

COUNTRY MEAT LOAF

THREE DIFFERENT KINDS OF MEAT ARE COMBINED WITH HERBS AND OTHER FLAVOURINGS TO MAKE THIS HEARTY AND APPETIZING TRADITIONAL MEAT LOAF.

SERVES SIX

INGREDIENTS

    30ml/2 tbsp butter or margarine
    115g/4oz/½ cup chopped onion
    2 garlic cloves, crushed
    50g/2oz/½ cup chopped celery
    450g/1lb lean minced (ground) beef
    225g/½lb minced (ground) veal
    225g/½lb lean minced (ground) pork
    2 eggs
    50g/2oz/1 cup fine fresh
      bread crumbs
    15g/½oz/½ cup chopped
      fresh parsley
    30ml/2 tbsp chopped fresh basil
    2.5ml/½ tsp fresh or dried
      thyme leaves
    2.5ml/½ tsp salt
    2.5ml/½ tsp pepper
    30ml/2 tbsp Worcestershire sauce
    60ml/4 tbsp chilli sauce or
      tomato ketchup
    6 bacon rashers (strips)

1 Preheat the oven to 180°C/350°F/ Gas 4. Melt the butter or margarine in a small frying pan over a low heat. Add the onion, garlic and celery and cook, stirring occasionally, for 8–10 minutes, until softened. Remove from the heat and leave to cool slightly.

COOK'S TIP
To test if the meat loaf is cooked through, insert a skewer. If the juices run clear and skewer comes out fairly clean, then it is ready.

2 In a large mixing bowl combine the onion, garlic and celery with all the other ingredients except the bacon. Mix together lightly, using a fork or your fingers. Do not overwork or the meat loaf will be too compact.

3 Form the meat mixture into an oval loaf. Carefully transfer it to a shallow baking tin (pan).

4 Lay the bacon across the top of the meat loaf. Bake for 1¼ hours, basting occasionally with the juices and bacon fat in the tin.

5 Remove from the oven and drain off the fat. Leave the meat loaf to stand for 10 minutes before serving.

Per portion: Energy 285Kcal/1188kJ; Protein 18.6g; Carbohydrate 11.9g, of which sugars 5.1g; Fat 18.4g, of which saturates 8.3g; Cholesterol 119mg; Calcium 62mg; Fibre 1g; Sodium 572mg.

TAMALE PIE

THIS IS A TEXAN VERSION OF A TRADITIONAL MEXICAN RECIPE, ALTHOUGH SO MANY VARIATIONS EXIST THAT BOTH SIDES OF THE BORDER CAN CLAIM THE ORIGINAL.

SERVES EIGHT

INGREDIENTS
  115g/4oz bacon, chopped
  1 onion, finely chopped
  450g/1lb lean minced (ground) beef
  10–15ml/2–3 tsp chilli powder
  5ml/1 tsp salt
  400g/14oz can tomatoes
  40g/1½oz/⅓ cup chopped
    black olives
  175g/6oz/1 cup corn kernels, freshly
    cooked or thawed frozen
  120ml/4fl oz/½ cup sour cream
  115g/4oz/1 cup grated Cheddar or
    Monterey Jack cheese
For the tamale topping
  250–300ml/8–10fl oz/1–1¼ cups
    chicken stock
  175g/6oz/1½ cups masa harina
    or cornmeal
  90ml/6 tbsp margarine or
    vegetable shortening
  2.5ml/½ tsp baking powder
  50ml/2fl oz/¼ cup milk
  salt and ground black pepper

1 Preheat the oven to 190°C/375°F/ Gas 5. Cook the bacon in a large, heavy frying pan for 2–3 minutes, until the fat runs. Pour off any excess fat, leaving 15–30ml/1–2 tbsp. Add the onion and cook, over a medium heat, stirring occasionally, for about 5 minutes, until just softened.

2 Add the beef, chilli powder and salt and cook for 5 minutes, stirring to break up the meat. Stir in the tomatoes and cook for 5 minutes more, breaking them up with a spoon.

3 Add the olives, corn, and sour cream, and mix well. Transfer to a 38cm/15in long rectangular or oval ovenproof dish. Set aside.

4 To make the topping, bring the chicken stock to the boil in a pan over a medium heat and season it with salt and pepper if necessary.

5 In a food processor, combine the masa harina or cornmeal, margarine or shortening, baking powder and milk. Process until combined. With the machine still running, gradually pour in the hot stock until a smooth, thick batter is formed. If the batter is too thick to spread, add additional hot stock or water, a little at a time.

6 Pour the batter over the top of the beef mixture, spreading it evenly with a metal spatula.

7 Bake for about 20 minutes, until the top is just browned. Sprinkle the surface evenly with the grated cheese and continue baking for a further 10–15 minutes, until the cheese has melted. Serve immediately.

Per portion: Energy 492Kcal/2044kJ; Protein 23.3g; Carbohydrate 26.6g, of which sugars 6.1g; Fat 32.1g, of which saturates 17.4g; Cholesterol 96mg; Calcium 206mg; Fibre 1.6g; Sodium 827mg.

PIZZAS, TARTS AND PIES

Although pizzas are now commonplace, filling supermarket freezers and fast becoming the world's favourite takeaway food, the home-made variety is almost always superior. Making your own dough enables you to tailor the toppings to the tastes of your guests. We've supplied recipes for basics like Fiorentina Pizza and Hot Pepperoni Pizza, but you can add extra ingredients or invite diners to invent their own combinations. This chapter also includes delectable pastries like Cheese and Onion Flan, Filo-wrapped Fish and Rich Game Pie.

SUN-DRIED TOMATO CALZONE

CALZONE IS A TRADITIONAL FOLDED PIZZA. IN THIS TASTY VEGETARIAN VERSION, YOU CAN ADD MORE OR FEWER RED CHILLI FLAKES, DEPENDING ON PERSONAL TASTE.

SERVES TWO

INGREDIENTS

    4 baby aubergines (eggplant)
    3 shallots, chopped
    45ml/3 tbsp olive oil
    1 garlic clove, chopped
    50g/2oz/⅓ cup sun-dried tomatoes
      in oil, drained
    1.5ml/¼ tsp dried red chilli flakes,
      if using
    10ml/2 tsp chopped fresh thyme
    75g/3oz mozzarella cheese, cubed
    salt and ground black pepper
    15–30ml/1–2 tbsp freshly grated
      Parmesan cheese, plus extra to serve
For the dough
    225g/8oz/2 cups strong white
      bread flour
    5ml/1 tsp salt
    2.5ml/½ tsp easy-blend (rapid-rise)
      dried yeast
    15ml/1 tbsp olive oil
    150ml/¼ pint/⅔ cup warm water

1 Make the dough. Place the dry ingredients in a bowl and mix to form a soft dough with the oil and water. Knead for 10 minutes. Put in an oiled bowl, cover and leave in a warm place until doubled in size.

2 Preheat the oven to 220°C/425°F/ Gas 7. Dice the aubergines. Cook the shallots in a little oil until soft. Add the aubergines, garlic, sun-dried tomatoes, chilli, if using, thyme and seasoning. Cook for 5 minutes. Divide the dough in half and roll out each piece on a lightly floured work surface to an 18cm/7in round.

3 Spread the aubergine mixture over half of each round, leaving a 2.5cm/1in border, then sprinkle on the mozzarella. Dampen the edges with water, then fold over the dough to enclose the filling. Press the edges firmly together to seal. Place on greased baking sheets.

4 Brush with half the remaining oil and make a small hole in the top of each calzone to allow steam to escape. Bake for 15–20 minutes, until golden. Remove from the oven and brush with the remaining oil. Sprinkle over the Parmesan and serve immediately.

Per portion: Energy 777Kcal/3259kJ; Protein 25.3g; Carbohydrate 92.2g, of which sugars 6.2g; Fat 36.7g, of which saturates 11.8g; Cholesterol 37mg; Calcium 494mg; Fibre 7g; Sodium 323mg.

CLASSIC MARINARA PIZZA

THE COMBINATION OF SIMPLE INGREDIENTS, FRESH GARLIC, GOOD QUALITY OLIVE OIL AND A TASTY TOMATO SAUCE GIVES THIS PIZZA AN UNMISTAKABLY ITALIAN FLAVOUR. ALTHOUGH PLAIN IN LOOKS, THE TASTE OF THE MARINARA IS UTTERLY DELICIOUS.

SERVES TWO

INGREDIENTS
   60ml/4 tbsp extra virgin olive oil or
      sunflower oil
   675g/1½lb plum tomatoes, peeled,
      seeded and chopped
   4 garlic cloves, cut into slivers
   15ml/1 tbsp chopped
      fresh oregano
   salt and ground black pepper
For the pizza base
   225g/8oz/2 cups plain (all-purpose)
      white flour
   pinch of salt
   10ml/2 tsp baking powder
   50g/2oz/4 tbsp margarine
   about 150ml/¼ pint/⅔ cup milk

1 Preheat the oven to 220°C/425°F/
Gas 7. Use non-stick baking parchment
to line a baking sheet. Sift the flour, salt
and baking powder in a bowl and rub
the margarine lightly into the flour until
it resembles breadcrumbs.

2 Pour in enough milk to form a soft
dough and knead. Roll the dough out to
a round about 25cm/10in in diameter.

3 Place the dough on the prepared
baking sheet and make the edges
slightly thicker than the centre.

4 Heat 30ml/2 tbsp of the oil in a pan.
Add the seeded and chopped plum
tomatoes and cook, stirring frequently
for about 5 minutes, until soft.

5 Place the tomatoes in a sieve over
a bowl and leave to drain for about
5 minutes.

6 Empty the juice from the bowl and
force the tomatoes through the sieve into
the bowl with the back of a spoon. You
may also use a food processor or blender
and process until smooth.

7 Brush the pizza base with half the
remaining oil. Spoon over the tomatoes
and sprinkle with garlic and oregano.
Drizzle over the remaining oil and
season with salt and pepper.

8 Bake for 15–20 minutes, until the
pizza is crisp and golden. Serve
immediately, while piping hot.

Per portion: Energy 858Kcal/3597kJ; Protein 15.6g; Carbohydrate 101.7g, of which sugars 16g; Fat 46.2g, of which saturates 4.5g; Cholesterol 4mg; Calcium 272mg; Fibre 6.9g; Sodium 266mg.

FIORENTINA PIZZA

AN EGG ADDS THE FINISHING TOUCH TO THIS SPINACH PIZZA; TRY NOT TO OVERCOOK IT THOUGH, AS IT'S BEST WHEN THE YOLK IS STILL SLIGHTLY SOFT IN THE MIDDLE.

SERVES TWO TO THREE

INGREDIENTS

45ml/3 tbsp olive oil
1 small red onion, thinly sliced
175g/6oz fresh spinach,
  stalks removed
1 pizza base, about
  25–30cm/10–12in diameter
1 small jar pizza sauce
freshly grated nutmeg
150g/5oz mozzarella cheese
1 egg
25g/1oz/¼ cup grated Gruyère cheese

1 Heat 15ml/1 tbsp of the oil and cook the onion until soft. Add the spinach and cook until wilted. Drain any liquid.

2 Preheat the oven to 220°C/425°F/Gas 7. Brush the pizza base with half the remaining olive oil. Spread the pizza sauce evenly over the base, using the back of a spoon, then top with the spinach mixture. Sprinkle over a little freshly grated nutmeg.

3 Thinly slice the mozzarella and arrange over the spinach. Drizzle over the remaining oil. Bake for 10 minutes, then remove from the oven.

4 Make a small well in the centre of the pizza topping and carefully break the egg into the hole.

5 Sprinkle over the grated Gruyère cheese and return to the oven for a further 5–10 minutes, until crisp and golden. Serve immediately.

VARIATION
Italians make a folded pizza called calzone. It is made in the same way as a pizza but is folded in half to conceal the filling. Add the egg with the rest of the pizza topping, fold over the dough, seal the edges and bake for 20 minutes.

Per portion: Energy 808Kcal/3377kJ; Protein 33.1g; Carbohydrate 72g, of which sugars 10.3g; Fat 44.8g, of which saturates 16.3g; Cholesterol 151mg; Calcium 640mg; Fibre 5.3g; Sodium 911mg.

PEPPERY TOMATO PIZZA

*PUNGENT ROCKET AND AROMATIC FRESH BASIL ADD COLOUR AND FLAVOUR TO THIS CRISP PIZZA,
A PERFECT ADDITION TO ANY PICNIC, BUFFET OR OUTDOOR MEAL.*

SERVES TWO

INGREDIENTS

10ml/2 tsp olive oil
1 garlic clove, crushed
150g/5oz can chopped tomatoes
2.5ml/½ tsp caster (superfine) sugar
30ml/2 tbsp torn fresh basil leaves
2 tomatoes, seeded and chopped
150g/5oz mozzarella cheese, sliced
20g/¾oz rocket (arugula) leaves
For the pizza base
225g/8oz/2 cups strong white
   bread flour
5ml/1 tsp salt
2.5ml/½ tsp easy-blend (rapid-rise)
   dried yeast
30ml/2 tbsp olive oil

1 To make the pizza base, place the
dry ingredients in a bowl. Add the oil
and 150ml/¼ pint/⅔ cup warm water.
Mix to form a soft dough.

2 Turn out the dough and knead until it
is smooth and elastic. Place in an oiled
bowl and cover. Leave in a warm place
for 45 minutes, or until doubled in bulk.

3 Preheat the oven to 220°C/425°F/
Gas 7. Make the topping. Heat the oil in
a frying pan and cook the garlic for
1 minute. Add the canned tomatoes
and sugar and cook for 10 minutes.

4 Knead the risen dough lightly, then
roll out to form a rough 30cm/12in
round. Place on a lightly oiled baking
sheet and push up the edges of the
dough to form a shallow, even rim.

5 Season the tomato mixture and stir in
the basil. Spoon it over the pizza base,
then top with the chopped fresh
tomatoes. Arrange the mozzarella slices
on top of the tomato mixture. Season
with sea salt and pepper and drizzle with
a little olive oil.

6 Bake for 10–12 minutes, until crisp
and golden. Scatter the rocket leaves
over the pizza just before serving.

Per portion: Energy 735Kcal/3087kJ; Protein 26.1g; Carbohydrate 93g, of which sugars 7.3g; Fat 31.3g, of which saturates 12.7g; Cholesterol 44mg; Calcium 459mg; Fibre 5.5g; Sodium 330mg.

PISSALADIÈRE

This famous onion and anchovy dish is a traditional market food of Nice in southern France. It can be made using either shortcrust pastry or, as here, yeasted dough, similar to a pizza base. Either way, it is most delicious eaten lukewarm rather than piping hot.

SERVES SIX

INGREDIENTS
250g/9oz/2¼ cups strong white bread
  flour, plus extra for dusting
50g/2oz/⅓ cup fine polenta
  or semolina
5ml/1 tsp salt
175ml/6fl oz/¾ cup lukewarm water
5ml/1 tsp dried yeast
5ml/1 tsp caster (superfine) sugar
30ml/2 tbsp extra virgin olive oil
For the topping
60–75ml/4–5 tbsp extra virgin
  olive oil
6 large sweet Spanish (Bermuda)
  onions, thinly sliced
2 large garlic cloves, thinly sliced
5ml/1 tsp chopped fresh thyme, plus
  several sprigs
1 fresh rosemary sprig
1–2 × 50g/2oz cans anchovies in
  olive oil
50–75g/2–3oz small black olives,
  preferably small Niçoise olives
salt and ground black pepper

1 Mix the flour, polenta or semolina and salt in a large mixing bowl. Pour half the water into a bowl. Add the yeast and sugar, then leave in a warm place for 10 minutes, until frothy. Pour the yeast mixture into the flour mixture with the remaining water and the olive oil.

2 Using your hands, mix all the ingredients together to form a dough, then turn out and knead for 5 minutes, until smooth, springy and elastic.

3 Return the dough to the clean, floured bowl and place it in a plastic bag or cover with oiled clear film (plastic wrap), then set the dough aside at room temperature for 30–60 minutes to rise and double in bulk.

4 Meanwhile, start to prepare the topping. Heat 45ml/3 tbsp of the olive oil in a large, heavy pan and add the sliced onions. Stir well to coat the onions in the oil, then cover the pan and cook over a very low heat, stirring occasionally, for 20–30 minutes. (Use a heat-diffuser mat to keep the heat low, if possible.)

5 Add a little salt to taste and the garlic, chopped thyme and rosemary sprig. Stir well and continue cooking for another 15–25 minutes, or until the onions are soft and deep golden yellow but not browned at all. Uncover the pan for the last 5–10 minutes' cooking if the onions seem very wet. Remove and discard the rosemary. Set the onions aside to cool.

6 Preheat the oven to 220°C/425°F/ Gas 7. Roll out the dough thinly and use to line a large baking sheet, about 30 × 23–25cm/12 × 9–10in. Taste the onions for seasoning before spreading them over the dough.

7 Drain the anchovies, cut them in half lengthways and arrange them in a lattice pattern over the onions. Sprinkle the olives and thyme sprigs over the top of the pissaladière and drizzle with the remaining olive oil. Bake for about 20–25 minutes, or until the dough is browned and cooked. Season with pepper and serve warm, cut into slices.

VARIATIONS
• Shortcrust pastry can be used instead of yeast dough as a base: bake it blind for 10–15 minutes before adding the filling.
• If you enjoy anchovies, try spreading about 60ml/4 tbsp anchovy purée (paste) – *anchoïade* – over the base before adding the onions. Alternatively, spread black olive paste over the base.

Per portion: Energy 431Kcal/1797kJ; Protein 9.9g; Carbohydrate 51.6g, of which sugars 10g; Fat 21.7g, of which saturates 3.1g; Cholesterol 8mg; Calcium 138mg; Fibre 3.8g; Sodium 825mg.

BRESAOLA AND ROCKET PIZZA

ALTHOUGH THE ARMENIANS ORIGINATED THE IDEA OF TOPPING FLATTENED DOUGH WITH SAVOURY
INGREDIENTS BEFORE BAKING IT, IT WAS THE ITALIANS — THE NEAPOLITANS IN PARTICULAR —
WHO DEVELOPED THE PIZZA IN THE 1830S.

SERVES FOUR

INGREDIENTS
  150g/5oz packet pizza base mix
  120ml/4fl oz/½ cup lukewarm water
  225g/8oz/3¼ cups mixed
    wild mushrooms
  25g/1oz/2 tbsp butter
  2 garlic cloves, coarsely chopped
  60ml/4 tbsp pesto
  8 slices bresaola
  4 tomatoes, sliced
  75g/3oz/⅓ cup cream cheese
  25g/1oz rocket (arugula)

1 Preheat the oven to 200°C/400°F/
Gas 6. Tip the packet of pizza base mix
into a large mixing bowl and pour in
enough of the water to mix to a soft, not
sticky, dough, following the instructions
on the packet.

2 Turn out the dough on to a lightly
floured surface and knead for about
5 minutes, or until smooth and elastic.
Divide the dough into two equal pieces,
knead lightly to form two balls, then pat
out the balls of dough into flat rounds
with your hands.

3 Roll out each piece of dough on a
lightly floured surface to a 23cm/9in
round and transfer to baking sheets.

4 Slice the wild mushrooms. Melt the
butter in a frying pan and cook the
garlic for 2 minutes. Add the mushrooms
and cook over a high heat for about
5 minutes, or until the mushrooms have
softened but are not overcooked.

5 Spread pesto on the pizza bases, to
within 2cm/¾in of the edge of each
one. Arrange the bresaola and tomato
slices around the rims of the pizzas,
then spoon the cooked mushrooms into
the middle.

6 Dot the cream cheese on top of the
pizzas and bake for 15–18 minutes, or
until the bases are crisp and the cheese
just melted. Top each pizza with a
handful of rocket leaves just before
serving. Serve immediately.

COOK'S TIP
If you are in a hurry, buy two ready-made
pizza bases instead of the pizza mix and
bake for 10 minutes.

Per portion: Energy 448Kcal/1873kJ; Protein 16.6g; Carbohydrate 34.7g, of which sugars 6g; Fat 28g, of which saturates 12.8g; Cholesterol 56mg; Calcium 179mg; Fibre 3.5g; Sodium 213mg.

HOT PEPPERONI PIZZA

THERE IS NOTHING MORE MOUTHWATERING THAN A FRESHLY BAKED PIZZA, ESPECIALLY WHEN THE TOPPING INCLUDES TOMATOES, MOZZARELLA CHEESE, PEPPERONI AND RED CHILLIES.

SERVES FOUR

INGREDIENTS
  225g/8oz/2 cups strong white
    bread flour
  10ml/2 tsp easy-blend (rapid-rise)
    dried yeast
  5ml/1 tsp granulated sugar
  2.5ml/½ tsp salt
  15ml/1 tbsp olive oil
  175ml/6fl oz/¾ cup mixed lukewarm
    milk and water
For the topping
  400g/14oz can chopped
    tomatoes, strained
  2 garlic cloves, crushed
  5ml/1 tsp dried oregano
  225g/8oz mozzarella cheese, grated
  2 dried red chillies, crumbled
  225g/8oz pepperoni, sliced
  30ml/2 tbsp drained capers
  fresh oregano, to garnish

1 Sift the flour, stir in the yeast, sugar and salt and make a well in the centre. Stir the oil into the milk and water, then stir into the flour. Mix to a soft dough.

2 Knead the dough on a lightly floured surface for 10 minutes until it is smooth and elastic. Cover and leave in a warm place for about 30 minutes, or until the dough has doubled in bulk.

3 Preheat the oven to 220°C/425°F/ Gas 7. Turn the dough out on to a lightly floured surface and knead lightly for 1 minute. Divide it in half and roll each piece out to a 25cm/10in round. Place on lightly oiled pizza trays or baking sheets. To make the topping, mix the strained tomatoes, garlic and dried oregano in a bowl.

4 Spread half the tomato mixture over each base, leaving a border around the edge. Set half the mozzarella aside. Divide the rest between the pizzas, sprinkling it over evenly. Bake for 7–10 minutes, until the dough rim on each pizza is pale golden.

5 Sprinkle the crumbled chillies over the pizzas, then arrange the pepperoni slices and capers on top. Sprinkle with the remaining mozzarella. Return the pizzas to the oven and bake for 7–10 minutes more. Sprinkle over the fresh oregano and serve immediately.

Per portion: Energy 631Kcal/2638kJ; Protein 28.8g; Carbohydrate 47.6g, of which sugars 4.7g; Fat 37.5g, of which saturates 16.8g; Cholesterol 80mg; Calcium 317mg; Fibre 2.7g; Sodium 1498mg.

CHEESE AND ONION FLAN

THE USE OF YEAST DOUGHS FOR TARTS AND FLANS IS POPULAR IN VARIOUS REGIONS OF FRANCE. CHOOSE A STRONG CHEESE SUCH AS LIVAROT, MUNSTER OR PORT SALUT IN THIS RECIPE.

SERVES FOUR

INGREDIENTS

15g/½oz/1 tbsp butter
1 onion, halved and sliced
2 eggs
250ml/8fl oz/1 cup single
    (light) cream
225g/8oz strong semi-soft
    cheese, sliced
salt and ground black pepper
salad leaves, to serve
For the yeast dough
10ml/2 tsp dried yeast
120ml/4fl oz/½ cup milk
5ml/1 tsp sugar
1 egg yolk
225g/8oz/2 cups plain (all-purpose)
    flour, plus extra for kneading
2.5ml/½ tsp salt
50g/2oz/4 tbsp butter, softened

2 Put the flour and salt in a food processor fitted with a metal blade and pulse to combine. With the machine running, slowly pour in the yeast mixture. Scrape down the sides and continue processing for 2–3 minutes. Add the softened butter and process for another 30 seconds.

3 Transfer the dough to a lightly greased bowl. Cover the bowl with a dishtowel and leave to rise in a warm place for about 1 hour, until the dough has doubled in bulk.

4 Remove the dough from the bowl and place on a lightly floured surface. Knock back (punch down) the dough by hitting it with your fist. Sprinkle a little more flour on the work surface and roll out the dough to a 30cm/12in round.

5 Line a 23cm/9in flan tin (quiche pan) with the dough. Gently press it into the tin and trim off any overhanging pieces, leaving a 3mm/⅛in rim around the flan case (pie shell). Cover with a dishtowel, set aside in a warm place and leave the dough to rise again for about 30 minutes, or until puffy.

6 Meanwhile, melt the butter in a heavy pan and add the onion. Cover the pan and cook over a medium-low heat, stirring occasionally, for about 15 minutes, until softened and lightly coloured. Remove the lid and continue cooking, stirring frequently, until the onion is very soft and caramelized.

7 Preheat the oven to 180°C/350°F/Gas 4. Beat together the eggs and cream. Season and stir in the cooked onion.

8 Arrange the cheese on the base of the flan case. Pour over the egg mixture and bake for 30–35 minutes, until the base is golden and the centre is just set. Cool slightly on a wire rack and serve warm with salad leaves.

1 To make the dough, place the yeast in a bowl. Warm the milk in a small pan until it is at body temperature and stir into the yeast with the sugar. Continue stirring until the yeast has dissolved completely. Leave the yeast mixture to stand for about 3 minutes, then beat in the egg yolk.

COOK'S TIP
If you prefer to use easy-blend (rapid-rise) yeast, omit step 1. Beat the egg yolk and milk together in a jug (pitcher). Add the dry yeast to the flour and salt in the food processor and pulse to combine. Pour in the egg and milk mixture and proceed with the recipe as normal.

Per portion: Energy 747Kcal/3113kJ; Protein 27.1g; Carbohydrate 49.6g, of which sugars 5.9g; Fat 49.2g, of which saturates 29.9g; Cholesterol 271mg; Calcium 619mg; Fibre 2.3g; Sodium 576mg.

TUNA AND EGG GALETTE

THIS FLAKY PASTRY TART COMBINES SOFT-CENTRED EGGS AND A SLIGHTLY PIQUANT FISH FILLING.
IT MAKES A WONDERFUL DISH FOR A SUMMER SUPPER AND IS ALSO A GREAT BUFFET-TABLE STANDBY.

SERVES FOUR

INGREDIENTS

2 sheets of ready-rolled puff pastry
plain (all-purpose) flour, for dusting
beaten egg, to glaze
60ml/4 tbsp olive oil
175g/6oz tuna steak
2 onions, sliced
1 red (bell) pepper, seeded
  and chopped
2 garlic cloves, crushed
45ml/3 tbsp capers, drained
5ml/1 tsp grated lemon rind
30ml/2 tbsp lemon juice
5 eggs
salt and ground black pepper
chopped flat leaf parsley, to garnish

1 Preheat the oven to 190°C/375°F/
Gas 5. Lay a sheet of pastry on a lightly
floured baking sheet and cut to a
28 × 18cm/11 × 7in rectangle. Brush
the whole sheet with beaten egg.

2 Cut the second sheet of pastry to the
same size. Cut out a rectangle from
the centre and discard, leaving a
2.5cm/1in border. Lift the border on to
the first sheet. Brush the border with
beaten egg and prick the base.

3 Bake the pastry case (pie shell) for
about 15 minutes until golden.

COOK'S TIP
If you are using fresh, unfrozen pastry,
the remaining rectangle of pastry can
be wrapped in clear film (plastic wrap)
and frozen. Allow to thaw at room
temperature for 1 hour before using.

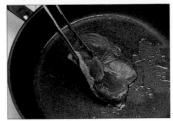

4 Heat 30ml/2 tbsp of the oil in a frying
pan and cook the tuna steak for
2–3 minutes on each side, until golden
but still pale pink in the middle. Transfer
to a plate and flake into small pieces.

5 Add the remaining oil to the pan and
cook the onions, red pepper and garlic
for 6–8 minutes, until softened, stirring
occasionally. Remove the pan from the
heat and stir in the tuna, capers and
lemon rind and juice. Season well.

6 Spoon the filling into the pastry case
and level the surface with the back of a
spoon. Break the eggs into the filling
and return the galette to the oven for
about 10 minutes, or until the eggs
have just cooked through. Garnish with
chopped parsley and serve immediately.

COOK'S TIP
To make sure the eggs do not become
hard on top during baking, cover the tart
with lightly oiled foil.

Per portion: Energy 544Kcal/2263kJ; Protein 21.7g; Carbohydrate 27.7g, of which sugars 4.7g; Fat 39.5g, of which saturates 10.1g; Cholesterol 260mg; Calcium 102mg; Fibre 1.9g; Sodium 320mg.

FILO-WRAPPED FISH

THIS DELICIOUS DISH COMES FROM JERUSALEM, WHERE WHOLE FISH ARE WRAPPED IN FILO PASTRY AND SERVED WITH A ZESTY TOMATO SAUCE. THE CHOICE OF FISH CAN BE VARIED ACCORDING TO WHAT IS IN SEASON AND WHAT IS FRESHEST ON THE DAY OF PURCHASE.

SERVES THREE TO FOUR

INGREDIENTS

450g/1lb salmon or cod steaks
  or fillets
1 lemon
30ml/2 tbsp olive oil, plus extra
  for brushing
1 onion, chopped
2 celery sticks, chopped
1 green (bell) pepper, diced
5 garlic cloves, chopped
400g/14oz fresh or canned
  tomatoes, chopped
120ml/4fl oz/½ cup passata
  (bottled strained tomatoes)
30ml/2 tbsp chopped fresh flat
  leaf parsley
2–3 pinches of ground allspice or
  ground cloves
cayenne pepper, to taste
pinch of sugar
about 130g/4½oz filo pastry
  (6–8 large sheets)
salt and ground black pepper

1 Sprinkle the salmon or cod steaks or fillets with salt and black pepper and a squeeze of lemon juice. Set aside while you prepare the sauce.

2 Heat the olive oil in a pan, add the chopped onion, celery and pepper and cook for about 5 minutes, until the vegetables are softened. Add the garlic and cook for a further 1 minute, then add the tomatoes and passata and cook until the tomatoes have softened and the mixture is of a sauce consistency.

3 Stir the parsley into the sauce, then season with allspice or cloves, cayenne pepper, sugar and salt and pepper.

4 Preheat the oven to 200°C/400°F/ Gas 6. Take a sheet of filo pastry, brush with a little olive oil and cover with a second sheet. Place a piece of fish on top of the pastry, towards the bottom edge, then top with 1–2 spoonfuls of the sauce, spreading it evenly.

5 Roll the fish in the pastry, taking care to enclose the filling completely. Arrange on a baking sheet and repeat with the remaining fish and pastry. You should have about half the sauce remaining, to serve with the fish.

6 Bake for 10–15 minutes, or until golden. Meanwhile, reheat the remaining sauce if necessary. Serve immediately with the remaining sauce.

Per portion: Energy 509Kcal/2135kJ; Protein 36.2g; Carbohydrate 37.2g, of which sugars 10.4g; Fat 25.1g, of which saturates 4.2g; Cholesterol 75mg; Calcium 137mg; Fibre 5g; Sodium 192mg.

SALMON <u>IN</u> PUFF PASTRY

THIS IS AN ELEGANT PARTY DISH, MADE WITH RICE, EGGS AND SALMON ENCLOSED IN PUFF PASTRY.

SERVES SIX

INGREDIENTS

450g/1lb puff pastry, thawed
    if frozen
1 egg, beaten
3 hard-boiled eggs
90ml/6 tbsp single (light) cream
200g/7oz/1¾ cups cooked long
    grain rice
30ml/2 tbsp finely chopped
    fresh parsley
10ml/2 tsp chopped fresh tarragon
675g/1½lb salmon fillets
40g/1½oz/3 tbsp butter
juice of ½ lemon
salt and ground black pepper

2 In a bowl, mash the hard-boiled eggs with the cream, then stir in the cooked rice. Add the parsley and tarragon and season well. Spoon this mixture on to the prepared pastry.

5 Roll out the remaining pastry and cut out a semi-circular piece to cover the head portion and a tail shape to cover the tail. Brush both pieces of pastry with a little beaten egg and place on top of the fish, pressing down firmly to secure. Score a criss-cross pattern on the tail.

1 Preheat the oven to 190°C/375°F/Gas 5. Roll out two-thirds of the pastry into a large oval, measuring about 35cm/14in in length. Cut into a curved fish shape and place on a lightly greased baking sheet. Use the trimmings to make narrow strips. Brush one side of each strip with a little beaten egg and secure in place around the rim of the pastry to make a raised edge. Prick the base all over with a fork, then bake for 8–10 minutes until the sides are well risen and the pastry is lightly golden. Leave to cool.

3 Cut the salmon into 2cm/¾in chunks. Melt the butter until it starts to sizzle, then add the salmon. Turn the pieces over in the butter so that they begin to colour but do not cook through.

6 Cut the remaining pastry into small rounds and, starting from the tail end, arrange the rounds in overlapping lines to represent scales. Add an extra one for an eye. Brush the whole fish shape with the remaining beaten egg.

7 Bake for 10 minutes, then reduce the temperature to 160°C/325°F/Gas 3 and cook for a further 15–20 minutes, until the pastry is evenly golden. Slide the fish on to a serving plate and serve.

COOK'S TIP

If the pastry seems to be browning too quickly, cover it with foil during cooking and remove from the oven for the last 5 minutes. It is important that the "fish" cooks for the recommended time, so that the salmon is sufficiently cooked through.

4 Remove from the heat and arrange the salmon pieces on top of the rice, piled in the centre. Stir the lemon juice into the butter in the pan, then spoon the mixture over the salmon pieces.

VARIATION

If time is short you may prefer to use this simplified method. Roll out the pastry into a rectangle, then make pastry edges to contain the filling. Part bake the pastry, add the filling, top with plain, rolled out pastry and return it to the oven.

Per portion: Energy 668Kcal/2782kJ; Protein 31g; Carbohydrate 36.6g, of which sugars 0.7g; Fat 45.3g, of which saturates 14g; Cholesterol 209mg; Calcium 98mg; Fibre 1.1g; Sodium 389mg.

CHICKEN-MUSHROOM PIE

THIS IS A GREAT FAMILY FAVOURITE, ESPECIALLY POPULAR ON A COLD WINTER'S EVENING. IT'S ALSO A GOOD WAY TO USE UP LEFTOVER ROAST CHICKEN.

SERVES SIX

INGREDIENTS

15g/½oz dried porcini mushrooms
50g/2oz/¼ cup butter
30ml/2 tbsp flour
250ml/8fl oz/1 cup simmering
  chicken stock
50ml/2fl oz/¼ cup whipping cream
  or milk
1 onion, coarsely chopped
2 carrots, sliced
2 celery sticks, coarsely chopped
50g/2oz fresh mushrooms, quartered
450g/1lb cooked chicken
  meat, cubed
50g/2oz/½ cup shelled fresh or
  frozen peas
beaten egg, for glazing
salt and ground black pepper
For the pastry
225g/8oz/2 cups plain (all-
  purpose) flour
1.5ml/¼ tsp salt
115g/4oz/½ cup cold butter, cut
  into pieces
75g/3oz/⅓ cup shortening
60–120ml/4–8 tbsp iced water

1 For the pastry, sift the flour and salt into a bowl. With a pastry blender or two knives, cut in the butter and shortening until the mixture resembles coarse breadcrumbs. Sprinkle with 90ml/6 tbsp iced water and mix until the dough holds together. If the dough is too crumbly, add a little more water, 15ml/1 tbsp at a time. Gather the dough into a ball and flatten into a round. Wrap in greaseproof (waxed) paper and chill for at least 30 minutes.

2 Place the dried porcini mushrooms in a small bowl. Add hot water to cover and leave to soak for about 30 minutes until softened. Lift out of the water with a slotted spoon, leaving any grit behind, and drain. Discard the soaking water.

3 Preheat the oven to 190°C/375°F/ Gas 5. Melt 30ml/2 tbsp of the butter in a heavy pan. Stir in the flour and cook, whisking constantly, for about 1 minute, until bubbling. Gradually, add the warm stock and cook over a medium heat, whisking constantly, until the mixture comes to the boil. Cook, still whisking, for 2–3 minutes more. Whisk in the cream or milk and season to taste with salt and pepper. Remove the pan from the heat and set aside.

4 Heat the remaining butter in a large, non-stick frying pan until foaming. Add the onion and carrots and cook over a medium heat, stirring occasionally, for about 5 minutes, until softened. Add the celery and fresh mushrooms and cook, stirring occasionally, for a further 5 minutes. Stir in the cubed chicken meat, fresh or frozen peas, and drained porcini mushrooms.

5 Add the chicken mixture to the cream sauce and stir to mix. Taste for seasoning. Transfer to a 2 litre/4 pint/ 10 cup rectangular ovenproof dish.

6 Roll out the dough on a lightly floured surface to about 3mm/⅛in thickness. Cut out a rectangle about 2.5cm/1in larger all around than the dish. Lay the rectangle of dough over the filling. Make a decorative edge, crimping the dough by pushing the index finger of one hand between the thumb and index finger of the other hand.

7 Cut several vents in the top of the pie to allow steam to escape. Brush the dough with the egg glaze.

8 Press together the dough trimmings, then roll out again. Cut into strips and lay them over the top of the pie. Glaze again. If you like, roll small balls of dough and set them in the "windows" in the lattice.

9 Bake for about 30 minutes, until the top of the pie is browned and the filling is piping hot. Serve the pie hot, straight from the dish.

Per portion: Energy 600Kcal/2501kJ; Protein 23.7g; Carbohydrate 38.8g, of which sugars 3.7g; Fat 40g, of which saturates 21.8g; Cholesterol 132mg; Calcium 92mg; Fibre 2.7g; Sodium 226mg.

RICH GAME PIE

TERRIFIC FOR STYLISH PICNICS OR JUST AS SMART FOR A FORMAL WEDDING BUFFET, THIS PIE LOOKS SPECTACULAR WHEN BAKED IN A FLUTED RAISED PIE MOULD. SOME SPECIALIST KITCHEN STORES HIRE THE MOULDS SO THAT YOU CAN AVOID THE EXPENSE OF PURCHASING THEM; ALTERNATIVELY A 20CM/8IN ROUND SPRINGFORM TIN CAN BE USED.

SERVES TEN

INGREDIENTS
    25g/1oz/2 tbsp butter
    1 onion, finely chopped
    2 garlic cloves, finely chopped
    900g/2lb mixed boneless game
        meat, such as skinless pheasant
        and/or pigeon (US squab) breast,
        venison and rabbit, diced
    30ml/2 tbsp chopped mixed fresh
        herbs such as parsley, thyme
        and marjoram
    salt and ground black pepper
For the pâté
    50g/2oz/¼ cup butter
    2 garlic cloves, finely chopped
    450g/1lb chicken livers, rinsed,
        trimmed and chopped
    60ml/4 tbsp brandy
    5ml/1 tsp ground mace
For the hot water crust pastry
    675g/1½lb/6 cups strong white
        bread flour
    5ml/1 tsp salt
    115ml/3½fl oz/scant ½ cup milk
    115ml/3½fl oz/scant ½ cup water
    115g/4oz/½ cup lard, diced
    115g/4oz/½ cup butter, diced
    beaten egg, to glaze
For the jelly
    300ml/½ pint/1¼ cups game or
        beef consommé
    2.5ml/½ tsp powdered gelatine

1 Melt the butter in a small pan, then add the onion and garlic and cook until softened but not coloured. Remove from the heat and mix with the diced game meat and the chopped mixed herbs. Season well, cover and chill.

2 To make the pâté, melt the butter in a pan until foaming. Add the garlic and chicken livers and cook until the livers are just browned. Remove the pan from the heat and stir in the brandy and mace. Process the mixture in a blender or food processor to a smooth purée, then set aside and leave to cool.

3 To make the pastry, sift the flour and salt into a bowl and make a well in the centre. Place the milk and water in a pan. Add the lard and butter and heat gently until melted, then bring to the boil and remove from the heat as soon as the mixture begins to bubble. Pour the hot liquid into the well in the flour and beat until smooth. Cover and leave until cool enough to handle.

4 Preheat the oven to 200°C/400°F/Gas 6. Roll out two-thirds of the pastry and use to line a 23cm/9in raised pie mould. Spoon in half the game mixture and press it down evenly. Add the pâté and then top with the remaining game.

5 Roll out the remaining pastry to form a lid. Brush the edge of the pastry lining the mould with a little water and cover the pie with the pastry lid. Trim off excess pastry from around the edge. Pinch the edges together to seal in the filling. Make two holes in the centre of the lid and glaze with egg. Use pastry trimmings to roll out leaves to garnish the pie. Brush with egg.

6 Bake the pie for 20 minutes, then cover it with foil and cook for a further 10 minutes. Reduce the oven temperature to 150°C/300°F/Gas 2. Glaze the pie again with beaten egg and cook for a further 1½ hours, keeping the top covered loosely with foil.

7 Remove the pie from the oven and leave it to stand for 15 minutes. Increase the oven temperature to 200°C/400°F/Gas 6. Stand the mould on a baking sheet and remove the sides. Quickly glaze the sides of the pie with beaten egg and cover the top with foil, then cook for a final 15 minutes to brown the sides. Leave to cool completely, then chill the pie overnight.

8 To make the jelly, heat the game or beef consommé in a small pan until just beginning to bubble, whisk in the gelatine until dissolved and leave to cool until just setting. Using a small funnel, carefully pour the jellied consommé into the holes in the pie. Chill until set. This pie will keep in the refrigerator for up to 3 days.

Per portion: Energy 731Kcal/3058kJ; Protein 44g; Carbohydrate 54.3g, of which sugars 2.5g; Fat 32g, of which saturates 17.9g; Cholesterol 223mg; Calcium 163mg; Fibre 2.3g; Sodium 444mg.

STEAK, MUSHROOM AND ALE PIE

THIS ANGLO-IRISH DISH IS A FIRM FAVOURITE ON MENUS AT RESTAURANTS SPECIALIZING IN TRADITIONAL FARE. PIPING HOT, CREAMY MASHED POTATOES OR PARSLEY-DRESSED BOILED POTATOES AND SLIGHTLY CRUNCHY CARROTS AND GREEN BEANS OR CABBAGE ARE PERFECT ACCOMPANIMENTS; FOR A BAR-STYLE MEAL, CHIPS OR BAKED POTATOES AND A SIDE SALAD CAN BE SERVED WITH THE PIE.

SERVES FOUR

INGREDIENTS
25g/1oz/2 tbsp butter
1 large onion, finely chopped
115g/4oz/1½ cups chestnut or button (white) mushrooms, halved
900g/2lb lean beef in one piece, such as braising steak
30ml/2 tbsp plain (all-purpose) flour
45ml/3 tbsp sunflower oil
300ml/½ pint/1¼ cups stout or brown ale
300ml/½ pint/1¼ cups beef stock or consommé
500g/1¼lb puff pastry, thawed if frozen
beaten egg, to glaze
salt and ground black pepper

1 Melt the butter in a large, flameproof casserole, add the onion and cook gently, stirring occasionally, for about 5 minutes, or until it is softened but not coloured. Add the halved mushrooms and continue cooking for a further 5 minutes, stirring occasionally.

2 Meanwhile, trim the meat and cut it into 2.5cm/1in cubes. Season the flour and toss the meat in it.

COOK'S TIP
To make individual pies, divide the filling among four individual pie dishes. Cut the pastry into quarters and cover as above. If the dishes do not have rims, press a narrow strip of pastry around the edge of each dish to seal the lid in place. Cook as above, reducing the cooking time slightly.

3 Use a slotted spoon to remove the onion mixture from the casserole and set aside. Add and heat the oil, then brown the steak, in batches, over a high heat to seal in the juices.

4 Replace the vegetables, then stir in the stout or ale and stock or consommé. Bring to the boil, reduce the heat and simmer for about 1 hour, stirring occasionally, or until the meat is tender. Season to taste and transfer to a 1.5 litre/2½ pint/6¼ cup pie dish. Cover and leave to cool. If possible, chill the meat filling overnight as this allows the flavour to develop. Preheat the oven to 230°C/450°F/Gas 8.

5 Roll out the pastry in the shape of the dish and about 4cm/1½in larger all around. Cut a 2.5cm/1in strip from the edge of the pastry. Brush the rim of the dish with water and press the pastry strip on it. Brush the pastry rim with beaten egg and cover the pie with the pastry lid. Press the lid firmly in place and then trim the excess from around the edge.

6 Use the blunt edge of a knife to tap the outside edge of the pastry, pressing it down with your finger as you seal in the filling. (This technique is known as knocking up.)

7 Pinch the pastry between your fingers to flute the edge. Roll out any remaining pastry trimmings and cut out shapes to garnish the pie, brushing the shapes with a little beaten egg before pressing them lightly in place.

8 Make a hole in the middle of the pie to allow steam to escape, brush the top carefully with beaten egg and chill for 10 minutes to rest the pastry.

9 Bake the pie for 15 minutes, then reduce the oven temperature to 200°C/400°F/Gas 6 and bake for a further 15–20 minutes, or until the pastry is risen and golden.

Per portion: Energy 1061Kcal/4423kJ; Protein 58.8g; Carbohydrate 59.3g, of which sugars 7.6g; Fat 65.3g, of which saturates 24g; Cholesterol 164mg; Calcium 129mg; Fibre 3.2g; Sodium 622mg

quiches 232–53
see also flans

rabbit: rich game pie 250
radicchio: 173
rainbow trout: pueblo fish
   bake 223
ravioli: lobster ravioli 96
red mullet: siniya 222
red wine sauce 221
rice 70–89
   basmati and nut pilaff 74
   beef biryani 88
   burritos with chicken and rice 86
   Caribbean peanut chicken 85
   chicken and mango salad with
      orange rice 65
   chicken and prawn jambalaya 84
   kedgeree 83
   lobster bisque 15
   mushroom pilaff 75
   Peruvian salad 52
   Provençal fish soup 19
   pumpkin, rice and chicken
      soup 24
   roasted squash 73
   roasted vegetables with salsa
      verde 192
   salmon in puff pastry 246
   seafood paella 82
   seared scallops with chive
      sauce on leek and carrot
      rice 80
   spinach and rice soup 14
   stuffed vegetables 72
   see also risottos
rice noodles with pork 107
rice vermicelli: seafood laksa 20
   Thai crispy noodles with
      beef 109
ricotta: leek roulade with cheese,
      walnut and sweet pepper
      filling 36
   risotto with ricotta and basil 79
   roasted ratatouille moussaka 214
rigatoni: with tomatoes and fresh
      herbs 93
risottos: osso bucco with risotto
      Milanese 147
   with four cheeses 78
   with four vegetables 77
   with ricotta and basil 79
roasts 190–211
Romanian kebabs 183
rösti: pork escalopes baked with
      apple and potato rösti 227
rouille 23
roulades: leek roulade with cheese,
      walnut and sweet pepper
      filling 36

sage and onion stuffing 204
salads 50–69
salmon: baked salmon with watercress
      sauce 224
   filo-wrapped fish 245
   salmon fish cakes 120
   salmon in puff pastry 246
   salmon mousse 49
   seafood lasagne 98
   striped fish terrine 46
   with tequila cream sauce 121
salsas: orange and chilli salsa 157
   red onion salsa 175
   sour green chilli salsa 180
salt cod fritters with aioli 116
sauces: Béarnaise 185
   cheese and chilli 186
   chive 80
   cranberry 202
   cream 208
   five willow 154
   mint 206
   mushroom 96
   Neapolitan tomato 94

onion and mustard 226
   red wine 221
   sesame 105
   tamarind and chilli 119
   tequila cream 121
   tomato 94, 98, 118, 194
   tomato and butter 103
   tomato, garlic and chilli 112
   watercress 224
   yakitori 176, 177
   yuan 205
sausages: cheese and leek
      sausages 112
   pork and leek sausages with mashed
      potato 181
   potato and sausage casserole 141
   Spanish pork and sausage
      casserole 140
scallops: insalata di mare 59
   Provençal fish soup 19
   seared scallops with chive sauce on
      leek and carrot rice 80
schnitzels: turkey or chicken
      schnitzel 124
sea bass: Chinese-style steamed
      fish 156
   with orange chilli salsa 157
sea bream: baked sea bream with
      tomatoes 220
   siniya 222
sea trout mousse 49
seafood: Louisiana seafood
      gumbo 134
   seafood laksa 20
   seafood lasagne 98
   seafood paella 82
sesame: sauces 105
shallots: caramelized shallots 210
   French mussels 153
   lamb stew with baby onions 144
   roasted vegetables with salsa
      verde 192
   seafood laksa 20
   shallot and herb dressing 68
   Thai prawn salad with garlic
      dressing 56
   vegetable-stuffed squid 115
shark: Yucatan-style shark
      steak 174
shellfish: pasta with tomatoes and
      shellfish 95
shiitake: fish pie 217
   pot-cooked duck and green
      vegetables 165
   pot-cooked udon in miso soup 26
   Thai beef salad 69
siniya 222
skewers: grilled chicken balls cooked
      on bamboo skewers 177
   grilled skewered chicken 176
smoked cod: fish pie 217
smoked haddock: omelette Arnold
      Bennett 43
   seafood lasagne 98
   smoked haddock and new potato
      pie 218
smoked whitefish salad 60

sole: quenelles of sole 48
   striped fish terrine 46
soufflé omelette with mushrooms 42
soufflés: classic cheese soufflé 40
soups 90–121
spaghetti: pasta with garlic and
      chilli 92
   pasta with tomatoes and shellfish 95
   with eggs, bacon and cream 100
spinach: Fiorentina pizza 236
   frittata with leek and spinach 35
   spinach and rice soup 14
   warm chicken and tomato salad
      with hazelnut dressing 64
squashes: risotto with four
      vegetables 77
   roasted 73
   roasted vegetables with salsa
      verde 192
squid: insalata di mare 59
   Italian fish stew 132
   seafood paella 82
   vegetable-stuffed squid 115
steaks: beef enchiladas with red
      sauce 169
   Cantonese fried noodles 108
   lone-star steak and potato
      dinner 188
   steak Béarnaise 185
   steak, mushroom and ale pie 252
   stuffed butterfly of beef with cheese
      and chilli sauce 186
   tacos with shredded beef 168
   Thai beef salad 69
   Thai crispy noodles with beef 109
stews 130–49
stove-top dishes 150–69
stuffed vegetables 72
stuffings: marmalade-glazed
      goose 200
   oatmeal and onion stuffing 223
   parsley stuffing 208
   sage and onion stuffing 204
sweet peppers *see* peppers
sweet potatoes: beef and grilled sweet
      potato salad with shallot and herb
      dressing 68
sweetcorn *see* corn
swordfish: seared swordfish with citrus
      dressing 63

tacos: soft tacos with spiced
      omelettes 38
   tacos with shredded beef 168
tagines: chicken and vegetable
      tagine 163
tagliatelle: warm salad with ham,
      egg and asparagus 67
taleggio: grilled polenta with
      caramelized onions, radicchio
      and taleggio cheese 173
   risotto with four cheeses 78
tamales: tamale pie 231
   tamarind and chilli sauce 119
tandoori chicken 162
tangier dressing 54
tanuki jiru 28
tarts 242–9
tequila: salmon with tequila cream
      sauce 121
terrines: striped fish terrine 146
thamin lethok 105
tofu: Indian mee goreng 104
tomatoes: baked sea bream with
      tomatoes 220
   cheese and leek sausages with
      tomato, garlic and chilli sauce 112
   chilli con carne 149
   clams with Neapolitan tomato
      sauce 94
   classic marinara pizza 235
   cod, basil, tomato and potato pie 216
   lamb, pot-roasted with tomatoes,
      beans and onions 166
   Mediterranean leek and fish soup

with tomatoes and garlic 22
   pasta with tomatoes and
      shellfish 95
   peppery tomato pizza 237
   red onion and tomato 127
   rigatoni with tomatoes and fresh
      herbs 93
   roasted cod with fresh tomato
      sauce 194
   sauces 94, 98, 118, 194
   seafood paella 82
   simple tomato and butter
      sauce 103
   spiced lamb with tomatoes and
      peppers 146
   sun-dried tomato calzone 234
   tamale pie 231
   tomato, garlic and chilli sauce 112
   tomato-corn salsa 179
   warm chicken and tomato salad with
      hazelnut dressing 64
trenette: pasta with tomatoes and
      shellfish 95
trout: bacon-wrapped trout with
      oatmeal and onion stuffing 223
   Chinese-style steamed fish 156
   pueblo fish bake 223
   sea trout mousse 49
   siniya 222
   smoked fish and asparagus
      mousse 45
   with tamarind and chilli sauce 119
tsukune 177
tuna: seared tuna steaks with red onion
      salsa 175
   tuna and egg galette 244
turbot: fillets of turbot with oysters 158
turkey: turkey breasts with tomato-corn
      salsa 179
   turkey croquettes 125
   turkey lasagne 101
   turkey or chicken schnitzel 124
   turkey patties 178
turnips: chicken and vegetable tagine 163

udon noodles: pot-cooked udon in miso
      soup 26

veal: country meat loaf 230
   escalopes of veal with cream
      sauce 208
   osso bucco with risotto Milanese 147
   roast veal with parsley stuffing 208
venison: rich game pie 250
vermicelli *see* rice vermicelli

walnuts: basmati and nut pilaff 74
water-crust pastry 250
watercress: baked salmon with
      watercress sauce 224

yakitori sauce 176, 177
yogurt: moussaka 228
Yorkshire puddings 210

zucchini *see* courgettes